DIANA: ONE OF THE FAMILY?

Other books by Paul James include:

Anne: The Working Princess
At Her Majesty's Service
At Home with the Royal Family
The Royal Almanac
Excuses, Excuses . . .
Prince Philip's 101 Great Games
It's a Weird World
The Laugh-A-Minute Book
The Fact-A-Minute Book
V.V.I.P. Diaries
Sleep at Last

DIANA: ONE OF THE FAMILY?

Paul James

SIDGWICK & JACKSON
LONDON

To Gwen and Denis Cockerton with love, for
the Sandringham years and all those since

First published in Great Britain in 1988
by Sidgwick & Jackson Limited

Copyright © 1988 by Paul James

ISBN 0-283-99667-6

Typeset by Hewer Text Composition Services, Edinburgh
Printed in Great Britain by
Butler & Tanner Ltd, Frome and London
for Sidgwick & Jackson Limited
1 Tavistock Chambers, Bloomsbury Way
London WC1A 2SG

Contents

Acknowledgments

In one of my previous books I likened writing about a member of the Royal Family as akin to writing of the dead. You cannot communicate easily with your subject. The attraction of the Princess of Wales, however, is not only that she is a warm human being, but that she lived on our side of the world before transcending to the realm she now inhabits. In this book I have attempted to discover not only what it is like on the *other* side, behind the palace walls, but more importantly what it has been like for a girl, who even now is under thirty, to climb up on to the first step of the throne; to be absorbed into the Royal Family. Although I have consulted books to check facts, figures, dates, places, the major instruments of my research were my eyes, and my ears. Any opinions expressed are my own, as are any unwitting errors or omissions.

In helping me get closer to the Princess of Wales, to better understand her character and behaviour, I would like to thank the many people who have given freely of their time to talk to me: people from the royal circle itself who have sat at the Wales' table, people who have provided a service for the Kensington Palace Household, people who in some way have come into contact with Her Royal Highness and have made observations.

My gratitude goes to the following for practical help and encouragement: the staff of the Press Office at Buckingham Palace who, as always, courteously answered questions despite the obvious limitations placed upon them; Miss Anne Beckwith-Smith, Assistant Private Secretary and Lady-in-Waiting to HRH The Princess of Wales; Sally Hughes, Secretary to Miss Beckwith-Smith; my agent, Andrew Lownie; the invaluable Trish, Patricia Reynolds; David Horne, for acting as guru; Deryn Cutting for being a fast and efficient secretary; Julian Clegg and the staff of

BBC Radio Sussex; my editors Carey Smith and Anne Cohen, for being so patient, and to my family and friends who put up with me being locked in my study for hours on end with 'Diana'.

Finally, my thanks must go to the Princess of Wales for being an inspiration to so many in the past, and for having a future that we all so anxiously await.

PAUL JAMES
Brighton, 1988

Introduction

The Queen smiled directly at me. That radiant smile which always seems to light up her entire face. Perhaps it was because I was dressed as Prince Charles had been as a child, right down to the velvet collared coat.

At a younger age than most children I became aware of the mystique and magic that surrounds the Royal Family. Born a mere stone's throw from their country retreat at Sandringham, Norfolk, I was taken in the early 1960s to watch the Queen and her children as they walked to church on a Sunday morning, in those glorious days when security appeared to be little more than the local village policeman. As Her Majesty walked past and smiled that incredible smile it was impossible not to be touched by her aura. As a child, I could not help but sense the reaction of the people around me, here was somebody special.

Not one of us knew, as we walked around the Sandringham estate that in nearby Park House lay a baby, christened in the same church where we always waited to see the Queen, whose smile would also capture hearts. A child who would *become* special.

It it unlikely that we ever saw the honourable Diana Frances Spencer in her pram. If we had, it would have seemed insignificant. Only two decades later when I became a professional royal observer did I become fully aware of the child born to be Queen. Only then did I realize that a member of my *own* family, employed by Queen Elizabeth the Queen Mother, had unknowingly been a colleague of the future Queen's grandmother, Lady Fermoy.

The impact that Diana had on the world in 1981 could not have escaped even the most ardent anti-monarchist: scarcely a magazine failed to feature 'Lady Di' on the cover; a million gallons of ink must have been used to describe every facet of her life; and as I wrote enthusiastically about every other member of the Royal

Family I vowed with all my heart never to write about the new Princess of Wales. Yet, whenever I stood a few feet from the Queen at a function, or followed the Princess Royal around for an afternoon, as to a magnet I seemed drawn to the Princess of Wales. It became impossible to talk to anyone at a royal engagement without the same topic arising: Diana. Contrary to popular belief at the time, interest in her has never waned. Even the Duchess of York has been unable to compete with the fairytale Princess.

I saw Lady Diana Spencer for the first time a few months after her engagement on her way to the Trooping the Colour ceremony in 1981. Seeing her at close range, I was entranced. Within minutes her enchantment was overshadowed when, a few yards from me, Marcus Sarjeant raised a gun, pointed it directly at the Queen, and fired. Never have I become so aware of the vulnerability of royalty. Had the bullets been real, the future Queen I had seen only moments before would have inherited the crown long before her time. Only those present will remember what the television cameras failed to see; the appalling sight of the Queen sliding from side to side as she miraculously brought her frightened horse, Burmese, under control, with an anxious glance over her shoulder to ensure that her husband and son were still alive. The momentary look of terror on Her Majesty's face will go with me to the grave. I went home and wept.

'Life must go on,' said the Queen philosophically, and even in 1987 when advisers suggested that the public be kept away from Buckingham Palace for security reasons, she vetoed the plans. 'I have to be seen to be believed,' she says, somewhat tongue-in-cheek, but for Diana the constant threat of assassination is at times unbearable. 'If someone really wants to kill you, there is nothing you can do about it,' says Princess Anne, whose own life has been threatened on numerous occasions, but for someone as young as the Princess of Wales the very idea that a terrorist might want to kill your husband or children for political reasons must be a horrifying prospect.

It was at this point that I began to look at the future bride as a person on the verge of some terrible realization. This was no normal marriage; Diana was not simply about to gain a husband. The greatest change was that she would become royal and have to reconcile herself with all that it entailed. Most of us at some time fear being robbed or mugged in the street, but Diana now had the worry that someone might kill or maim a member of her own family simply to cause deliberate outrage. It was the first of many changes that this new royal was forced to accept.

It is now seven years since Diana joined Britain's most élite family, during which time we have seen her blossom from a slightly plump teenager into a sophisticated beauty. Few would have thought a decade ago that the popularity of the Queen and Queen Mother could be overshadowed by a non-royal. Not only has Diana, since her marriage to Prince Charles, captured the largest slice of media attention, she has forced the Family to sit up and take stock of themselves and their image. Whereas words like 'glamour', 'fashion' and 'beauty' were seldom spoken in the same breath as royalty, even the Queen has now tucked in some shoulder pads, albeit discreetly . . .

That someone so young and inexperienced can cause what is little short of a revolution amongst royalty is an intriguing concept. 'Di-mania' was never deliberately calculated. Whoever married the heir to the throne was an inevitable target for attention, but all assumed that once the honeymoon was over, interest would wane. The Royal Family were prepared for a six-month upheaval; no-one could have anticipated its permanency. What began to fascinate me very early on, and has continued to do so, is not only the effect Diana has had on the Royal Family at a time when they were in danger of becoming an anachronism, but what it has done to her. From the very outset she found herself in a unique position with incalculable pressures from all sides. The psychological effect that this must have had on a girl then only nineteen and even today still under thirty, was surely devastating. As a very immature teenager, already emotionally scarred and insecure as a result of her parents' divorce, she was pushed overnight into womanhood. Not only did she need to find her feet, she had to grow up in a glare of publicity. No error of judgment on her part could go unnoticed. What began as a fun episode in her life turned into something so serious and demanding that it pushed her to the verge of a nervous breakdown.

For a long time Diana must have felt an outsider in a very élite circle. To the public she was the diamond amid the pearls; to the royals themselves she was the uncut stone whose rough edges needed polishing. A great deal of hewing was required before the brilliant gem could emerge. As a result she is today an accepted member of the Family, having come through relatively unscathed though far removed from the shy young woman she would still be had she not married the Prince of Wales.

In 1981 I began to follow our future Queen; I kept Press cuttings until the sheer volume meant one had to be selective, and having had the privilege to attend a large number of royal engagements over the years I have been able to talk to hundreds of people. It still surprises me that people *are* happy to talk, but then Diana is a favourite topic of conversation for so many. Gradually this has enabled me to draw up a portrait of a girl in a unique position. I have tried to discard the myths, and have not dwelt on aspects of the Princess' life that have been so often repeated that they are as familiar as if we had lived them ourselves. Inevitably there are details that have been written about before, but I have used them only to illustrate the effects that they have had on the Princess herself, events that have brought her to the point she is at today. Not only have I stated facts, but I have also raised questions. Questions to be pondered rather than answered. No-one else for several decades will find herself in Diana's position – we may have to wait for the bride of Prince William of Wales. It is this individuality that has turned the former Lady Diana Spencer into an enigma.

As a biographer I came to find Diana an irresistible subject. She has inspired dozens of slim books, filled mostly with photographs, that tell us again and again of her first meeting with Prince Charles in a ploughed field, his proposal of marriage, the detailed intricacies behind their wedding preparations as well as providing blow-by-blow accounts of her pregnancies. I wanted instead to get deeper into the heart of Diana and get to know the woman who will, after all, one day be Queen. I have attempted to get beneath the skin of one of the world's most glamorous women, to assess her true character, her achievements, and ultimately her future. My goal has been to find the real person behind the hype and the myth. I began studying Diana with a feeling of euphoria; I ended up feeling sad for her.

When writing once about Queen Elizabeth II, I was told by one of Her Majesty's aides that although we, the public, often express the notion that we would not wish to change places with her, equally she would not wish to change places with us. She has never known any life other than a royal one, it is not a role that can be switched on and off, and she would simply be unable to cope with anything different.

For our future Queen, however, the situation is reversed. Those close to Diana know only too well that at times she would give a King's ransom to change places with us.

❧ 1 ❧

No Footsteps To Follow

The great tragedy of the ninth Princess of Wales is, to echo the sentiments of both Oscar Wilde and George Bernard Shaw, that she achieved her heart's desire. In winning the heart of a Prince, the riches of royalty and the adulation of the world, she unwittingly relinquished her most valued possession: liberty. At the tender age of nineteen she was proffered a crown, security for life and an assured place in the annals of history as Queen Consort to the forty-third Sovereign of England since William the Conqueror. She grabbed the opportunity with both hands. Only then did she discover that amid the jewels was a crown of thorns.

Four years into her marriage Diana publicly admitted that she had not realized the full implications of becoming royal. So vehement was her tone, she could not fail to imply that had she been older and more mature when Prince Charles proposed marriage she might have, like her sister Sarah before her, opted for a quieter life. Certainly, she would have thought twice about the consequences. Possibly, she would still have taken the same path, but she would have been more adequately equipped for the road that lay ahead.

In February 1978 Lady Sarah Spencer said: 'Charles is a fabulous person, but I am not in love with him. I would not marry a man I did not love, whether he was a dustman or the King of England. If he asked me I would turn him down.' There are many who insist that Charles' was an arranged marriage. Sarah Spencer was the original choice; when she failed to live up to expectations and talked publicly to the Press (a cardinal sin) her younger sister took her place. The more romantic insist that Diana had her sights set on Prince Charles from an early age and

1

married him eventually because of love. It is believed that Diana fell in love with Charles when she was sixteen. From the age of twelve she had slept beneath his portrait on the dormitory wall at West Heath Boarding School in Kent but contrary to romantic belief she did not place the photograph there herself. Was it merely in fun though that she would joke with friends that she would one day be Princess of Wales long before it became a practical possibility?

Cynics who suggest that Diana deliberately planned to catch her Prince, then the most eligible bachelor in the world, emanate from the same school of thought that condemns Wallis Simpson, the divorcee who married Edward VIII, as a calculating social climber. Unlike Diana, Mrs Simpson had a 'past' that prevented her from becoming Princess of Wales and later Queen, but both women married ultimately for love and took the consequences.

Born on the fringes of the Royal Family inasmuch as the Spencers have long been part of the hallowed inner circle of intimates, Diana must have been well aware of the pros and cons of their lifestyle. Yet from an aristocratic background herself it is highly probable that she seldom looked beyond the benefits. With an army of servants, now at her beck and call, cars, planes, boats, trains, helicopters at her disposal and the top designers longing to make her clothes, on the face of it she must have thought it would all enhance her lifestyle enabling her to do *everything* that she wanted. She forgot that nothing in life comes for free and loss of freedom was a high price to pay. Lord Forte once said that a rich person is only a poor person with money. In gaining wealth, you lose something in return.

By their very nature there is an inherent difference between those born royal and those, even from aristocratic or well-to-do families, who marry royalty. Such partnerships invariably experience problems because of this essential difference: Princess Margaret and Lord Snowdon were at loggerheads whenever she attempted to pull rank on him or he overplayed the role of Earl; the Princess Royal and Captain Mark Phillips have suffered when royal duty has kept them apart; Prince Michael of Kent and more recently the Earl of St Andrews had to renounce their rights to the throne to marry Catholic commoners. Again and again, the battle between true blue-blooded royals and the innocent infiltrators goes on. True acceptance takes decades, if indeed you survive the course. Few today would consider Queen Elizabeth the Queen Mother to be anything other than royal, but she encountered blatant hostility in the early years of her marriage as Lady Elizabeth Bowes-Lyon – not from the general public, but from the Family who felt that she was 'not like us'.

The fact that Diana was not like a Princess was her trump card when it came to the media and the public. Looking like the girl-next-door, and not being a seasoned personality, were endearing traits. Before she had undertaken one official duty or made a public speech she was an international superstar, and nearly a decade later even though she has gained the gloss and style expected of a star she has not lost that early captivating charm, the underlying uncertainty that she is doing the right thing.

Walking past some ornamental fountains on an official tour she turned to her host and said, 'I wish they'd turn those off. They make me want to go to the loo.' Such a statement would never come from the Queen, nor even the plain speaking Princess Royal, but because of her unaffected approach and relative inexperience, the Princess of Wales could get away with it. It was wrong, muttered her aides, to publicly describe herself as being 'thick as a plank' however much in jest, but again it showed a human touch that royalty in the past has failed to display. Although the Princess might not be academically brilliant and would be the last to describe herself as an intellectual, these apparently throwaway remarks about having nothing inside her head are not entirely off-the-cuff. They achieve their intended purpose, for as long as people are prepared to accept the slightly dumb-blonde image, Diana has the upper hand. She *can* sometimes let the dignity slip, or kick out at royal protocol and succeed much of the time in getting her own way by using inexperience and naivety as a tool.

As a Princess without a precedent and the newest addition to the Royal Family, this approach worked well until 1986 when Prince Andrew married the Duchess of York. *One* royal who could occasionally be immature and rebellious, the public would tolerate; *two* proved unacceptable and for the first time Diana toppled too far on her pedestal and suffered harsh criticism, at times justified.

Prince Charles has joked that he learned his job 'the way a

monkey learns, by watching its parents,' and for the role he has now and the future he can expect, there was no better model to emulate. His brothers and sister again were initiated through a lifetime's experience and were allowed to enter royal duty at a slow and steady pace. Diana was thrown in at the deep end and found herself facing a formidable career with no training and no real guide to offer help. The Princess Royal has said that you cannot give any advice other than to recount your own experiences and that it is simply a case of finding your feet, which inevitably takes time. Diana did not have the time to make the mistakes that other members of the Royal Family had made during their gentle initiation into the round of engagements because of the constant and exacting scrutiny to which she was subjected.

The most recent addition to the Family at that time was Princess Michael of Kent, the former Mrs Thomas Troubridge, but a seventeen-year age gap instantly set her apart from Diana. The two were relative strangers as the Queen did not ever include Prince Michael and his wife on the Balmoral guest list, even though Princess Michael might well have been able to offer very practical advice from her first hand experience of joining the British Royal Family. Diana privately dismissed the Princess as being 'too horsey', a surprising comment considering the fact that her future husband spent much of his time preoccupied with equestrian events.

In crossing the great divide that separates the aristocracy from royalty, Diana's progress has been described by one of her former flatmates as like 'walking on a tightrope'. She had to tread very carefully so as not to offend her prestigious in-laws, upset Palace staff by being too authoritative or lose their respect with overfamiliarity, and more importantly she could not publicly fall in any respect that would provide the eager Press with much sought-after stories of an embarrassing nature. In the five months prior to her marriage, Diana may not have toppled off the tightrope completely, but she did sway at times. If she giggled while the National Anthem was played she would receive a frosty reproachful glance from the Queen; when she borrowed jewellery that had been offered to her, she was quickly told by royal advisers to return it. 'I'm not royal yet,' she had grumbled, but as fiancée to the Prince of Wales she was forced to comply. Even on the eve of her wedding when she wanted to spend her remaining few hours as a single girl with her former flatmates, looking nostalgically back to carefree teenage days, she was firmly informed that she should instead have a quiet dinner with the Queen Mother and Lady Fermoy.

Having had a long association with the Spencers and Fermoys herself, the Queen Mother was particularly delighted by Prince Charles' choice of bride. Indeed there is a school of thought that believes that the grandmothers of Charles and Diana pushed the two together. Although the Queen Mother and her lady-in-waiting were probably less calculating, they certainly did much to encourage the relationship and it was to Clarence House that Diana was destined after leaving Coleherne Court on the day of her engagement. Although nearly six decades had passed since the Queen Mother, as Lady Elizabeth Bowes-Lyon, had been in an identical position to Diana – that of marrying a future King – it was nevertheless considered that she better than anybody else was qualified to give Diana advice and encouragement. To this day many believe that Diana spent five months at Clarence House receiving lessons in royal etiquette and protocol, safely protected by the quiet chintzy atmosphere that this early nineteenth-century building exudes. Nothing could be further from the truth.

Still only nineteen and very much in love with her future husband, Diana did not relish the thought of spending so much time with the two formidable ladies at Clarence House and quite naturally expressed a preference for Buckingham Palace where she could be close to Prince Charles. It was one of the earliest displays of her strong character and Diana, quite surprisingly in this instance, got her own way and spent only two nights at Clarence House before taking up residence further down The Mall. It was, it must be said, with the Queen's permission but at the time the very fact that Charles and Diana were sleeping under the same roof had to be kept from the Press for fear of misinterpretation. With royal engagements usually lasting only a few months, the Queen encouraged the couple to spend as much time together as possible so that Prince Charles could make quite certain that his choice of bride was right before it was too late. Equally the Queen was happy for Diana to be resident at the Palace to ensure that the young girl could cope with the life ahead of her. It was not, however, as one might perhaps expect, a period in which the Queen got to know her future daughter-in-law. Although the Queen has a busy working schedule, there were ample opportunities for a quiet lunch together, or a cosy evening in front of the television, but Her Majesty remained totally aloof and not once in the weeks prior to the marriage did the Queen and the future Princess of Wales dine alone together. Even stranger, were the numerous occasions when Prince Charles would have lunch with his mother, on the pretext of discussing 'royal business' while Diana remained alone in her room.

Throughout this period of adjustment, Diana must have felt very much alone, not yet officially royal but nevertheless unable to continue with her old life as before. With no engagement diary of her own it was not always considered suitable or practical for her to accompany the Prince of Wales and so she remained in her small suite of rooms in the nursery wing, once occupied by a succession of royal nannies. The fact that Diana had been a kindergarten teacher was purely coincidental in the choice of rooms. It was a time of watching television, reading, and undertaking a vast amount of shopping to build up the trousseau and necessary wardrobe for the life ahead. To occupy her time she visited her mother's flat in Warwick Square, only a short drive from the Palace, and made many trips to see her sisters, Jane, who lived at Kensington Palace in a grace-and-favour apartment, and Sarah, who had a flat in nearby Chelsea. Again, it might have been a period when Diana could have been given a guided tour of Buckingham Palace, which could one day be considered her main residence, or been given valuable lessons in the intricacies of royal duty and the vast amount of planning that goes into any engagement, but this opportunity was denied her.

Although no stranger to the splendours of Buckingham Palace and not in awe of priceless treasures, having been used to living amid the stately interiors of Althorp House, in Northampton-shire, she nevertheless felt intimidated by the building and the museum-like atmosphere that seems to pervade many of the state rooms and corridors. Unlike at Althorp, Diana could not visit the Palace kitchens and chat to the staff or help herself to a sandwich. Here she was expected to ask the young footman assigned to her for anything that she needed. As the refrigerator in her apartment was constantly restocked with food, even the footman's visits were brief and infrequent. 'I'm quite all right, thank you,' Diana would nervously reply if he ever checked to see if she needed anything, and she would carry on counting the hours until Prince Charles' return.

Through the very nature of their position many members of the Royal Family are loners, their friends few, and it is a fact of life that they have grown to accept. The Queen has been described as one of the loneliest women in the world, and many people are shocked to discover that as she seldom attends evening engagements or dinners she spends many evenings alone, watching television with a supper tray on her lap. Having lived a gregarious existence until now, Diana at times found this ritual imprisonment in a gilded cage intolerable. Even today Diana finds that she often spends evenings alone at Highgrove in Gloucestershire once the children are in bed, and if Prince Charles has guests for dinner whom she finds boring, she will excuse herself from the table and listen to music privately.

In the very early days during the period of limbo between engagement and marriage it was one of the Queen's Women of the Bedchamber, Lady Susan Hussey, a long-standing and highly respected member of the Royal Household, who became Diana's confidante and adviser. Assigned to Diana as a lady-in-waiting the gentle Lady Susan, whose husband Marmaduke is chairman of the BBC, became a valued friend and later, in 1982, was chosen to be a godmother to Prince William. In the first public engagements that Diana undertook with Prince Charles, it was Lady Susan Hussey who could be seen in the background as a dedicated supporter of this new addition to the Royal Family and after years of accompanying the Queen it must have been something of a novelty for her to attend someone at the opposite end of the spectrum.

Although everyone in the royal household appears outwardly to have remained unemotional and cool towards Diana, it is not to say that she was unpopular. Quite the reverse, in fact, and even the austere Edward Adeane, then the Prince of Wales' Private Secretary, quickly warmed to her and admitted that she was a 'lovely girl'. Secretly, however, officials at the Palace began monitoring Diana's progress and reactions, her successes and errors. From the moment of her engagement a file was opened, cataloguing exactly what she wore publicly, who she met, what she said, how she reacted, not only for the essential records, but so that Diana could, it was hoped, learn from any mistakes. Again this appears to place an enormous burden on one so young to be conscious that not only the media and the public were watching but that those who were supposedly confidantes and supporters appeared at times to be like spies, reporting back to base on her every move. Being informed that this study was for her own good can have been of small comfort. To anyone with the wrong temperament, this could easily have led to paranoia and it is hardly surprising that in the first few months as Princess of Wales, when approached about attending a public function, Diana's first words were often, 'Do I *have* to go?'

The greatest terror at this time for the Princess was not so much meeting individuals at a reception or dinner and making small talk, but facing large crowds. Her eyes often reflected sheer panic as thousands chanted her name. 'We want Diana!' was always the predominant cry; they never called for Charles. Her obvious vulnerability on these occasions, the embarrassed look from under her fringe, the blushing cheeks, the head bowed nervously, only made her even more appealing. Faced with a new situation Diana seldom knew how to react. Ultimately she ended up showing her own emotions, not necessarily those expected of her. On one walkabout a small boy gave her flowers, at the same time constantly trying to feel the buttons on her dress and touch her face. When she realized that the child was blind, she fought back the tears and allowed him to touch her face and hands. It was a natural reaction and the people loved her for it. The Queen under similar circumstances would undoubtedly have betrayed no emotion, but Diana refused to control hers.

Diana is renowned for her love of children, and will even today head straight for youngsters on a walkabout because they put her immediately at ease by their open reactions. Fame meant that adults stopped treating her as a normal human being. A few months before her engagement Diana could meet people at parties, talk to shop assistants, travel on the London Underground and be accepted as an equal. It is not easy to accept that overnight almost every person that you meet is treating you with awe and reverence. Prince Charles has said that he is very used to people's reactions when he walks into a room. Some become tongue-tied, others tremble with nervous excitement and their handshakes become clammy, for no reason other than because he is royal. For Diana it must have felt as if she had grown an extra head to suddenly experience a room full of people go silent as she entered, to find people extending a trembling hand or performing an unsteady curtsey as she approached. In that unnerving position it can only be a slow realization and acceptance that everyone you meet, other than members of the Family, is going to treat you with veneration for the rest of your life. Today if Diana visits, for example, an old schoolfriend privately, protocol dictates that this contemporary, no matter how close, must curtsey when they first meet. For this reason it is children, unimpressed and unbound by diplomatic etiquette, that Diana will always head for. As she kneels beside them, accepts wilting posies of flowers and shakes sticky fingers, for a few fleeting cherished seconds she must think back to those carefree days at the Young England Kindergarten in Pimlico when her world was so very different.

The greatest realization of her new found status came within hours of the announcement of her engagement to the Prince of Wales when Diana went to get into her own car. She opened the door and a detective got in with her. 'I can drive myself,' she announced firmly. 'Sorry,' said the detective, appropriately called Paul Officer, 'We're part of your life now.' With such finality Diana was thus forced to accept without question this new fact of life. Although resigning herself to the inevitability, receiving constant surveillance, like a prisoner on remand, is not something that she takes lightly and it is characteristic of her underlying determination that it was not long before her first detective was released from duty. Diana found him oppressively overprotective, she insisted, and the diligent man was transferred to duties in South London. Were it not for Detective Chief Inspector Paul Officer, however, Diana might not today be Princess of Wales: it was in 1974 that Prince Charles was attacked by an armed assailant at two o'clock one morning while serving in the Navy at Portland barracks in Dorset. Hearing a struggle, Paul Officer rushed to the Prince's aid just as the attacker, a deranged lieutenant from the base, was about to hit him over the head. This was one of the few attacks there have ever been on the Prince's life. It was the loyal detective also who was chosen in 1979 to break the tragic news to the Prince that his favourite uncle and 'honorary grandfather', Lord Mountbatten had been assassinated by the IRA. Diana's attitude towards Officer was, therefore, most certainly upsetting to the Prince.

The autocratic display on Diana's part was not, however, as some might suppose, the cause of an early rift between the Prince and Princess. During the initiation period Diana was only able to survive because of Prince Charles' love and devotion throughout, without which she might not have stayed the course. There was no greater evidence publicly of this bond than two days after the engagement when the Prince left England for a five-week tour of Australia, New Zealand, Venezuela and the United States. For such a long tour, meticulously planned months in advance, it was not practical for Diana to accompany the Prince and she made no attempt to hide her tears as they parted at the steps leading up to the aircraft. With typical control Charles betrayed no emotion.

These were not the last tears that Diana was to shed before the wedding, for just five days before the big event the strain of the previous five months began to take their toll. On a private visit to watch Prince Charles play in a polo match at Tidworth, she sat calmly with Earl Mountbatten's daughter-in-law, Lady Romsey, when unexpectedly a barrage of photographers turned and focused their lenses on the then most newsworthy girl in the world. Taken completely by surprise Diana burst into tears and ran with Lady Romsey to the back of the enclosure before being driven swiftly back to Windsor Castle. It was obvious to all present that her acceptance of this permanent intrusion in her life was far from complete. Diana still lacked confidence and had a tendency to crack under severe pressure, in absolute contrast to Sarah Ferguson, now Duchess of York, who five years later not only coped well with the media but positively enjoyed the attention of the cameramen, even engaging in a witty repartee with journalists. Both girls disliked intensely the nicknames given to them by the tabloid press of 'Di' and 'Fergie', but whereas Sarah has the personality to laugh off the tag, the Princess can still attack any recalcitrant scribe with, 'My name is Diana, *not*

Di,' not unlike her sister-in-law the Princess Royal who turned sharply on a photographer in Australia who shouted, 'Look this way, love,' with the retort 'I am not your love, I am your Royal Highness!'

It was not until after the wedding, when Diana officially became Princess of Wales, that she could in any way begin to adjust to the new role and lifestyle. Once married, instead of being the future royal, someone who had little more than curiosity value, Diana became one of a pair and suddenly had a very specific job to fulfil. Still unsure of herself, completely inexperienced and ill-at-ease, she now had much more of a purpose. She was no longer literally a lady in waiting, but a full-blown Princess with a mission. The first major change on marriage was a change of title. The Honourable Diana Spencer, had found it 'a bit of a giggle' when at fourteen she became a 'Lady' through her father's inheritance. It was a change in style and seemed a glamorous one for a teenager, but it made little or no difference to her way of life. The new 'handle' of Princess of Wales had more dramatic implications. At first it was mooted that Diana should officially be styled as 'Princess Charles' – just as Marie-Christine von Reibnitz was forced to adopt her husband's name to become Princess Michael of Kent. Although the media, and even books by well respected writers, use the name 'Princess Diana', in terms of protocol it is incorrect although say Debretts, the authority on titles, it should 'be made acceptable'. Publicly Diana, and the media as a whole, quickly adjusted to calling the much dubbed 'Lady Di' Princess of Wales, except in the United States where the former nickname seems to have remained. Far harder for the new royal was the acceptance of being called 'Ma'am' (pronounced 'Mam' deriving from the word 'Madam', never 'Marm') by anyone other than very close friends and members of the Family. Even Prince Charles will refer publicly, and to the staff in private, to his wife as 'the Princess', never simply 'Diana'.

Marrying a Prince, and the heir to the throne at that, was quite unlike becoming the wife of any other man in the country. The key to being royal is the quality of being able to place duty before personal desire. Prince Charles admits that he has no material or financial worries, currently estimated to be worth £340,000,000, but that his conscience 'takes a constant battering' because of the privileges he has in life. He feels continually that he must work hard and 'help people' almost as a penance for royal birth. Although she has never spoken publicly about it, the Princess Royal can equally identify with him and works above and beyond the call of duty to justify her birthright. Diana has no such twinges of conscience. She is affected visibly by the handicapped, the dying, the physically disadvantaged, but does not share her husband's guilt complex about money and possessions. Prince Charles continuously attempts to put something back into society and relishes any opportunity to work on a farm or a remote croft in a very real attempt to understand different standards of living. Although Diana enjoys her royal work more today than when she began it, her attendance at functions is still often out of necessity rather than desire. Off duty, she does not share her husband's desire to experience hardship and lack of creature comforts.

One of the most daunting prospects on becoming Princess of Wales was being given an engagement diary to fill, putting her in the unenviable position of knowing exactly where she will be on any given day up to twelve months ahead. There are key dates in the diary for annual functions that she will attend *for the rest of her life*. It is not surprising that sometimes the whole situation has in recent years turned the Princess into a royal rebel, and, greatly influenced by the Duchess of York, Diana has kicked back at tradition and what she calls the 'pomposity' of some of the people she meets. When Diana visited the BBC 'Breakfast Time' studio, presenter Selina Scott attempted to be witty and complained to the Princess that she gets fan mail from 'a lot of old men'. 'You should think yourself lucky,' said Diana sharply, 'I have to sit next to them at dinner!'

Although unquestionably a hard worker – in 1987 she under-took 180 engagements in the United Kingdom and 86 abroad – Diana still undertakes only a third of the duties that her sister-in-law the Princess Royal fulfils (704 engagements in 1987) and finds it a struggle to place duty before personal desire, an ability that the Royal Family really do need in abundance and one of the Queen's earliest lessons. When as a child she complained of being tired, Queen Mary rebuked her with, 'We are Royal, we are *never* tired.' In her grandmother the Queen had an excellent teacher; Diana had no such mentor. Unlike the stalwarts of the Royal Family, Diana is unable to conceal the look of boredom that crosses her face at less interesting functions. The Queen can sit impassively through endless hours of tribal dancing, reception committees and exhibition tours and only those closest to her know whether she is really enjoying herself or simply going through the mechanics of appearing interested. On the 1988 tour of Australia television cameras clearly captured the Princess' look of dismay as she raised her eyes heavenwards when confronted with a seemingly endless line of handshaking.

It is noticeable that foreign tours in latter years have become much shorter, rarely longer than ten days, since the Princess complained of the long and punishing schedule that she had to endure. The couple's first tour of Australia and New Zealand in 1983 lasted for seven weeks, after which Diana returned home so exhausted that she refused ever to undertake such a lengthy visit again. Before aircraft were widely used for visits, the Royal Family were forced to spend many weeks away because of the travel time involved. Now that Australia is only thirty hours away, the Princess had a reasonable argument in questioning the length of such visits. When she collapsed in Canada during the Expo '86 visit, it was officially stated that the heat and lack of air had taken its toll on Diana and that she was physically tired. Tired she may well have been, but a member of the Princess' staff insists that the fainting fit was a result of sheer boredom. Although refusing to admit that it was a deliberate act, it was pointed out that Diana coincidentally fainted at a spot where the cameras were not on her. Only one television camera from a long distance managed to take a split-second blurred shot.

Diana's early difficulties in coping with royal duty did not become publicly apparent for several months. In the late summer of 1981, the Prince and Princess took up residence in their Gloucestershire home, Highgrove. This was their first real home together, the honeymoon was over and Diana hoped that she and her husband could relax together in private and *off duty*. Looking out of a first floor window she quickly became aware that they were being watched. The position of the house meant that it was, unfortunately, close enough to the road, a public road, for zoom lenses to be focused on her. One single photograph could be syndicated around the world for thousands of pounds and cameramen were prepared to wait for days if necessary to obtain pictures. Quickly Diana became conscious of never going near windows that faced a road or public footpath. If she left the grounds of Highgrove, even to drive to the local newsagents she had the unappreciated detective at her side and the unwanted Press photographers all around her. The pressure never seemed to abate, even after the Queen's much publicized intervention in which Fleet Street editors were summoned to Buckingham Palace and told politely but firmly to leave the girl alone. Her Majesty's then Press Secretary, Michael Shea, informed the formidable gathering that Diana lacked the formal qualifications to be a secretary to any one of them and needed time to adjust to her new position. 'She's very young,' said the Queen, 'she's not like the rest of us,' implying subtly and succinctly that the Princess lacked royal training. By this time Diana had been married for five months and was well and truly a Princess, yet the Queen's unprecedented mediation must have served only to make her feel even more of an outsider and *still* not one of the Family. Even if you are unable to cope with pressure, it comes as small consolation to have your mother-in-law and monarch publicly, in essence, say: make allowances for her, she's not one of us. The most dramatic evidence of the pressure manifested itself on the eve of Remembrance Sunday in 1982 when the Princess failed to appear with other members of the Family at the Royal Albert Hall for the Festival of Remembrance. It was a very different scene to the previous year when she won herself an ovation with the crowds singing *You Made Me Love You* to the Royal Box and the bands striking up *The Lass that Loves a Sailor* leaving no doubts as to who the tune was aimed at. This time she arrived late and flustered, driving herself to the Albert Hall after the Queen and the rest of the Royal Family had arrived. The annual British Legion Festival had special significance in 1982 because of the Falklands War that year in which Prince Andrew had fought. More members of the Family than usual were present and naturally Diana was expected to be one of the party. The royal cars arrived on time, with one noticeable absence. Doormen were informed that the Princess would not be coming, her chair was hastily removed from the Royal box, and Prince Charles impressed upon everyone within earshot that his wife was unwell. Five minutes later, unheralded and obviously unhappy, Diana pulled up outside the Albert Hall and her seat had to be unceremoniously returned. No word of explanation was given, and Diana looked depressed and on the verge of tears throughout most of the evening. 'The Princess is in the best of health; I expect it is a domestic mix up', said a Buckingham Palace spokesman, uncharacteristically contradicting the Prince of Wales' story.

Predictably the Press immediately began to speculate about a marital rift. The tabloids noticed the Princess' weight loss and declared that she was suffering from the dreaded slimmer's disease anorexia nervosa, others asked 'Is it all becoming too much for Diana?'

The Albert Hall incident was the public culmination of a number of events over the preceding months. In little more than a year Diana had become a wife, a Princess and a mother. As a wife she had to adjust, as all married couples do, to living with someone, difficult in any relationship and even more so with the added burden of running a royal household. As a Princess she faced the glare of publicity and lived almost her entire life under the scrutiny of cameras. She wanted to please her husband and was determined not to let him or the Royal Family down, and she knew that she had to live up to very high expectations and standards. As a mother she not only had to adjust to life with a baby, but had to quickly regain her beauty-queen figure to return to the image that the media had created for her. Beneath all this was an underlying fear for the safety of her husband and child. Shortly after Charles and Diana met President Sadat of Egypt, he was assassinated. In 1982 the unthinkable happened when intruder Michael Fagan broke into the Queen's bedroom at Buckingham Palace, having penetrated what was then considered to be the tightest possible security. Two weeks later IRA bomb explosions in Hyde Park and Regents Park killed eleven of the Queen's men of the Household Cavalry. Seven horses were killed and over fifty people were injured in the blasts. Since the assassination of Lord Mountbatten any outrage caused by the IRA has understandably deeply upset the Prince of Wales, and therefore his wife at a time when she could so easily have been suffering from postnatal depression. In September Princess Grace of Monaco died after a car crash and this too distressed the Royal Family. Diana attended the funeral; it was her first solo royal duty abroad and she was visibly moved, wiping away tears throughout the Archbishop of Monaco, Monseigneur Charles Brandt's words: 'Her lovely eyes will not be seen again here, but through our tears we shall never forget her.' As Diana left the cathedral her moist cheeks glistened beneath her black veil. It was in happier times with Princess Grace that Diana had made her stunning début at the first formal evening engagement with Prince Charles just a few days after it had been announced that they would marry. The glamorous Princess Grace, former actress Grace Kelly (also a commoner who had married a Prince), was overshadowed by the then Lady Diana Spencer's revealing black dress.

Ahead of her lay the prospect of the gruelling seven-week Australian tour and a battle against royal tradition to take the baby Prince William with her. After the fullest, most demanding year of her life, and *still* only twenty-one, there came times when Diana began,to kick back at the people around her. 'Why should I have to go?' she would occasionally shout at her husband when she felt that she would prefer a quiet evening at home with her baby son. 'Because it's expected of you,' – words that would haunt her.

Finally, on Saturday 13 November 1982, Diana, not surprisingly, broke down. She was forced to attend an engagement that she would have to attend every year for the rest of her life. The Festival of Remembrance also meant inevitably contemplating death, thinking of the dying. Remembering the funeral of Princess Grace. 'They shall not grow old, as we that are left grow old . . .' On top of everything else this was a *Family* event, one of those rare occasions in the year when almost the entire Royal Family would be present. Still Diana did not feel that she was one of the Family.

Conscious that she was losing her own identity and in danger of having her personality crushed unnaturally to fit in with everyone's expectations of a Princess, Diana put her foot down and declared that she would not attend the Festival of Remembrance. Only after Prince Charles had left Kensington Palace for the Albert Hall did she feel pangs of guilt and realize the possible consequences of her outburst. Hastily she rushed out to her car,

16

with detective Alan Peters in hot pursuit, still buttoning up his coat, hoping that she would arrive unnoticed directly behind the royal party. Unfortunately the five-minute delay caused a public outcry. 'Nobody, but nobody, arrives after the Queen,' declared one outraged journalist. On American television, gossip columnist Nigel Dempster described Diana as 'a wilful and spoilt girl . . . a fiend and a little monster.' For the first time the Princess who could do no wrong began to topple on her pedestal. In characteristic fashion the Press had built Diana up so high that eventually the time had to come when they would knock her down.

Only Prince Charles realized that the Remembrance weekend was a crisis point for his wife, a time when she finally revealed an ever-increasing feeling of isolation. The signs had been there for some time. Her smile had become more tense and her eyes seemed harder. Apart from attending a Service of Remembrance for the men who gave their lives in the Falklands Conflict at which there was another mass turnout of royals, she declined all other invitations both public and private. Instead she tried to spend as much time as possible with Prince William, not simply because of the mother/baby relationship, but because he was the *one* thing that was hers, her greatest achievement in the eyes of the Family, and more importantly he was someone who needed her.

The temporary absence of the Princess of Wales from public life created an enormous gap in the lives of the media. Since the end of 1980 Diana had dominated the headlines and feature pages, and without her there was an empty space. When there is no news the simplest ploy is to invent some. So as the Princess worked hard to regain her figure through dancing, swimming and tennis, the anorexia rumours abounded, fuelled by the fact that her sister, Lady Sarah Spencer, had once suffered from the disease and had gone down to five and a half stone in weight. Diana's absence also gave journalists time to look through photographs of the previous year's engagements and make wild calculations as to the estimated cost of her wardrobe. 'The Princess spends over £2,000 a week on clothes and shoes,' penned one royal correspondent, grossly exaggerating the cost. 'Sometimes when I see the things that are written about me I don't want to go out and do my morning's engagement,' she has since said; the wild reports did nothing to boost her confidence during this time of depression.

For a change of environment Prince Charles insisted that she and the baby Prince join the rest of the Royal Family for the annual Balmoral holiday. No sooner had they flown to Scotland than the Press criticized the fact that Prince Charles had been the pilot on the trip. 'If the plane had crashed, two heirs to the throne could have been killed in one fell swoop,' they grumbled, 'Surely the Queen should have put her foot down?'

Hardly relishing the thought of two months on her best behaviour with her husband's family, the Princess became more and more depressed as each morning she awoke in the unspectacular castle to find that the heavens opened daily bringing torrential rain. Eventually it became too much and Diana decided to return to London with Prince William. Inevitably in media terms this meant 'a major argument with Princes Charles' and even 'reliable sources' wrongly revealed that Diana had swept out of Balmoral leaving her husband *and son* behind.

Back home, Diana became obsessive about doing everything right so that no criticism could be aimed at her. If the staff put her shoes back untidily in the cupboard, there was trouble. At times those closest to her described her behaviour as irrational and unpredictable, and Diana noticeably became more of a perfectionist than usual, pushing herself to extremes. Unwisely, she insisted on reading practically every article written about her, which is frustrating for a royal who is not allowed to answer back. The resulting crisis seemed inevitable.

What really happened between Charles and Diana on that November weekend in 1982 is their own personal secret. Speculatively, it was a time for bringing grievances, regrets and fears out into the open. Certainly it appeared to bring the couple much closer together, and it was a more relaxed and confident Diana who appeared in public two days later to greet Queen Beatrix of the Netherlands on a four-day state visit to Britain. The Prince and Princess waited over forty minutes in the bitter cold on Westminster Pier, during which time Prince Charles was extremely attentive towards his wife. For someone as concerned as Diana about putting a foot wrong in public and making a fool of herself, Queen Beatrix's arrival must have been a tonic to her, for twice the Dutch Queen nearly lost her balance walking up the gangplank, almost toppling into the River Thames and causing much controlled amusement among the waiting reception committee of British royalty. If a blue-blooded Queen could make an undignified entrance, a young Princess of non-royal birth need have no worries!

Over the next two and a half weeks Diana threw herself into her work, undertaking more engagements than any other member of the family, twice as many as Prince Charles, even more than Princess Anne. She toured her favourite radio station, Capital Radio, outshone the cast of the film *Gandhi* at a première, paid a two-day visit to North Wales, visited hospitals and playgroups, and on each occasion proved to be resounding success. Remarkably transformed into a working Princess, a succession of solo engagements proved to be the answer to Diana's problem. 'Her formal training inside the Royal Family is over and she has now thrown herself in at the deep end,' said the *Daily Express*, full of admiration. 'The Princess has travelled hundreds of miles, her performance is remarkable.' This was the kind of morale-boosting report that the Princess needed. Throughout her eight-hour days people shouted: 'We love you Diana.' Gone was the look of panic that once shadowed her face. With new found confidence she began to enjoy engagements. Now she felt needed for herself and who she was. Diana still had a long way to go, but the first stage of the battle was won.

∝ 2 ∝
New Blood

Diana giggled girlishly. 'I'd walk miles for a bacon sandwich,' she said, causing consternation among the health conscious who in the past have classed the Prince and Princess of Wales as paragons of virtue when it comes to healthy eating, in the light of Charles' public confession that he is 'practically vegetarian', preferring fish to meat. To courtiers of long standing it was another un-royal quote that was destined to be bandied around the tabloids; for ever more 'bacon' will feature in lists of Princess Diana's 'Favourite Things' – the kind of feature that eventually drives many members of the Royal Family to distraction. When the Princess Royal once revealed that she could be a truck driver, she found herself inundated with offers of vehicles to drive and, inevitably, the words 'Had Princess Anne not been born royal, she would like to be a truck driver,' were to haunt her in articles for years to come.

Still relatively new to royal engagements, compared with old hands like the Queen and the Princess Royal, Diana invariably speaks her mind without thinking. An endearing trait to members of the public; a fault as far as the royal household are concerned. In many ways the Princess has brought about a revolution in the art of being royal, and as time progresses she refuses to let her position swamp her personality. On numerous occasions Diana has kissed her husband publicly at polo matches, something the Queen never did when Prince Philip used to play. Likewise, although we are aware that Her Majesty likes lemon barley water, Dover sole, saddle of lamb, and Bendicks Bittermints, we know only because others have told us; such snippets of information have never been heard from the Queen's own lips.

The intrinsic unwritten rule that members of the Royal Family remain aloof and never reveal too much, is one to which Diana does not adhere. When President Jimmy Carter gave the Queen Mother a kiss on the mouth, Britain's favourite grandmother was horrified: 'He's the first person to kiss me on the lips since the King died,' she tutted. It would seem unthinkable for her to stoop and kiss children on a walkabout as the Princess of Wales has done so many times. After her first official engagement Diana announced loudly: 'What a long time to sit! I've got pins and needles in my bottom.' No other member of the Family could have got away with such informality at that time.

'Like a piece of unseasoned natural wood, she is ready to be fashioned into a stately and polished figurehead,' said *Woman's Own* magazine shortly after Charles and Diana's engagement in 1981, mindful that in the past those who marry royalty are quickly taught to conform. The genteel Miss Katherine Worsley, now Duchess of Kent, for example, has become so regal that she now epitomizes everything that is royal with a gracious dignity. Those who fail to conform quietly, as in the case of Princess Michael of Kent, always seem to remain outsiders. Diana's public success is that she is without precedent: she works hard to fit the royal mould, but her endearing human lapses have so far kept her with one foot in each camp. The very fact that she has breathed new life into the monarchy and in so doing has given the Royal Family greater popularity than probably at any other time this century saves her from condemnation.

On the surface many would say that Diana's youth and girlish charms have much to do with her own popularity, and yet it goes much deeper. Each new addition to the Royal Family this century has been firmly in vogue until they are superseded by the next. In 1934 the beautiful Greek Princess Marina captured the imagination of the British people with her style when she married the then Duke of Kent in Westminster Abbey. Her arrival into the country wearing a pillbox hat immediately started a new fashion, and within days the 'Marina Pillbox' was in the shops at two shillings and elevenpence; the soft blue that she wore was christened 'Marina Blue', just as Lady Elizabeth Bowes-Lyon a decade earlier had popularized 'Powder Blue', and yet the novelty soon

wore off once Marina was firmly established as the Duchess of
Kent. Were the interest in Diana of the same type, she would
certainly have been overshadowed by the vibrant personality and
titian locks of the Duchess of York in 1986. By then Diana had
completed a five-year reign as Princess of Wales, surely the public
needed someone new? Not so, it seemed. Although the Duchess
remains in the headlines, especially with her first pregancy in
1988, she finds it difficult to compete with Diana. Youth and
personality alone are obviously insufficient. Opinion polls in 1988
placed Diana in second place behind the Queen as the most
popular member of the Royal Family, no mean feat, especially in
the light of the Princess Royal's much admired status today. The
Marplan poll conducted amongst 1,500 adults at ninety-three
points throughout Britain posed identical questions to those
asked in 1981. The Queen was only one point ahead of the
Princess of Wales in the question, 'Which member of the Royal
Family would you most like to see?' Significantly there was a large
increase in the number of people, now 59 per cent, in favour of the
Royal Family speaking their minds unreservedly in public – a
major change since the advent of the unaffected Princess.
Unknowingly perhaps, the Princess has saved the Royal Family
from becoming an anachronism, bringing them forcibly into the
nineteen eighties. One thing is certain. With Diana came
noticeable changes.

In the words of *The Times*, Diana had the effect of 'badly needed
fresh air blowing through the stuffy court'. In a world dominated
by archaic tradition and strict protocol, many found it refreshing
to see a future Queen of England who tentatively chose not to be
swamped by it. Although uncertain of herself at first, it says
something about Diana's character that she has not been totally
swallowed up by royal convention. She could in theory have
remained in the shadow of the Prince of Wales, quietly fulfilling
only the necessary duties as his wife. That she has ultimately
allowed her own personality to influence life at court can only
have been to the good. A member of her staff admits that Diana
appears 'sweet and shy' in public, but is 'strong-willed and
stubborn' in private, and a visit to either Highgrove or Kensington Palace leaves you in no doubt as to who is in control.

Kensington Palace has jokingly been referred to as the Windsor

Council House, as it houses so many of the family. Princess Margaret and her family were the longest established residents, before being joined by Prince and Princess Michael of Kent, the Duke and Duchess of Gloucester, and the Prince and Princess of Wales and their respective offspring. Although Kensington Palace is Princess Margaret's main residence, the others all have country houses that they call 'home', using the Palace as an office and London apartment. In this most exclusive apartment block, Charles and Diana occupy apartments 8 and 9 which they see only as a base for their working lives. Although the Palace upkeep is officially in the hands of the Department of the Environment, as soon as the couple took up residence in 1981 Diana employed the South African designer, Dudley Poplack, to decorate the rooms to her taste, greatly influenced by her mother, Mrs Shand-Kydd who was conveniently married to a wallpaper heir.

Diana chose her favourite shades of pastels and beiges while much of the dark woodwork, especially banisters, received a coat of white paint, giving a warm but modern touch to their rooms in this seventeenth-century Wren building. Although the main sitting-room is dominated by many valuable pieces of furniture from the royal collection, it is unlike that of any other royal residence because of its quite obvious modern touches. The Queen's apartments at Buckingham Palace, the private rooms at Windsor, Sandringham and Balmoral, all have a very distinctive chintzy, homely feel. Once spectacular carpets are now slightly threadbare with the years, chairs are well used, and a slightly jaded air pervades. Only state rooms retain their former glory and elegance. Princess Margaret's apartment at Kensington Palace, number 1A Clock Court, has an instant feel of warmth and taste. The ground floor drawing-room is decorated in an eighteenth-century style with pale grey curtains and kingfisher blue walls, the large doors displaying intricate cornicing. Yet, the rooms influenced by the Princess of Wales in her own homes have a very distinctive twentieth-century feel: the Wales' drawing-room at Kensington Palace has soft antique gold walls to set off the gilt mirrors, picture frames, and more importantly a vast medieval tapestry that dominates an entire wall. Sofas are piled with modern cushions in beige, yellow and green to complement the colours in the tapestry. On the mantelpiece is a colourful china cockerel, something Diana specifically placed on her wedding list, along with other china birds, and on either side of the fireplace stand two modern round tables draped with floor length cloths, making it look for all the world like any Sloane Ranger room featured in *House and Garden* magazine. A feature in most royal houses is a large selection of family photographs and Charles' and Diana's highly polished Broadwood grand piano is adorned by a large collection of framed pictures: a delightful portrait of the Queen Mother in Venice; Prince Charles and Prince Andrew with their favourite grandmother; a Spencer/Shand-Kydd photograph of Diana's mother with her husband and three non-royal children. All photographs are characteristically formal, many with the Prince of Wales' crest surmounting the frame. Inevitably there are photographs of Princes William and Harry, as in Diana's own study, which again is highly individual.

At Kensington Palace Diana's light, airy study looks out onto the gardens. The modern blue curtains have been teamed with an exclusive wallpaper pattern featuring a design that looks uncannily like the Prince of Wales feathers and that seems to dominate the apartment, having even been woven into some of the carpets. Quite unlike the Queen's study at Buckingham Palace, Diana's is bright and modern, with comforting touches from her former life: a small trunk with 'D. Spencer' in large black letters on the side stands permanently on the window sill as a reminder of school days, a disc of stained glass with the letter 'D' hangs on one of the windows; and on the desk is a basket frog, a creature that the Princess has a fondness for. Those close to her reveal that Diana can do an expert imitation of Kermit the Frog's voice, and it is no coincidence that the mascot on her car is one of her favourite amphibians. Characteristically again, there often seem to be as many piles of material samples and swatches dotted around as there are notes about future engagements.

Highgrove House, the Wales' real home for the time being, was purchased by Prince Charles in 1980 for £800,000, quite obviously with marriage in mind. Until moving to Highgrove, Diana's home had been a first-floor, three-bedroomed flat in South Kensington. At £100,000 it was out of reach of most nineteen-year-old girls, but Diana had inherited some money and had three flatmates to help out with the bills. The Coleherne Court building is unimposing from the outside and has a somewhat clinical feel inside. The corridors and staircases leading to the flats are unwelcoming, and the interiors themselves have a relatively cold and gloomy feel, many have ancient wooden panelling. Flat number 60 on the corner of Block H, must now seem a million miles from Highgrove House, set in 347 acres of Cotswold countryside. Previously Prince Charles had leased Chevening House, a 100-room mansion near Sevenoaks in Kent. It was an uninspiring building which he seldom visited and of which he gave up the tenure on purchasing Highgrove. When compared with the Chevening mansion Highgrove is a medium-sized family home. There are nine main bedrooms, six bathrooms and a nursery wing, four reception rooms, a staff block and stables. The garden covers around seven acres, the rest of the adjoining land being made up of arable crops and a diary unit, so that if necessary the Wales could be self-sufficient.

Diana was not impressed when she first saw their new home, some ninety miles away from her beloved London. Practically the entire house, however, needed redecorating which gave the Princess an opportunity to make it a home indelibly her own. It would have been much harder for her to settle in had she been faced with a house fully furnished in a predetermined style. Again the Princess opted for pastel shades throughout, resulting in an elegant country home. The second-floor nursery at Highgrove, and the nursery suite above their own bedroom at Kensington Palace, are in a very marked contrast to those that both Diana and Charles occupied as children. Blue for boys has been consciously avoided and neutral, restful colours have been adopted with plump sofas in cream and pink and a pine table and chairs in close proximity to a small kitchen so that the Princes can both eat and play in the nursery. There are also scaled down tables and chairs for the boys to sit at and draw, paint, and do jigsaws, and large areas of cream carpet with a pattern of strawberries in geometric squares on which toys can be spread. Completely modern in design and decoration the nursery, at Kensington Palace for example, could easily be a modern attic at first glance, free from any grandeur, giving no hint of royal ownership. Perhaps this is deliberate on Diana's part. She cannot shield her children totally from their future, and she cannot keep them from royal duty as sons of the heir to the throne, but at all costs Diana attempts to maintain as normal and as carefree a life as possible for them. The pressures will come all too soon.

Within the first year the new Princess of Wales, with the help of Dudley Poplack, was able to establish two homes in her own taste, the first real security that she had ever known, certainly the first since earliest childhood. Amid the Laura Ashley prints in Wild Cherry with plum ruffles, the General Trading Company vases, the Liberty fabrics, Diana had a real home of her own, a far cry from Prince Charles' bachelor tastes and the style of Chevening. Having quietly watched the running of her own mother's households and the organizational skills of her step-mother Raine at Althorp, these new royal households are most certainly run along Spencer rather than Windsor lines.

A new broom sweeps clean and it came as something of a shock to many of Prince Charles' staff to find someone else taking control of him and attempting discreetly to change many of the systems that had worked so well for years. Once master in his own house, it is now a firmly established fact that Diana controls the household and that Prince Charles is in charge of 'external affairs', a regime that works well. The Prince is a keen gardener and has greatly enjoyed designing and establishing the garden at Highgrove, from formal vegetable plots to a stretch of wild flowers. In recent years he has actively involved himself in architecture and design, having been notoriously critical of many post-war buildings, and has practised what he has preached. The Prince has completely redesigned the frontage of Highgrove, resulting in an elegant façade complete with columns, that completely enhances the somewhat plain Georgian house that was the original building. It is a project that he has enjoyed undertaking and an area that Diana leaves totally in his control. In return he would not dream of choosing the wallpaper for their bedroom, or a bathroom carpet.

One 'home' that Charles and Diana visit less frequently is their small holiday bungalow named Tamarisk, situated on the main Scilly Isle – St Mary's. The Scilly Isles are part of the Prince of Wales' Duchy of Cornwall, and before his marriage the Prince enjoyed the bleak ruggedness of his island retreat where security was almost unnecessary and he could go for long hikes unhampered by onlookers. Diana is not quite so enthusiastic about the wild surroundings and the remoteness of this small modern building from which her husband once derived such pleasure.

Noticeably, many of the Prince's former staff have resigned since the time of his marriage. Some lay the blame at Diana's door and insist that she deliberately ousted the men who had too much control over her husband, and who influenced his every day life. For her such accusations are obviously distressing, but secretly she is delighted to employ new staff who have only ever worked for them as a couple. People who cannot mutter 'in the old days, we used to . . .'

Diana is essentially a nest-builder. Her home and immediate members of the family take priority over everything else in her life. Any cuckoo in the nest has to be quickly ejected and the status quo restored. It is not insignificant that some thirty members of the Wales' staff have left the household in the last seven years. Not always because they have failed to see eye to eye with the Princess, and never have they been sacked amid a blazing row as has been suggested. 'I do *not* sack my staff,' said Diana angrily at a Press call after reports had appeared stating that she personally fired a number of her staff. It is true to say, however, that those whose faces have not fitted have been frozen out until they eventually felt obliged to resign as if it had been their own decision. Bodyguards were the first to go – three in the first year – until the Princess found someone with whom she could feel comfortable, someone who did not treat her like a priceless object, but as a human being. Detectives who have been assigned to protect other members of the Royal Family have learned to treat them with reverence, to speak when spoken to and concentrate on the job in hand. Diana prefers a more personal relationship, addressing her staff by their Christian names, and likes people with a sense of humour. When she does find someone on her wavelength, the working relationship is a happy one and she commands intense loyalty. With new staff Diana can maintain a good relationship, but those that had been employed by Prince Charles for many years before his marriage were less ready to accept the non-royal approach.

One of the first to leave was Oliver Everett, Diana's first Private Secretary, who had been Prince Charles' Assistant Private

Secretary for four years. Acting as an adviser to the raw Princess would to an outsider seem to be a most enjoyable challenge, but Everett found Diana's inexperience difficult to cope with after the Prince's hardened professionalism. After over twenty years of royal engagements Prince Charles obviously knows his job backwards, but the uncertain Princess often changed her mind at the last moment causing endless headaches for the person co-ordinating royal affairs. With the Princess came endless sacksful of mail from around the world which all had to be replied to, and again it was up to her Private Secretary to take control. The mounds of sometimes trivial and often ingratiating mail resulted in an unenviably increased workload with no extra income. Eventually Everett, a former diplomat, sought a quieter job, which he found amid the peace of the Royal Archives as the Queen's Deputy Librarian, where he is still employed today.

On the domestic front, Kensington Palace butler Alan Fisher resigned officially through boredom. 'There simply wasn't enough for me to do,' he says. Those who work for the Prince and Princess at the Palace disagree. There is always plenty to do in any royal household but Fisher was, it seems, disappointed that being butler to the world's most glamorous duo was in fact anything but glamorous from the inside. Alan Fisher had previously been employed by the Duke and Duchess of Windsor in their days of stylish entertaining, followed by a period as manservant to 'the old groaner' Bing Crosby. Disappointed when working for royalty failed to live up to expectations, Fisher returned to the bright lights of the United States. It is said that the Princess was not saddened by Fisher's departure.

Many who join the royal household are disillusioned. The income is low, the work is demanding, the hours are often long and unsociable. Employees tend to fall into two categories: those who quickly realize that they could be earning more in a domestic capacity at any nearby hotel, and those who remain for years through job satisfaction and unswerving loyalty to their employers. For many of the latter it is a labour of love, spurred on by the aura of royalty. It was when employees such as this began to resign that questions were asked and eyebrows raised.

The most controversial departure was that of Prince Charles' Private Secretary, Edward Adeane in 1984. The Adeanes have had a long and illustrious reign in royal service. The late Michael Adeane, Edward's father, had been Private Secretary to Her Majesty the Queen and Assistant Private Secretary to King George VI, and his grandfather Lord Stanfordham in turn had been Assistant Private Secretary to Queen Victoria before being appointed Private Secretary to King George V. Edward Adeane's resignation ended more than a century's royal employment for his family.

For the Prince of Wales the departure was a serious and much lamented loss. Adeane, still only forty-five, returned to his former career in law, preferring to inhabit a traditional serious world. Edward Adeane has been called a 'courtier of the old style'. No doubt using his own father and grandfather as role models, he was the stereotyped image of a royal aide. Quiet, austere, totally discreet, efficient and precise in his work, he found the change in Prince Charles from mature bachelor to a less formal family man difficult to accept. Where work once took priority, the Prince now gave more time to his wife and any changes that she wished to make to her schedule affected the Prince and therefore Edward Adeane. Like Oliver Everett, Adeane found unpredictability an anathema. After the birth of Prince Harry in 1984 the constant preoccupation with children was part of an alien world to this confirmed bachelor. Diana and Adeane had nothing in common; he found her informality and youth created a gulf between them, and in turn the Princess found her husband's right-hand man 'stuffy'. Although the blame for Adeane's departure, like so many things, has been laid at Diana's door it was as much the changes in Prince Charles that tipped the balance. In recent years the Prince has had his social conscience pricked, has tried to get close to nature, better able to 'understand the ordinary people' and break out of the closeted world traditionally associated with the heir to the throne. No longer could his Private Secretary of the old school identify with him and they began to grow apart.

An important figure in any royal household is the Comptroller. Charles and Diana's first, Lieutenant Colonel Philip Creasy was pushed out because he was 'too formal, too much of a military man'; the household accountant, Michael Colbourne, who played an equally important role, relinquished his post in 1985 officially because he 'wanted a change of scene' but inwardly because he disliked the unsettled atmosphere amongst the Wales' household.

Disenchantment appears to have been the key factor in the departure of such a large number of employees. Perhaps in private the royal duo fail to live up to expectations. Someone who was not impressed by the new Princess of Wales was Prince Charles' valet, Stephen Barry. The changes in the Prince's marital status affected Barry more than any other member of staff because for so many years he had been as much adviser and confidante to the heir to the throne as a valet. Having first become a member of the Buckingham Palace household as a footman in 1967, Barry was appointed valet to Prince Charles in 1970, and for a decade became as close to the Prince as his own family. Unlike most royal valets, Barry often accompanied the Prince on royal engagements fulfilling the duties of an equerry. He took charge of certain financial arrangements, dealt with the entire official and off-duty wardrobe (the Prince has more than one hundred uniforms that have to be kept in order), and when Charles first purchased Highgrove House Barry helped with the practical arrangements, often cooked for the Prince and dined alone with him.

In such a privileged position, Stephen Barry felt in many ways superior to Diana. He had, after all, dealt with the more intimate side of the Prince's life for so long, from laying out clean underclothes in the mornings, to running the bath, often even selecting which shirt and tie would be worn at a particular function. In some respects Barry took on the duties of a wife: he gave support to the Prince in times of distress, he was the first person who Prince Charles saw when he woke up in the morning, and frequently the last to say goodnight to him before he went to bed. He became the person on whom Prince Charles knew that he could rely. When Diana came on the scene there were very obvious changes to be made. No longer was Barry called upon to wake the Prince up in the morning; gone were the days when he selected what the Prince would wear, and even more distressing for the once indispensable valet, Diana now helped choose her husband's clothes. She detested the staid and conservative style that Charles had long adopted, the 'royal' style that Stephen Barry encouraged. In many respects Prince Charles dressed like his father, looking much older than necessary. One immediately apparent change that Diana brought about was to smarten her husband up in a more modern style. Coloured shirts replaced the once popular crisp white ones, ties became modern in width and design, trousers and suits became more tailored with far less material than the baggy ageing suits that he had worn before. Even shoes became a bone of contention and the Prince's classic hand-made leather Bond Street shoes were phased out on the introduction of Gucci slip-ons and ready-to-wear Country House shoes from Paul Wildsmith in Jermyn Street. Some of Prince Charles' shoes had cost over £450 to make while the ready-mades that the Princess encouraged cost under £150. The Prince wore them not only to keep his wife happy, but also in the name of economy. Stephen Barry raised his eyes in horror.

Barry was one of the breed of staff who enjoyed their royal lifestyle, not always because of the work involved but the benefits that it brought to his private life. To be able to give your address as 'Buckingham Palace' in a club or shop would give anyone a feeling of grandeur. On my first visit to the Palace, the taxi driver's face was a picture when I gave him my destination! One perk of being a part of the royal household is that seats are always kept free at West End theatres, cinemas and the opera just in case a member of the Royal Family decides to go unexpectedly. If not used, members of the respective households can take advantage of the seats if they have no other duties. Stephen Barry frequently entertained guests of his own in the royal box at the ballet or opera at Covent Garden. With the arrival of the Princess of Wales in 1981 came the beginning of the end for Stephen Barry's self-induced lifestyle. His duties became more and more mundane, and gone were the days when he could accompany the Prince on a private outing for the day. From friend and confidante he was reduced to his former level of valet, and the fall from favour was not appreciated.

Throughout royal circles it was common knowledge that Stephen Barry was a homosexual. This did not raise a single eyebrow in the household. At the time Prince Charles had six gay members of staff, the Queen ten times that number amid her large household. At one time the Queen Mother had thirty gay members of staff and seemed to relish their company. When she returned to Clarence House one day to find two footmen trying on one of her tiaras, it is said that she merely laughed, and the much told story of Her Majesty shouting: 'Is there any old queen down there who can bring an old Queen up here a gin and tonic?' is no myth. When the Queen's bodyguard, Michael Trestrail, was forced to resign because of the threat of blackmail regarding his homosexuality, the Queen was extremely sad that he had to leave and tried to prevent the story from becoming common knowledge. When a footman was sacked by the Master of the Household after a failed suicide attempt resulting from a broken gay love affair, Her Majesty asked that he 'be given another chance'. As long as their gay members of staff are discreet royalty almost prefer employing them, not least because family life and children do not predominate, enabling them to work unsociable hours.

The arrival of AIDS has not changed the Royal Family's open acceptance of homosexuality, but for the sake of her children Diana seems far more concerned now with the sexuality of her household. 'The Princess always wants to know whether or not someone is gay,' says a member of her staff. When Stephen Barry's private life became less discreet after an incident in a gay club dominated the gossip columns, Diana was not happy for him to be in close proximity to the Prince. Again, there was no great argument – he simply felt obliged to go, although secretly Prince Charles was saddened by his valet's departure. He may not have approved of Stephen Barry's promiscuity, but Prince Charles appreciated familiarity. In a world that is dominated by strangers, with only close members of family in whom to confide, the Prince appreciates stability in his own home. Stephen Barry obviously knew the Prince's ways, likes and dislikes, even better than Diana. When he left after twelve years' service (the Prince was only twenty-two when his valet was appointed) it must have been difficult for the Prince to start from scratch with a member of staff on such an intimate level; but Diana was happy.

On leaving London Stephen Barry went to America where he made over a million dollars through his memoirs *Royal Service* and *Royal Secrets*, banned in the United Kingdom under the Official Secrets Act. The harmless, comparatively unrevealing books, were actually totally in praise of Charles and Diana and attempted to quash any rumours that he had left under a cloud. Although the income from these books helped Barry maintain a royal lifestyle, he contracted AIDS in the United States and died in October 1986 at the age of thirty-seven in a clinic just a short distance from Buckingham Palace where his service had begun. The sensitive Prince confessed that he felt remorse over his former valet's death. Perhaps if he had remained in the royal household he would not have caught the killer disease in America. Perhaps it is coincidental, but since Barry's death, both Charles and Diana have taken a much closer interest in AIDS and on 9 April 1987, the Princess opened Britain's first purpose-built ward for AIDS sufferers, the Broderip Ward at the Middlesex Hospital in London. In a year dominated by public information campaigns about the disease, Diana's visit to the hospital was said to have dispelled more myths about the transmission of the disease than any amount of Government advertising. She did not wear gloves on that day deliberately so that she could shake hands with sufferers in a very public attempt to end misconceptions. As a member of the Royal Family the future Queen of England can be confident that she will not catch the disease through contaminated blood but nevertheless on a semi-private visit to Spain that same month, the Prince and Princess had, for the first time, a special AIDS prevention kit in their luggage. Costing £140 each, the packs contained blood plasma, sterile syringes and needles and medical equipment that would, if necessary have kept them alive without a blood transfusion until they could have been flown back to London. Such kits are now standard for all royal travellers, so that in the event of an accident members of the Royal Family would not have to be admitted into a hospital in a country where levels of hygiene and blood screening might be below standard. Whenever the subject is raised, Stephen Barry must inevitably come into Charles' and Diana's minds. It has been said that by the end of the century no family in Britain will not in some way have been touched by the AIDS virus; we will all know someone who has been a victim. When the statement was made, however, few would have suspected that the Royal Family would have experienced this sooner than most.

Until she found her feet as a Princess and mistress of the house, Diana found dealing with staff difficult. Having staff – all royals hate the word 'servant' – was nothing new to her, the houses in which she had lived as a child and teenager had had cooks and housekeepers, but someone else had always been in control. The main bone of contention among staff as a whole seems to be overall disorganization or general discontentment. Their first cook, Miss Roseanna Lloyd, left within the first couple of months of employment because the Wales did not entertain in the lavish style that she had expected. Constantly watching her weight, Diana requested mainly salads and omelettes, never using Miss Lloyd's capabilities to the full.

Many of Diana's maids and dressers left in succession because of the constant pressure imposed upon them of looking after the country's greatest leader of fashion. Other staff left when they were forbidden to bring their girlfriends or boyfriends back to their rooms at Kensington Palace for reasons of security. Cleaner Sheila Tilly was the first of several domestic staff to leave because of 'superiors with power complexes', and above stairs a number of senior staff quit after only a few months. Diana's equerry, Lieutenant Commander Peter Eberle, returned to the Navy; Prince Charles' equerry, Major John Winter, went back to the Parachute Regiment, and the Princess' Assistant Private Secretary, Francis Cornish, left to join the Foreign Office, all within the space of a few months.

After Stephen Barry's, the most publicized departure was that of the once popular nanny to Princes William and Harry, Barbara Barnes, who left when her methods of training failed to comply with what the Prince and Princess wanted for their sons. Her liberal approach to discipline and informal style had not curbed the defiant and difficult streak in Prince William. Prince Charles felt that Miss Barnes, totally devoted to the Princes, let them have their own way too often. She finally incurred her employers' wrath when she was seen at a party holidaying with Lord Glenconner in the Caribbean. Even in the 1980s there is a very definite pecking order and no member of staff should be seen to be getting ideas above their station. Her departure from the nursery happened swiftly in January 1987. A few months later a more mature nanny, Olga Powell, was seen admonishing a sullen Prince William in public on the polo field at Windsor for bad behaviour in an obvious return to a stricter, more traditional approach.

For the many staff who have left Kensington Palace or Highgrove House under a cloud, there are just as many who have remained and have proved loyal and efficient. As the new mistress

Diana inevitably took time to find her feet and unavoidably made mistakes not only in her choice of staff but on occasions in her handling of them. The title 'Princess' is not automatic grounds for respect. More experienced staff at times resented this twenty-year-old girl's intrusion; those who had previously worked for the Queen and the Prince of Wales were unimpressed by Diana's meteoric rise to fame and megastardom and objected to taking orders from her. There were those, now ex-members of staff, who would have been happy to see her fall flat on her face. For the Princess it created a situation that she found difficult to handle; she knew that she could not command instant loyalty and it has taken several years to finally gather together a united household.

At Kensington Palace and Highgrove there is now comparative domestic bliss, with an efficient team of staff that has Diana's approval. 'I won't deny that in a subtle way she's weeded out quite a few hangers-on that she found around her husband and family,' revealed Diana's forthright brother, Viscount Althorp, in a recent interview: butler Alan Fisher has been replaced by the genteel Harold Brown, who happily carries in breakfast trays or a light luncheon snack when required, seemingly without missing helping out at large banquets. To compensate for his employers' relatively quiet lifestyle Mr Brown always has the opportunity to work for other people on a casual basis when not required for duty, and may at times be called in to assist other members of the Royal Family with their entertaining. The dining-room at Highgrove is small and rarely do the Prince and Princess ever entertain more than six to eight guests. The more formal dining-room at Kensington Palace with plain mustard coloured walls and burgundy curtains is just as likely to be used as a workroom, because of the large table, than for eating.

Those who work for and with the Princess today have nothing but admiration and praise for their employer. 'She is much more together these days,' says one member of staff, 'and now has experience, which was the essential ingredient that she lacked at the start. No amount of advice can take the place of experience, and she has had to find her own way, but she's getting there.' Those who have helped Diana along the way when she was new and green, have in turn benefited from her friendship. There is more laughter on the Princess' engagements than with any other member of the Royal Family, and those members of staff who leave through illness or retire due to age or family commitments continue to receive letters, cards and occasional visits from the Prince and Princess.

The circle of royal intimates is restricted to such a degree that occasionally a close and well trusted member of staff will receive friendship. In the Queen's case this happens rarely, only 'Mrs' Margaret MacDonald – known affectionately as 'Bobo' – has really become a friend. Now in her eighties and living in a grace-and-favour apartment at Windsor, 'Bobo' first joined the Royal Household when the Queen was a child and continued in service as Her Majesty's dresser and closest confidante, even though Miss MacDonald (given the courtesy title of 'Mrs') assumed an air of grandeur that many of her colleagues despised. Some feared the wrath of 'Bobo' more than that of the monarch. At Highgrove, Charles and Diana had great affection for Paddy and Nesta Whiteland who worked as steward and housekeeper. The couple lived and worked on the estate before Prince Charles purchased the property, and were kept on when he married, even though Paddy had already turned sixty-seven. In a very short time a great bond was built up between the newly married couple and their cheerful housekeeper. When Nesta developed cancer and had to leave because of it, Charles and Diana were frequent visitors. Occasionally they would arrange for transport to bring Nesta to Highgrove to see the young Princes, and when she died at the end of 1986 it was Diana who held Paddy's arm throughout the funeral. Their wreath read 'In grateful and affectionate memory – Charles and Diana'. 'There could be no greater tribute to my wife than to have the future Queen of England at her funeral,' said Mr Whiteland afterwards. Having interrupted the annual summer holiday at Balmoral to attend the funeral, Diana insisted that Paddy accompany her back to Scotland. Although the public assumed that she was sunbathing or playing with the children that holiday, only those present saw how the Princess helped Mr Whiteland through this period of grief. At twenty-five Diana brought comfort to the seventy-two-year-old man, not something that every young girl could do, but it proved her worth as Patron of Help the Aged. It was also a new departure for a member of the Royal Family to take a member of staff under their wing at this most quintessential family holiday, and thus, a display of Diana's new found confidence. Five years earlier she dreaded the Balmoral holiday and felt a newcomer among the regal houseparty. She longed to return to Highgrove to her own home where she could be in control and not dominated by the traditions of her mother-in-law. Mr Whiteland made her feel needed and gave her a purpose, so much so that she felt enough in control to take the situation into her own hands, subconsciously accepting that Balmoral Castle will one day be another of her homes anyway.

When Diana first joined the Royal Family she found being the Queen's guest at Balmoral difficult to cope with. Eventually realizing that this was another royal ritual that she could not avoid, Diana has made the holiday bearable by creating a home of her own on the Balmoral Estate. When walking with the Prince they used to pass a dilapidated cottage, a single storey fishing lodge on the River Dee called Delnadamph Lodge. It had no electricity or running water and needed to be completely rebuilt and redecorated. Work began in the autumn of 1987 and provided the ideal project to amuse the Princess during her stay. The end result means that Charles and Diana can be close to the Castle, so keeping the Queen and the Family happy, but have complete privacy. The restoration of a crumbling building also appealed to the Prince's passion for architectural matters and maintaining British heritage. Although Balmoral Castle is relatively large with 180 windows, 67 fireplaces and a 100-foot-high tower, accommodation is surprisingly limited with only five guest rooms that have their own sitting-room and bathroom. The Queen Mother has long used Birkhall on the edge of the Balmoral Estate, on the walkers' route to the summit of Lochnagar (which inspired Prince Charles to write a book, *The Old Man of Lochnagar*, 1983) so no objections were raised to Diana's suggestion about a house of their own. Only she knows that even if Balmoral Castle had 200 guest rooms, she would *still* prefer a home of her own.

Paddy Whiteland still works as a caretaker at Highgrove, a job he has for as long as he wants it. He is by far the oldest person that the Prince and Princess employ; if gathered together the staff collectively appear much younger than in previous times and in other royal households. Diana feels more comfortable with people of her own age group if they are fulfilling an official capacity, and has encouraged the Prince to steer clear of the 'old school' of courtier whom she finds intimidating yet who are so favoured by the Queen. The formidable bachelor Edward Adeane has been substituted by Sir John Riddell as Prince Charles' Private Secretary, dealing with the Princess' work as well. The Northumbrian Sir John has three young children of his own which gave him an immediate common ground with the Princess. Diana's equerry is now the jovial Lieutenant-Commander Richard Aylard, who accompanies the Princess on official engagements along with the equally jolly lady-in-waiting Anne Beckwith-Smith, nicknamed 'Tubby' by Diana. Ten years older than Diana, she too is a former pupil of West Heath School and the member of staff closest to the Princess, having been lady-in-waiting since 1981. Although this position is usually unpaid, probably because it is invariably only undertaken by very close friends from the royal circle so that a lady-in-waiting is regarded as a companion rather than a member of staff, Miss Beckwith-Smith does in fact receive a salary because she works full-time for the Princess, acting as much as a personal secretary as a supporter on official engagments. The Princess has four other ladies-in-waiting, Mrs George West, Viscountess Hampden, Mrs Max Pike, and Miss Alexandra Loyd. They receive nothing more than their expenses for the duties that they undertake. They work one at a time and arrange a rota between themselves under the watchful eye of Anne Beckwith-Smith to ensure that the Princess always has someone in attendance. Because the very nature of the job requires such close personal involvement with the Princess all ladies-in-waiting are now carefully handpicked by Diana herself. This is not an area in which mistakes can be made. Of ladies-in-waiting, the Princess Royal has said, 'they must be good at chatting to people and making them feel comfortable because that helps me really. It's no good at all if you get somebody turning up in the morning looking like death, and furious and ratty about life and uncommunicative and when they go out on a trip they're standing in a corner looking glum and bored. That's no help to anyone.' Establishing a team of ladies with whom she feels at ease has proved to be an enormous advantage to the Princess of

Wales; with equerry Richard Aylard and a friendly lady-in-waiting, she never now feels that she is attending an engagement alone.

Having also become Queen of Style, two of Diana's most important employees are her dressers Evelyn Dagley and Fay Marshalsea. As the Princess often has three changes of clothes a day, including accessories, keeping the wardrobe in order, planning and packing it up for foreign tours, and seeing that all is laundered and pressed is a full-time job in itself. With these two young ladies permanently in charge of her clothes Diana has added confidence that she will always look good.

The whole style of the Wales' staff has altered in a comparatively short time: in the stables at Highgrove Marion Cox, still in her twenties, is employed as a groom; it comes as a surprise to many to see that the chef is the equally youthful Richard Brooks. Had Princes Charles been totally in control, his household would still consist of faithful old retainers and would take the form of a scaled-down version of his mother's staff. That such a major change in direction has occurred can be due only to Diana. In the space of a few years she has introduced informality into her household, a foretaste certainly of the direction she will take when the Prince of Wales eventually succeeds to the throne. Who can say what will happen to Buckingham Palace and Windsor Castle during the reign of King Charles III, but it will be a far cry from the style of its present incumbent. However much Charles attempts to cling on to the past, his wife will ensure that he keeps at least one foot in the present.

There are those who pour scorn on the Diana revolution, who reject the changes that she has made in Prince Charles, and the innovations she has introduced into the heart of the Royal Family. The more optimistic feel, however, that this young girl with impeccable ancestry has ensured the continuation of the monarchy but with a new image. Genealogically her blood is as royal as many a prince and princess of the past, who decades later now appear the very personification of royalty. It has been pointed out that when Prince William finally inherits the crown he will be the most British sovereign since James I in 1566, thanks to Diana's aristocratic lineage, English, Scottish and Irish blood. Setting trivia aside, it is Diana's character that is changing the shape of the royal mould. Not drilled for royal duty from an early age like her husband, Diana is still able to let her hair down, and introduce a more humanized approach to the monarchy.

In a life that is organized at least six months in advance, a job that can keep husband and wife at opposite ends of the country for days on end, it would be easy to lose touch with reality. On some public engagements the Queen can walk around an exhibition and appear impassively distant; although alert Her Majesty can have a dream-like quality. With Diana there is an earthy straightforwardness. At a briefing in America before a fact-finding mission on architecture, the Princess had other priorities. 'What will my hubby be doing then?' she asked, determined to know not only what was expected of her, but where the Prince would be at the same time. It was the reaction, not of a Princess, but of a working wife.

The effect of Diana on the Royal Family was shown in a six country poll, when people from Australia, Japan, South Africa, Spain, West Germany and the United States were asked to name their top ten Britons. The Princess held first place in every country, except America where she came second to the Prime Minister, Mrs Thatcher's support for the US bombing of Libya having put her at the top. It was the first time that a member of the Royal Family had taken top position in five countries, including Australia where Republicanism is rife. This new popularity and international appeal must have been a comfort to the Queen, who monitors public opinion very closely. If one member of the family is getting too much adverse publicity, Her Majesty makes certain that they know of her displeasure. Not by personal approaches, but through the subtle intervention of her Private Secretary who makes the Queen's feelings known. Although Diana will be a great contrast to Elizabeth when she becomes Queen, she has at least ensured the survival of the next generation of the House of Windsor.

Looking back it seems hard to imagine that in 1980 we had no Princess of Wales. In a short space of time, the former Lady Diana Spencer has firmly established herself as a leading member of the Royal Family. 'All by herself she has given the monarchy new magic and brought it much closer to the people,' said the Managing Director of Debrett's on the occasion of Diana's

twenty-third birthday – praise indeed from someone so passion-
ately concerned with tradition and protocol. 'It's been difficult,
but I am learning to cope,' revealed Diana privately to an
Australian journalist at a Press reception, who then syndicated
the Princess' words around the world . . .

3

The Throne Rangers

On Tuesday 24 February 1981, some five months before her marriage, Lady Diana Spencer was regarded as being royal in everything but title. At precisely 11 a.m. three policemen took up their positions outside Coleherne Court, and the soon-to-be dismissed detective Paul Officer acted as a personal bodyguard twenty-four hours a day. For Diana, that precise moment signified the eternal loss of privacy, the relinquishment of her independence.

As she left the South Kensington apartment for the final time, destined for the protection of Clarence House and her first taste of royal life at Buckingham Palace, it was no cursory parting line when she pleaded with her flatmate Virginia Pitman, 'For God's sake ring me up, I'm going to need you.' Closeted in a new world she craved the company of friends in the outside world and faced the dilemma that confronts all members of the Royal Family – just how do you make *new* friends? From the first moment of her entanglement with the Prince of Wales, Diana became increasingly aware of this problem. Officially she met people once, and only once. Any members of staff to whom she felt that she could chat without airs and graces were not considered as suitable friends for a Princess, and the age-old problem that has always faced anyone royal is just who can you *really* trust? 'It's absolutely maddening seeing things written about me without my having said anything', Diana confided in a neighbour as early as August 1980; the neighbour then sold the story and the conversation became a full-page news article. Because even the most genuine individual might eventually be tempted to reveal stories to the Press, the Princess has to remain continually on her guard.

It takes any member of the Royal Family a long time to make friends. *You* cannot choose to be close to them, *they* learn to confide in you. Ultimately they have to decide who holds the promise of true friendship, and who is interested in them only because of who they are so that they can boast royal connections. Having been free to talk to anyone for the first twenty years of her life, it was a difficult lesson for Diana to learn. Inevitably royal circles become very small and closeted. Close courtiers of the Queen and their families are introduced to other members of the Royal Family, and eventually it becomes a very insular, single-class world. Unfortunately for Diana, she had little in common with the 'horsey' set that made up her husband's circle. Horses are the Royal Family's overriding passion, be it steeplechasing, racing, three-day eventing, polo matches, gymkhanas or carriage driving, a true blue-blooded royal is keen to participate, and if unable to do so is happy to spectate. Horsey events bored Diana rigid, and she was frightened of riding herself. Thrown from her horse, Romany, at the age of ten, Diana admitted that she 'lost her nerve'. Until then she had not disliked the animals and had a Shetland pony called Soufflé, but she had never really enjoyed riding and the fall provided an excellent excuse. After the accident, which left her momentarily unconscious, she was examined by a doctor who discovered nothing more than bruising. Diana went away for the weekend with her mother and returned wearing a sling. From that day onwards she refused to ride, and despite polite invitations from the Queen, Diana has only rarely been on horseback and then only for fear of offending her mother-in-law by refusing.

Many of Prince Charles' friends are older than himself and are either connected with his own hobbies or are old family friends. Invariably they are people with whom Diana feels that she has nothing in common. At Kensington Palace the Prince will frequently have small lunch or drinks parties for friends entertaining them himself while the Princess eats alone elsewhere. On public engagements she is forced to make smalltalk, but does not relish the thought of having to do so off duty.

Of all her former flatmates, Diana has remained closest to Virginia Pitman, the only remaining 'bachelor' girl of her old crowd. From cosmopolitan Earls Court she has now moved to a more fashionable terraced house in Fulham and is one of the privileged few to have the private telephone number of the future Queen of England. Dark-haired, fun-loving Virgina is still able to treat Diana as a non-royal. She does not have to call her ex-landlady 'Ma'am', but has made one necessary concession to royal etiquette in that she always curtseys on meeting Diana, be it at Kensington Palace for an all-girls lunch, or on one of the less common occasions when the Princess can find the time to make a personal call at Virginia's home. Although Diana may drive herself to Fulham, the ubiquitous police detective will be beside her all the way.

Once a restorer of antique china, Virginia Pitman is now an interior designer and no doubt an invaluable source of reference for Diana for any changes that she wishes to make to Highgrove House or the Kensington Palace apartment. Although Virginia has never been given *carte blanche* to design whole rooms for the Wales family, her former flatmate's situation has obviously provided an unusual opportunity for her as a designer to be consulted about a royal residence.

One advantage from Diana's point of view is that Virginia is a valuable contact in the outside world: someone who can shop where Diana cannot go, who knows the Princess' taste in furnishings, and can search the stores to find the finishing touches that make Diana's homes complete.

Carolyn Pride, another of the ex-Coleherne Court clan, is a less frequent visitor since her marriage to William Bartholomew, but she was chosen to be a godmother to Prince Harry in 1984. She and the Princess share a love of opera, Carolyn having studied singing at the Royal College of Music. Her husband, in complete contrast, runs a mobile discothèque called 'Juliana's', despite being heir to a brewery empire. Carolyn is working her way up the operatic ladder and in the summer of 1988 sang in two operas at Glyndebourne as part of the Festival Opera Chorus. Earlier in the year official duties and pleasure combined when in April, Diana, as Patron of the Malcolm Sargent Cancer Fund for Children, attended a concert organized by Carolyn's mother Sally in St Nicholas' parish church, Newbury. Although Diana has publicly declared her adoration of opera, those closer to her feel that this has occasionally been said to please her husband and that secretly she would prefer William Bartholomew's discothèque.

In the pre-royal days the girls had all agreed that whatever happened to them in the future, they would all attend each other's weddings. When this was initially discussed in the late 1970s, not one of the four could have predicted who would marry first, nor the family that she would marry into. When the girls first heard of Diana's engagement they admit that they cried with 'joy and excitement', although for a long time even they could not be party to Diana's secret; initially she told them that she was going out with Baron Renfrew, which was quite correct, that being one of Prince Charles' lesser known titles. After the wedding, all assumed that the pressures of royalty would not enable Diana to fulfil her old promise, but true to her word, Diana attended Carolyn's marriage ceremony, and on 6 November 1983, drove herself to the tiny hamlet of Deene in Northamptonshire for the wedding of Sophie Kimball, her childhood friend and third ex-flatmate. The daughter of former MP Sir Marcus Kimball, Sophie married old Etonian farmer Reuben Straker and accepted the fact that one of her guests would upstage her, on this of all days. Already it was becoming a hard fact of life for Diana that friends whom she could once meet and talk to as equals suddenly found themselves overshadowed by her. No matter how discreet, informal or anonymous she attempted to be there was no escape from the glare of the media, and no forgetting that she was now a Princess. Even at Carolyn Pride's wedding exactly one year earlier, newspaper headlines had shrieked: 'Lovely Di for a Wedding . . . her saucy style stole the show.' For many, having the Princess of Wales as a friend would appear a distinct disadvantage.

If old friends have retreated or become overshadowed following Diana's elevated social standing, the royal tag has opened doors for the Princess to make new friends from the entertainment world – colourful characters who have themselves experienced both sides of the fence, climbing from obscurity to superstardom. Not everyone can cope with being constantly in the public eye and it is people from the world of showbusiness with whom the Princess can most identify. Fame affects everyone differently. Some shun the limelight, others bask in its glory. Child star Lena Zavaroni became anorexic and suffered a nervous breakdown as a direct result of the pressures of celebrity status while contemporary Bonnie Langford laps up every ounce of public exposure and even craves for more. It takes a certain kind of personality to live in the limelight, a personality that Diana did not at first possess. It is not unnatural, therefore, that when she began to lose weight after the birth of Prince William she was thought to be suffering from anorexia nervosa.

Today Diana has not only learned to overcome her natural shyness, but positively revels in the opportunities that royal status offers. Marriage may have closed a great many doors, but equally it has opened others. It is probably no mere coincidence that her associates from the world of entertainment are extroverts for whom timidity has never been an option. Diminutive dancer, Wayne Sleep, naturally flamboyant, has been a firm royal favourite ever since he helped the Princess spring a surprise on Prince Charles. At Diana's instigation Sleep choreographed a short routine *Uptown Girl*, and the couple rehearsed in secret before appearing in front of an astonished audience at a Royal Opera House Gala in 1985. They received seven curtain calls. Never before had a member of the Royal Family danced on a stage in front of a paying audience, apart from the pre-war Windsor Castle pantomimes when the young Princess Margaret decided that family and friends should pay for the privilege of watching. Absent television moguls kicked themselves at missing Diana's Royal Variety Performance of the decade. As a child she had longed to be a ballet dancer, but as she herself has admitted, she 'grew too tall'. So she was obviously delighted at the opportunity to dance with Wayne Sleep. As for Sleep, he had wanted to dance permanently with the Royal Ballet, but did not grow tall enough; he is best known today for his outrageous balletic impersonations. For Diana, the Covent Garden dance was a major display of confidence. Before her marriage, if she had seriously been asked to dance in public she would have blushed with embarrassment, yet suddenly she was not only performing in public but was also placing her own head on the block with both dignity and reputation at stake. In an unconscious gesture she was also kicking back at the restrictions on royalty that never permit them to let their hair down or allow the mask to slip and reveal a chink of emotion in public. She danced unashamedly, won herself a standing ovation, and loved every second of it. It is no surprise that Wayne Sleep has been the personal guest of the Princess at dinner on several occasions and she attends his shows, whenever possible. In April 1988 she visited the Bristol Hippodrome to see him perform again in Andrew Lloyd Webber's *Song and Dance*, a production she has seen on numerous occasions.

In contrast to Sleep's overt flamboyance, a more recent associate in the future Queen's little black book is the zany comedienne Pamela Stephenson, noted for her outlandish sense of humour. Some would say that eccentric Pamela and demure Diana are worlds apart, with little more in common than the fact that they are slim blondes and mothers of two children, yet the Australian import, who in the 1987 General Election stood for the 'I-want-to-drop-a-blancmange-down-Terry-Wogan's-trousers Party', was a guest in the royal box at an Elton John concert as far back as 1984. Possibly Diana envies her friend's ability to publicly shock and cock a snook at convention, going beyond the levels of taste and acceptability. At a Savoy luncheon, Stephenson told risqué jokes in front of Princess Michael of Kent. When Jack Tinker, diminutive *Daily Mail* theatre critic slated her performance as Mabel in the 1982 West End production of the Gilbert and Sullivan operetta *The Pirates of Penzace*, she sent him a gift of an expensively wrapped cowpat. Could it be that Diana longs to do the same to journalists of the gutter press? Would she secretly love to shock everyone at a State Banquet with a bawdy song? Miss Stephenson feels a great desire to send everything up, never taking life too seriously. Even her biography in theatre programmes is a parody of theatrical people's personal details, stating her hobbies as reading, knitting and pulling the legs off frogs, and thanking the management for redecorating the dressing-room to match her eyes – sludge green. In more recent times, Miss Stephenson gained notoriety when she joined the Princess and the then future Duchess of York in the 'policewoman prank' on Prince Andrew's stag night, when all three of them went to a London nightclub dressed in police uniforms. Later when Diana met actress Anna Carteret, the star of a BBC television series about policewoman Juliet Bravo, Diana asked: 'Did you know that I once dressed up as an officer too? Of course, I didn't look as good as you did', she added with a giggle. Courtiers muttered their disapproval at this undignified display. The Press, for whom Diana could once do no wrong, advised against acting up for the cameras and turning the Royal Family into a comic soap opera.

It is Diana's blossoming friendship with the Duchess of York that has indeed caused the most concern, and it has marked the final departure of the 'shy Di' image. Slowly as the Princess found her feet in the Royal Family, accepted that she was the media's darling, and began to actually *enjoy* the attention, she became surprisingly more self-assured, 'to an irritating degree' revealed one of her ex-members of staff. Prince Andrew's engagement to the forthright Sarah Ferguson came at the exact moment when Diana had finally relaxed into her role of wife, mother and working royal, and she relished having someone of her own age in whom to confide. For the Princess of Wales, the announcement that Sarah Ferguson was to join the Family was a godsend. Both had been acquainted for several years through Major Ronald Ferguson, Prince Charles' polo manager. High-spirited, non-royal Sarah found herself in exactly the same position as Diana, having to adjust to a very different lifestyle on marriage. Being older and with a stronger, more outgoing, personality Sarah found the transition easier than Diana had done although even now she finds it hard to come to terms with what's expected of her in the role of a Duchess. Never has Sarah suffered from embarrassment and insecurity though, or the lack of self-confidence that plagued the Princess of Wales in the first years.

The relationship between Diana and Sarah is close, but certainly not a 'sisterly' one. They are more 'best friends' than relatives and any suggestion that there is rivalry between the two is pure fabrication. Diana has never seen Sarah as a threat, and it comes as a surprise to many who know of the Duchess' strong, ebullient image that it is actually Diana who is the boss. She will go along with Sarah's frivolity when it suits her, but she is equally capable of pulling rank and almost seems to enjoy the fact that she is no longer the newcomer in the Family. Their different personalities and lifestyles keep them apart socially, but on family occasions, be they private or official, Diana enjoys having Sarah as a friend and ally. If Sarah's personality appears outwardly to overshadow her sister-in-law it serves as an excellent cover for Diana to hide behind if she wishes to do so. In turn the Duchess respects the Princess and looks up to her as a role model. Just as Diana feels slightly in awe of Princess Anne's achievements, so Sarah feels that she has a long way to go to keep up with Diana's track record.

The Duchess of York has not been worried about the lack of privacy that comes with being royal, although even she is irritated by the constant security protection and restricted freedom. 'She wants to be able to eat in a restaurant, or enjoy a day out with friends, off duty and without being hampered by cameras', her father Major Ferguson has said, but he of all people should know that when in public a royal is never off duty. Marriage for both Sarah and Diana changed their lifestyles drastically in small personal ways that the public seldom realize. On becoming royal Diana and Sarah were assigned personal maids, people who would deal with the very intimate side of their lives such as personal items of laundry and generally attending to their needs. For Diana, who for a number of years had been used to doing her own washing, ironing her own blouses, and at the very least having the bedroom as a sanctuary, it was not an easy adjustment to make. No longer could she rinse out tights in the bathroom. Her laundry, like that of all other members of the Royal Family, is put into drawstring bags and these go collectively to the laundry, unidentifiable to those taking charge. Each item is accounted for on a laundry list so that it can be checked off on its return, to prevent anyone stealing and parading the Princess' undergarments. Much of the Kensington Palace laundry is now undertaken on the premises, but larger items and staff uniforms go away to the Sycamore Laundry in Clapham, south London.

The Duchess of York has coped much quicker with domestic routines at the Palace than Diana did, and certainly has fewer inhibitions. Sarah from the start enjoyed the new lifestyle and privileges that being royal affords. Inside the Palace many feel that the friendship between the exuberant Duchess and the once reserved Princess has been destructive to the image of royalty. Suddenly, it seems that the younger members of the family have blossomed and formed their own 'Sloane Ranger' branch of the Windsors. Lady Helen Windsor, Lady Sarah Armstrong-Jones, Viscount Linley, James and Marina Ogilvy, all enjoy the bright lights of London life and outlandish partying – a lifestyle which Diana feels closer to and sometimes tires of watching from the periphery. When she first became engaged, Prince Charles' brothers and cousins were still under twenty-one and students, not yet old enough to take control of their lives. Now all are in their mid- to late twenties, they can spend an evening out on the town, and make the gossip columns, but it does little to dent their image because of their distance from the throne. Lady Helen Windsor, for example, the daughter of the Duke and Duchess of Kent is considered to be 'rather racy' by the Queen. Nicknamed 'Melons', the gregarious Lady Helen works in Christie's modern art department, has had a succession of boyfriends, and has been photographed topless on a beach in Corfu. Twentieth in line to the throne, and recently pushed down a place by the Duke and Duchess of York's baby she will continue to be pushed further away by any future Wales or York children, and thus there are no pressures upon her to change the lifestyle that she so obviously enjoys.

The Duchess of York is a linchpin between the two worlds; she has to curb her behaviour because she is married to the Queen's second son, yet it is so unlikely that Prince Andrew will ever become King that Sarah is able to adopt a freer approach. If she makes a *faux pas* in public it is more forgivable and even though she has now been a member of the Family for two years, the public are still prepared to use the 'new to the job and still learning' excuse, that is no longer valid for Diana. The Princess should, it is muttered in high places, act like a future Queen at *all* times.

Throughout 1987 rumours abounded that the Duchess of York had led Diana astray, introducing her to people of dubious reputation. When they giggled and poked their friend, the late Hugh Lindsay, on the bottom with an umbrella and laughed like a couple of high school teenagers at Royal Ascot, more than a few eyebrows were raised. Major Ronald Ferguson, always available to offer quotes whatever the situation, leapt to their defence by commenting that Diana and Sarah were simply having fun. 'It so happened that the person they jabbed was a great friend of theirs', he said. 'He was just in front and a very natural reaction from them was to have a bit of fun. The Press says that you can't behave like that, which is ludicrous.' The Major might not have found the high jinks so acceptable had the Queen jabbed Viscountess Rothermere with a parasol at the Derby, or if the Queen Mother had poked the Duke of Buccleuch in the ribs at the Coronation; the lack of dignity would have been condemned.

The scene at the Derby in June 1987 displayed better than any other the gulf between the former nursery school teacher princess,

As a member of the Family, Diana poses with Prince Charles for an informal official photograph before embarking on the 1988 bicentennial celebration tour of Australia *(Camera Press)*

Diana at work in her study at Kensington Palace where the past mingles with the present – a memento of her schooldays sits permanently on the window ledge, while the wallpaper incorporates a Prince of Wales feathers design (*Tim Graham*)

In a country where women usually take second place, Diana enjoyed the attention she received on a visit to the Middle East in 1986; she certainly seems to be treated as an equal by Prince Saud Faisal (*Syndication International*)

The Princess appears unimpressed whenever Charles refers to her in one of his speeches *(The Photo Source)*

Undertaking engagements in her own right, as at this charity ball in 1986, Diana's conversation proves that she has done her homework *(The Photo Source)*

Making small talk with strangers, especially important figures like Emperor Hiro Hito, is a skill that takes time to develop but one that Diana has now mastered *(The Photo Source)*

As Princess of Wales, Diana is rarely required to curtsey. She did not, however, forget to pay homage to Queen Sofia on a visit to Spain in 1987 *(Photographers International)*

Diana joins other members of the Family for the annual Service of Remembrance at the Cenotaph in London; it is an event that she will attend each year for the rest of her life *(Syndication International)*

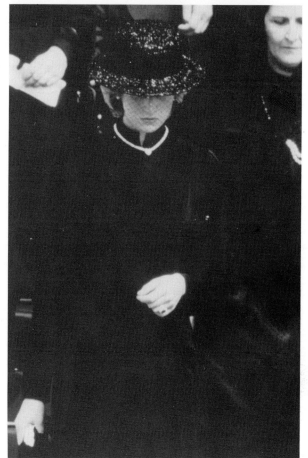

First royal duty abroad: at Princess Grace of Monaco's funeral Diana found it impossible to hide her emotions – a human 'lapse' that endeared her to the public *(Anwar Hussein)*

Princess Anne enjoyed competing with her sister-in-law in the fashion stakes at the Royal Film Première of *A Passage to India* in 1985 *(The Photo Source)*

Chief lady-in-waiting, the indispensable Anne Beckwith Smith, relieves Diana of a bouquet *(Anwar Hussein)*

'The wind is my enemy' says Diana but with the Queen *(below)* and Princess Anne *(below left)* she seems to be in good company *(The Photo Source)*

Diana's and Charles' opposing
interests are quite apparent at
this Elton John concert in 1987
(Syndication International)

Diana tries her hand at
basketball at Brixton Police
Station in 1987 *(Syndication
International)*

A rare escape for the royals: skiing in Klosters before the tragedy of 1988 *(Anwar
Hussein)*

the publishing house Duchess, and established members of the Royal Family. On one side stood Sarah and Diana, both clutching their large brimmed hats, laughing uproariously over something that had amused them while next to them stood the Queen and the Queen Mother, valiantly looking as if they were at a society wedding in their classic suits with matching hats, concentrating solemnly on the race with great propriety, apparently oblivious to the raucous girls at their sides. In the midst of the four women stood the Prince of Wales looking completely lost and out of place, tightlipped with embarrassment, glowing uncomfortably in his formal morning dress. Typifying 'Dignity and Impudence', nobody could fail to spot the commoners amid the Majesty.

At Royal Ascot later in the same month as the Princess and the Duchess tottered across the turf in their high heels, within yards of the Queen someone caught their eye. Without hesitation the Duchess let out an ear-piercing wolf whistle. 'Isn't it an extraordinary coincidence,' wrote Sir John Junor, 'that the problems with the Princess of Wales should have started from almost the same moment that Fergie became part of the Royal Family?' He suggested that Sarah begin to act more like a Duchess and less like 'an over-eager contestant in a TV talent show'.

With Sarah as part of the team, Diana appeared to blossom. She noticeably put on weight and began drinking alcohol, developing a liking for Pimms. Although no-one suspected for one moment that Diana was an alcoholic, she strangely felt the need a couple of months later to publicly deny that she had a 'drink problem': after being made an honorary freeman of the City of London in July 1987 Diana said, 'Contrary to recent reports in some of our more sensational Sunday newspapers, I have not been drinking and I am not, I can assure you, about to become an alcoholic.' It was a peculiar outburst from a princess. Fabricated stories about the Royal Family are written all the time, but seldom do they answer back or publicly deny rumours. Still unable to shrug off false rumours, Diana constantly feels a need to strike back and defend herself. 'Sarah and Diana both like a drink, but I'm sure that they never drink to excess,' Major Ferguson continued to twitter.

On a state visit to Portugal later in the year, Diana tweaked the blue braces of President Soares, obviously adopting the 'Fergie' informal approach to royal engagements. It is said elsewhere that Sarah encourages the giggles of Diana much to the displeasure of the Prince of Wales, who in the wake of the *Royal It's a Knockout* television game began to feel that his brother's wife let the side down. It is well known that the Queen and Princess Margaret are excellent mimics; the Princess Royal has a deadpan wit that causes her ladies-in-waiting to have fits of uncontrollable laughter, but they let their hair down *in private*. Diana has been encouraged to play the fool in public.

Before entering the Royal Family, Diana moved in 'Sloane Ranger' circles, adopting the discreet, stylish clothes that have become her trademark. She has revolutionized the fashion industry to the extent that fashion follows her. Yet more recent influences have encouraged her to extend the 'fun' approach into her wardrobe, getting away from the regal image of more mature members of the Family. The Princess Royal can adopt shoulder pads, go more daring with her hairstyles once a year at the BAFTA Award ceremonies where she now seems to select a different style on each occasion, and look sophisticated. Towards the end of 1987 Diana began to turn the Palace into *Dallas* with a new television soap opera look. 'Why does the Princess of Wales occasionally dress, and even behave, so unlike a princess?' asked author and journalist Suzy Menkes, after Diana had attended a performance of *Phantom of the Opera* wearing a tight black leather skirt and black lace tights. She has told friends in private that she detests being considered an unpaid fashion model, yet it must originally have been her own decision to dress for the cameras.

Since the arrival of the Duchess of York there has been competition. To match her boisterous personality the Duchess has made giant bows and hair ornaments her trademark; from imitation birds in a nest of hair, to aircraft shaped hairslides when she received her wings. On a visit to Los Angeles in February 1988 Sarah had the large letters 'L.A.' on the end of hat pins on a broad-brimmed black hat, and has even added false curls to her already thick titian mane. Diana has so far adhered to public opinion as regards her hairstyles. Two major attempts at a change of style were greated with such disfavour and criticism that she now stays within the bounds of the famous 'Lady Di' cut. Sarah takes full advantage of her curvaceous figure when selecting clothes, not always with success (one journalist described the Duchess as looking like 'a pig in the parlour curtains'), and it has not gone unnoticed by senior household staff that Diana's wardrobe has become 'sexier and slinkier'. Some feel that Diana's curvaceous look is a direct result of what has now commonly become known as 'The Fergie Factor'; with Sarah and her full figure, Diana no longer feels a need to be pencil slim. Whether or not the Duchess of York's influence has brought about a marked change in personality, however, is pure conjecture. It could be that Diana has simply relaxed into her role.

The Queen has been amazingly tolerant of Sarah's behaviour. Perhaps this is because of her less important rank in the royal structure, but certainly because of her love of royal pursuits such as riding and shooting. Sarah is far luckier than Diana because she has her sister-in-law to use as a role model, someone who had to go through the very exacting process alone. They come from similar backgrounds, both have fathers who have been employed by royalty and mothers who have left home, but Sarah has lived and seen the world to a far greater degree than the young Diana had been able to do in her pre-Princess days.

Although Sarah's past fits in with Prince Andrew's former playboy image, it is not a history that would have been suitable for the heir to the throne's partner. Twenty-six at the time of her engagement, Sarah had already had relationships with millionaire Paddy McNally and old Etonian Kim Smith-Bingham, before becoming involved with Prince Andrew. The virginal Diana Spencer had all the necessary qualities that jolly-hockey-sticks 'Fergie' lacked. Sarah can now turn to Diana for guidance; Diana can turn to her royal chum for fun and sympathy. In America the couple have been dubbed 'The Merry Wives of Windsor' through their skittish behaviour. The fact that they were born commoners has enabled the American public to identify with them, royalty themselves being too remote. Sarah has been described as wholesome, sincere, warm and big-hearted, and the Americans like the fact that she has problems with her weight and obvious lack of dignity – characteristics that Britons are less enthusiastic about. One senior member of the Royal Household confessed: 'Both girls are still young and any faults can still be put down to immaturity. Eventually they will grow up and realize the seriousness of their roles in British history, but I don't think that their characters will ever change. I think as the Duchess becomes older she will turn into an eccentric Margaret Rutherford type.'

Tolerant the Royal Family may be of Diana's and Sarah's friendship, but one recent addition to Diana's circle has been treated with less enthusiasm. In June 1987 the Princess was seen openly flirting with whiz-kid merchant banker Philip Dunne throughout the night at an exclusive wedding reception. The old Etonian, whose father is Lord Lieutenant of Hereford and Worcester, has been mixing in royal circles since the early 1980s, but only in 1987 did he appear to be so obviously close to the Princess. They were initially introduced by another of the Princess' close friends, Dunne's sister Camilla, known to Diana as Millie. Millie is the full-time organizer of the charity Help a London Child at Capital Radio.

In January 1987 Philip Dunne joined the royal skiing holiday at Klosters. Later he acted as host when Diana stayed at the family mansion for a weekend, and he became her escort at Royal Ascot for one day that year – the very week in which the changes in the Princess became most noticeable and the twelve-year age gap with her husband never more apparent.

'Far better to get it out of her system now than breaking out, as she surely otherwise would, at forty,' wrote Lynda Lee-Potter in the *Daily Mail*. 'It's not good that the name of the Princess of Wales should be coupled with the handsome young men with whom she dances the night away, while her middle-aged husband goes to bed,' commented Sir John Junor, echoing the sentiments of many national newspapers. Journalists' ink began to boil when the Princess was apparently spotted with Dunne once again at a David Bowie concert, but words had to be retracted when it was revealed that her escort was David Waterhouse, a friend of the Duchess of York, a nephew of the Duke of Marlborough and a Philip Dunne lookalike.

Waterhouse was not the first of the Duchess' friends with whom Diana was seen at this time. A Somerset county cricketer turned stockbroker, Charles Carter, jived energetically with Diana at a charity ball, the couple having been first introduced at a pre-wedding party organized by the Duchess herself. 'I'm delighted if she wants to dance with him,' said Carter's wife through gritted teeth.

It quickly became common knowledge that Prince Charles was unhappy about his wife's choice of company. Initially he allowed Diana to socialize with people who were happier attending pop concerts, all night parties and discothèques than himself. In October 1987 Charles and Diana spent three weeks apart while the Prince took a solo holiday in the Scottish highlands, not the first time that year that they had spent 'breathing spaces' away from each other. It is thought that during this period Philip Dunne was banned from contacting the Princess. Involved for three years with Lord St Just's elder daughter Katya Grenfell, until the relationship came to an end at the beginning of 1988, Dunne is known as a 'ladies' man'. Close friends call him 'Bungalow Phil' after Joan Collins' ex-Romeo Bill Wiggins, an image considered unsuitable for a companion of the Queen-in-waiting.

1987 was clearly a year of self-assessment for Diana, a year in which she temporarily broke out after what has now been termed her seven-year-itch. Of the Duchess of York Major Ronald Ferguson has said, 'I think there are times when she would like to break quietly away from the shackles, but she knows she can't. One difficulty is that she doesn't have the freedom now that she did; everywhere she goes she is accompanied by a bodyguard.'

If the strong-willed Duchess occasionally feels trapped it is not suprising that Diana still seeks relief in a lifestyle that she might at heart prefer. Most of the time Diana is able to accept fully her position, responsibilities and duty, but every so often one event, a single television programme, a conversation on a walkabout, gives her pangs of longing for her former life. Her fun to date has always been harmless, her circle of friends are from suitable backgrounds, and she is sensible enough never to allow any of her actions prove a threat to her marriage or endanger the monarchy. Were the Princess having an extra-marital relationship, which the gutter Press have wrongly suggested that she might, she would certainly have had the discretion to carry it out less publicly. Perhaps naïvely, Diana danced the night away with her young escorts, innocently enjoying herself assuming that her actions would be taken at face value. She should have known. Some blame Prince Charles for surrounding himself with friends who are older than himself, such as the octogenarian writer Sir Laurens Van der Post, twice the Prince's age. It is not unnatural for his wife to seek the companionship of her contemporaries.

The difficult autumn of 1987 made Diana even more conscious of public opinion and concerned about restraining her self-indulgences. Not wishing to bring embarrassment to her husband or the Royal Family, she now surrounds herself with inoffensive intimates, although still angry that she is not free to select friends without fear of misinterpretation. Her elder sister, Jane, married the Queen's Assistant Private Secretary, and the couple now have a grace-and-favour flat in Kensington Palace itself. She and her husband, Robert Fellowes, have seen more of the Princess recently. Since Robert's promotion to Deputy Private Secretary in 1986 there have been greater demands on his time, leaving the two sisters more time to be together. The advantage of this sisterly friendship is that Jane understands the royal way of life only too well through her husband. She had also worked as an editorial assistant for *Vogue* magazine, and was therefore able to introduce Diana to the top fashion designers; she must now in some way be given credit for her sister's style. The two obviously have a great deal more in common than just the sisterly connection.

Natalia Phillips, the wife of Gerald Grosvenor, the sixth Duke of Westminster, is someone else whose friendship has been rekindled in recent years. Having known each other since they were teenagers, Diana and 'Tally' have only really become close since they both had two children. Whereas Diana produced two boys and secured the line of succession, the Duchess of Westminster has so far had only girls and has not yet produced an heir to continue the line that dates back to 1622. Natalia has all the right credentials to befriend the Princess of Wales as granddaughter of the Queen's aunt Lady Zia Wernher. Before her marriage she too worked for *Vogue* magazine. An estimate at the beginning of 1988 put Gerald Grosvenor's fortune at £1,400,000,000, which is said to increase at the rate of £5 per second. Both the Prince and Princess of Wales spend weekends at the Grosvenor family seat at Eaton Hall, near Chester, set in 13,000 acres of grounds. Like Diana, Natalia enjoys letting her hair down and both can gossip over lunch in the secure knowledge that the conversation will never be leaked.

Other friends of long standing are beginning to find themselves once more part of the Diana set. Alexandra Loyd, a prep' school pal, whose father is land agent at Sandringham, lost touch with Diana for a while but has now been raised to the coveted rank of lady-in-waiting – an honour that only the closest friends can fulfil. As a child Alexandra lived on the Sandringham estate at Laycocks and used to play with the future Princess, along with the local rector's daughter, Penelope Ashton. In 1968 both Alexandra and Diana began attending the small Silfield School in King's Lynn, Norfolk, a private day school. Until this time Diana had been educated by a governess, Miss Gertrude Allen, known as 'Ally'. She left in November 1967 soon after Diana's mother left home, and on the recommendation of her godmother, Carol Fox, Diana moved on to the small school. It must have been a proud moment when years later Gertrude Allen heard that the young girl that she had taught to read and write was engaged to the Prince of Wales, and she lived just long enough to see the wedding. Because this was Diana's first real venture into the outside world, Alexandra Loyd's presence at Silfield made the transition much easier. It was a family-run establishment and Diana found herself in a class of just fifteen children, learning the three R's on very traditional lines.

When Diana moved on to board at Riddlesworth Hall in 1970, now introverted and emotionally insecure, she again found the new experience much easier to bear because Alexandra went too. Five years later Johnny Spencer inherited the title of Earl and Diana's main home and security at Park House was packed into cases and transported to the grand stately home of Althorp in Northamptonshire. Unable to face the trauma that her father's inheritance meant, Diana rang up Alexandra and the two fourteen-year-old girls raided the Park House larder of peaches and went to the Spencer family beach hut at Brancaster where they spent the entire day. It was a typical reaction of Diana's at this time, that when a crisis occurred in her life she ran away from it. She fled to somewhere where she felt safe and hoped that the situation would go away. Always, of course, she was eventually forced to face reality. Throughout the emotional upset of her parent's divorce, she would often spend entire days in the swimming pool at Park House, getting rid of her aggression in the water. After leaving West Heath school in 1977 Diana moved into her mother's house in Chelsea, but with four spacious floors she chose another school friend to share with her, Laura Grieg, who was then undertaking a Cordon Bleu cookery course. Later they were joined by Sophie Kimball. It was during this time in London that Diana's main circle of friends developed, people with a similar background and education, who remain close to her today. Many are ex-schoolfriends who have kept in contact, Theresa Mowbray, Mary-Ann Stewart-Richardson, Caroline Harboard-Hammond, and Henrietta Scott who once shared a flat with Diana's sister Jane. Such friendships are maintained by the Princess because they form a much valued link with the past.

Newer friends include Catherine Soames, the wife of Prince Charles' friend Nicholas Soames, who frequently accompanies the Princess to watch tennis at Wimbledon in July; Lady Alexandra Tollemache, wife of a brewery heir who shares Diana's sense of humour; Kate Menzies, daughter of the newsagent-chain boss and a friend of Viscount Linley's, and Julia Dodd-Noble, a friend of the Duchess of York's. Twice a week the Princess also visits the ultra-modern Vanderbilt Racquet Club to play tennis, just a short drive from Kensington Palace. This is one of the most expensive tennis clubs in Britain with a £500 membership fee, a £475 annual subscription fee (plus VAT), and court fees ranging from £10 to £17 each time you play, depending upon whether you play at peak or off-peak times. Although the Princess could easily play on the courts at Buckingham Palace, the Shepherds Bush club provides an excellent opportunity to meet friends and keep fit, as well as providing yet another link with the non-royal world. The visits to the club are as much an escape as a desire for sport. Seldom does Diana ever play tennis with other members of the Royal Family, even though many are keenly involved with the sport; Princess Michael of Kent plays regularly herself, but at another exclusive club. The Queen's Club in West London is Princess Michael's haunt, with a higher membership fee than the Vanderbilt, but a lower annual subscription.

Although other members of the Family stick together through the uniqueness of their position, Diana regards very few of them as friends. Prince Charles is naturally very close to Lord and Lady Romsey (pronounced 'Rumsi') who inherited Broadlands in

Hampshire on the death of Earl Mountbatten of Burma, the house where Charles and Diana spent their wedding night. As Norton Knatchbull, Lord Romsey was a contemporary of the Prince's at Gordonstoun school (although he is a year older than the Prince) and Charles was best man at his wedding to ex-deb Penelope Eastwood in 1979. Because of her husband's obvious closeness to the Mountbatten clan, Diana cannot help feeling an outsider and has been known to call this branch of the Family 'part of the Mountbatten Mafia'. When Charles and Diana spend off-duty time apart, which always results in gossip about a breakdown in communications, it is because they are happy for each other to spend time alone with their respective friends. Just as the Prince would feel an outsider chatting about William Bartholomew's mobile discothèque or reminiscing about West Heath days with Carolyn, so Diana feels decidedly bored by the huntin', shootin', fishin' set amid which Charles feels most relaxed. Although she has to an extent learned to enjoy watching the Prince play polo, she will never feel completely at ease doing so, and knows too little about equestrian sports to talk knowledgeably to fellow spectators in the royal box.

When a close study is made of the Prince and Princess of Wales' circle, it is conspicuous that far more of Charles' friends have disappeared since the time of his marriage than Diana's. It is no coincidence either that some of the more glamorous female friends of the Prince's made a very sudden exit from his life, as if they had been given firm marching orders. Most noticeable was the absence of Lady Tryon, nicknamed 'Kanga' by the Prince because of her Melbourne upbringing. The Prince first met the former Miss Dale Harper in the 1960s on a visit to Australia and obviously admired her bubbling personality. After a subsequent move to London, Dale married Lord Anthony Tryon, whose late father was formerly Keeper of the Privy Purse to the Queen, and the Prince became a frequent visitor to their Knightsbridge home. Unusually for him, he would often turn up unannounced and seemed to be able to confide totally in his Australian friend. Fun-loving 'Kanga' offered relief from an otherwise formal life and it is thought that he sought her advice on his current girlfriends. Many have suggested that their relationship was of a more intimate nature, a conjecture that will never be proved and one photographer was offered £50,000 if he could take an exclusive picture of the Prince and Lady Tryon together. Before marrying Diana, Charles used to join the Tryons for salmon fishing in their Icelandic holiday home at Vopnafjördur, and spent many weekends pheasant-shooting with them in Wiltshire. Obviously Lord Tryon was happy with the friendship, but Diana could not cope with the threat of another woman in her husband's life no matter how platonic the relationship.

Many myths have arisen regarding the Princess and Lady Tryon. Depending upon who you talk to the ladies range from being bosom buddies to sticking pins in wax models of each other. Certainly they have never been at each other's throats, Diana is after all no threat to Lady Tryon, but they are not the closest of friends. One common misconception is that 'Kanga' organized Diana's holiday in Australia prior to the engagement to give her a breathing space to contemplate her future. On 24 January, 1988, for example, Lady Olga Maitland, a gossip columnist on the *Sunday Express* newspaper, wrote of the Prince and Princess of Wales' forthcoming tour of Australia and inevitably mentioned Charles' Australian friend: 'It was Lady Tryon who arranged for Lady Diana, as she then was, to spend a reflective holiday in Australia with her mother before she accepted Prince Charles' proposal.'

This is an error typical of many gossip columnists. The truth comes from Lady Tryon herself that she did not arrange the holiday; Diana went to stay with her mother, Frances, who deliberately made a false statement to the Press to prevent her daughter from receiving further harassment: 'She is not in Australia. She is not even in this part of the world.' Unfortunately for Lady Tryon, she happened to be in Australia at the same time and the ever-anxious Press put two and two together only to make six.

Not only was Lady Tryon unaware that Prince Charles' future bride was in the country, but ironically the two had not met. Diana and 'Kanga' did not meet until after the wedding, a surprising fact considering that the Prince had supposedly consulted his antipodean confidante about every other prospective bride. 'That's because Charles was certain about Diana,' says a close friend, 'For the first time in his life he knew that he had found the right girl. He had no need to seek confirmation.' In the knowledge that Lady Diana Spencer was 'Miss Right', that he was not only in love with a girl, but that she also had the right credentials and the royal seal of approval there may have been an underlying fear that Lady Tryon might disapprove.

Jealous at first of her husband's closeness and empathy with Dale Tryon, Diana discouraged Charles from continuing the friendship at such an attentive level. It is wrong, however, to suggest that 'Kanga' was prevented completely from ever meeting the Prince – another media myth. As she is part of other regal circles it would have been impossible for them not to meet, and farcical to suggest that they could avoid each other at polo matches, receptions and private parties. What *did* come to an end were Charles' private, unannounced visits to the Tryon's home. Lord and Lady Tryon have been guests at Kensington Palace, and Diana's growing confidence is displayed in the tolerant way she now accepts the Prince's relationship as innocent; in the last year he has been able to enjoy 'Kanga's' company once again without guilt. Any initial jealousies on Diana's part have faded, despite their unquestionable strength throughout the first insecure months of her marriage. Here was yet another example of someone who had known the Prince since Diana was herself only a child, someone with whom Charles had private jokes and happy memories to which she was not privy. Even worse, the Tryons' eldest son had been named after his godfather, the Prince of Wales. Deep down must have been the secret fear and grievance, before the birth of Prince William, that she might herself only have daughters, or no children at all, and there would be Lady Tryon with a son and heir named Charles. Not until after the birth of two healthy sons could Diana accept this fact. Now it no longer matters that the Tryons have a son. With motherhood came the end of Diana's worst fears.

It is a sad fact of royal life that close friends can only remain anonymous until there is a scandal or a tragedy, then their privacy is gone. Such events can have some benefits: in times of scandal the ranks close in and royalty become aware of friends' trustworthiness; under tragic circumstances they receive and give support and strength. When their housekeeper, Nesta Whiteland, developed cancer the Prince and Princess of Wales did everything within their power to help, displaying the humanity of royalty that sometimes gets lost beneath the majesty and protocol. It came as a great shock to Diana when she learned that yet another close friend and member of her staff was also suffering from the dreaded disease. Someone half Nesta Whiteland's age.

For three years Fay Marshalsea had been one of Diana's dressers. She is only five years older than the Princess, and the two struck up an instant rapport. Few were more excited than Diana when Fay announced in 1987 that she was engaged to be married to handsome RAF pilot, Steven Appleby. The excitement soon turned to sadness though when just two weeks before her wedding day, Fay was told that she had cancer. She had noticed a small lump under her tongue and could scarcely believe the results of the routine biopsy: if left untreated it could be fatal.

Stunned by the news Fay told only her husband-to-be, her parents Bill and Marion, and the Princess. Determined that she would go ahead with the planned wedding she put on a very brave face, despite intensive radiation treatment, which left her face painfully burned, preventing her from wearing make-up. She continued to work as Diana's dresser until the strain became too much for her to carry on, but Diana insisted that she remain at Kensington Palace so that it would be easier for her to travel daily to St Bartholomew's hospital for treatment. Throughout the long battle Diana gave continual support and practical help, encouraging Fay to fight on. On the wedding day itself Diana arrived discreetly and unannounced with just a detective in tow, at the North Street Congregational Church in Taunton, Somerset. From past experience, the Princess was wary not to overshadow the bride and wore a sombre black and white check suit by Alistair Blair, and sat in the third row with other guests. Afterwards she acted as one of the witnesses and joined in the reception, never once betraying the secret that had been confided in her.

As a close member of the Princess' staff, Fay Appleby, as she is called today, will always remain discreet about the part Diana played in her return to health, but it was certainly a major one, even to the extent of accompanying her to the hospital on occasions for treatment. It is easy at times like this for Diana to forget that she is Princess, to set aside protocol, and help someone in need because she truly cares. It would be just as easy for a member of the Royal Family to express regret, send words of sympathy, but nevertheless continue with their hectic schedule, but Diana always wants to give practical help. It is a character trait that will never change.

Scarcely had Diana's dresser returned to health than a more public tragedy befell the royal circle. Thursday 10 March, 1988, is a day that will be etched in the minds of Charles and Diana for the rest of their lives, when an avalanche at the Swiss resort of Klosters killed their close friend and former Equerry to the Queen, Major Hugh Lindsay, and seriously injured Mrs Patti Palmer-Tomkinson. The Prince escaped death himself, it has been said 'more by luck than judgment.'

By coincidence that day, the fourteen-week pregnant Duchess of York had fallen heavily in the snow and Diana had returned with her to their holiday chalet. Had this not happened, both Sarah and Diana could well have joined the six-strong party headed by Prince Charles, who had decided to ski off-piste on one of the steepest and most dangerous runs in the Alps, the Gotschnawang, nicknamed 'The Wang'. It was a bright clear winter's day and despite avalanche warnings the party ventured further to find deeper fresher snow. The Prince has ski'd there before, and all members of the party were skilled sportsmen. This was their first full day of skiing and as they paused to take breath an avalanche rumbled towards them, caused it is believed by snow that they had themselves disturbed. Major Lindsay and Mrs Palmer-Tomkinson were swept away in a whirling maelstrom as the entire mountainside seemed to vanish.

Although deeply shocked and distressed by the disaster – eye witnesses say that the Prince broke down and wept when he learned of Major Lindsay's death – he played a vital part in the rescue operation, digging frantically in the snow with his bare hands despite the intense cold while shouting orders to the others. After the initial drama, when the true horror of the situation became apparent, it was the Prince who calmed hysterical members of the party. Mrs Palmer-Tomkinson was taken by the Swiss Air Rescue Service to hospital, where the Prince rang every two hours to monitor her condition and went to see her the next day, before the sombre royal party returned home with the body of Major Lindsay. A few days later the Prince returned alone to Switzerland to visit his friend.

For Diana, it was the first serious calamity that she had experienced as Princess of Wales. Nothing had caused the Prince so much distress since the assassination of his 'honorary grandfather' Lord Mountbatten nearly ten years earlier, and it proved to be a time when he needed the support of his wife. Charles' temperament, making him withdrawn and silent, requires careful and sympathetic handling on Diana's part.

Major Lindsay's death was equally upsetting for Diana; she had known him since 1983 when he became Equerry to the Queen, and also his wife, Sarah, who works in the Press Office at Buckingham Palace. Ironically Sarah Lindsay was on duty in the Press Office when news of the tragedy reached the Palace. Diana had attended their wedding in July 1987 and was particularly excited to learn that the couple were expecting their first child in May 1988. Diana's fond memories of Hugh Lindsay will always be of the man who advised her about the pitfalls of being royal when she was having problems. As a close friend he will be sorely missed.

The annual Klosters holiday has often been fraught with drama. For Diana it was always a *private* holiday. She hated being photographed and resigned herself to the inevitable photo-call on the first day. It was one of the rare events on the royal calendar when husband and wife could have fun on the ski slopes, enjoying the company of their closest friends. Now the future for this holiday looks bleak and possibly even these few weeks of freedom each year will be denied them. If they were to return in the winter of 1989 as if nothing had happened, criticism would land on them like a ton of bricks for being heartless and unfeeling; if they let the tragedy keep them away from the sport it will be the end of just a tiny piece more of their liberty and a further tightening of the circle.

The 1988 skiing holiday began well; Diana posed for photographers cheerfully, and even when she fell flat on her back she simply dusted herself down with a blush and a grin. It was the first time that she had appeared so relaxed and carefree, a mood that was fated to change. As she landed with her husband and sister-in-law at RAF Northolt, Diana must have cursed that even royal grief cannot escape public scrutiny.

ॐ 4 ॐ

Mrs Charles Windsor

Surrounded by Marriage Guidance Counsellors, the Princess of Wales listened attentively. Six months earlier her own marriage had, according to the media, been heading for the rocks. She and Prince Charles seemed to be leading increasingly separate lives; throughout 1987 they spent more time apart than any other year of their marriage. Maybe after six years together the relationship *was* beginning to lose some of its sparkle. As autumn approached, the gossip increased. The only consolation to any royal is that such rumours are always transitory unless fuel is foolishly added to the fire, and after the Prince and Princess' carefully stage-managed season of official trips together to Germany, Australia and Thailand the news stories quickly became unconvincing. So much so, that when Diana visited the National Marriage Guidance Council Headquarters at Rugby, Warwickshire, in March 1988 and watched a mock row between two members of staff pretending to be a couple raking through the ashes of their crumbling marriage, few noticed possible parallels. Had the visit been on the Princess' agenda a few months earlier, every national press photographer in the country would have been present to take the picture of the year.

Diana's image as a wife was destined to be tarnished from the start. In 1981 she was too much of a fairytale bride to continue living happily ever after. The Duchess of York, on the other hand, received her share of criticism from the moment she stepped into the limelight and so expectations were lower. Diana could do no wrong, she had led a virginally pure existence with no skeletons in the closet other than George Plumptre, the third son of Lord Fitzwalter, who is the only 'old flame' that even the most ardent of muckrakers have ever been able to unearth. Even so, nothing more sordid happened than the fact that Diana used to allow George to put his dirty laundry in her Coleherne Court washing machine. Plumptre, now living on his father's estate at Goodnestone Park, near Canterbury, is married to White Russian, Alexandra Cantacuzene-Speransky, the proud father of two boys, Wyndham and Piers, and has not seen Diana personally since the announcement of her engagement.

With a history but no past, Lady Diana Spencer was the perfect bride and Charles and Diana were seen as a real life 'Romeo and Juliet', an image to which they were happy to play up. And they did so literally, when at a charity Christmas Gala at the Royal Opera House in 1982, before Diana's routine with Wayne Sleep, Prince Charles appeared on stage dressed as Romeo, while Diana in the Royal box pretended to be Miss Capulet and laughingly lowered a rope down over the side of the box on to the stage. The Prince produced a ladder as the audience roared helplessly with laughter. Here were the Prince and Princess of Wales acting out the charade of the world's most famous lovers, although less 'starcrossed' and determined to omit the tragic ending. This small public spectacle embodies the nature of their relationship; publicly they feel the need to put on a show, to play up the loving image. Throughout their 1987 tour of Germany, royal watchers noted that the 'happy couple stance', the affectionate touches, the terms of endearment, appeared to be just a little too deliberate, calculated and overplayed. 'The affair smacked of Di-liberate strategy,' punned *Sunday Express* reporter, Louette Harding. At the time when their marriage was under the microscope, whatever moves they made were open to misinterpretation. Had they not touched each other, had the Prince not put his arm around Diana's waist, total lack of physical contact would have been noted and recorded. The great mistake that Charles and Diana made is that they did not allow themselves to relax and act naturally. They gave photographers poses that they *wanted* to see. Playing to the cameras always smacks of insincerity.

In July 1988 the Prince and Princess of Wales celebrated their seventh wedding anniversary, just four weeks after Diana's twenty-seventh birthday. Today she has the confidence she sorely lacked in 1981. She has grown up and instinctively acts out the role of Princess as she has learned to play it. Those who work for the Royal Family insist that it is an acting job for royalty and staff alike. At a State Banquet the staff, resplendent in their uniforms, are not merely serving a meal but are playing their part in the spectacle. For the leading players, the Queen, the Queen Mother and even Prince Charles, this is not a role that can be switched on and off. They may behave differently in private and put on a publc persona, but it is now such an intrinsic part of their lives that it comes naturally. Sitting in the back of her car, the Queen Mother often wears slippers and has a rug wrapped around her knees until she nears her destination, then on will go the high heeled shoes, off comes the rug, and Her Majesty emerges smiling and waving and always playing to the camera. And the people love her for it.

The Queen is a hardened professional when it comes to the theatricality, forever conscious of the standards she has to set and maintain, eschewing the artificiality of a film star while upholding the image of the monarchy. Nevertheless, she does enjoy some of the stage illusions that her life provides. One special effect that would thrill any Broadway audience is that of the Queen appearing from behind a secret panel in the White Drawing-Room at Buckingham Palace prior to a State Banquet. Before joining the main guests, the Queen and the immediate members of the Royal Family always assemble in a smaller drawing-room known as the Royal Closet, a misleading title for the large, elegant room with its crimson damask walls and decorous chimneypiece. Here the Royal Family have a pre-prandial drink, waiting in the wings to make a grand entrance. When the Queen gives the signal, a footman pulls a lever and startled guests in the White Drawing-Room attending their first formal function at the Palace, are astonished to see an apparently solid section of the wall swing open as the Royal Family parade through it. This extravagant artifice can have an unnerving effect on those who have never before seen the Queen or Diana at close quarters, and it is not unknown for gin and tonics to hit the blue and crimson Axminster carpet!

Such obvious theatricals are rare, but the Royal Family by the very nature of their job have to give an impression of dignity and grace. It is a skill that Diana is only now beginning to master, but the transition from wife and mother as she is at home, to leading member of the Royal Family as she is in public has still to be worked at. It is unnatural to control her emotions among people, and equally unnatural to display false emotions for the camera. After seven years of marriage Diana, like many wives, has grown accustomed and attuned to her husband but it is a sign of her ever-increasing sense of security that she no longer needs to constantly feel the closeness of her partner in public.

In the early days of her marriage and prior to the wedding, Diana was very insecure; she needed the comfort of Charles beside her. Psychologists see Diana's need to touch the Prince when in the company of others as an unconscious way of saying 'this is mine'. For Charles, who had always been discouraged from being demonstrative, it was a new experience. If he had girlfriends in the past he was not allowed to hold hands with them at the racecourse, canoodle on the dancefloor, or link arms after a polo match, in the certain knowledge that the media would intrude. Throughout his youth and early twenties he had been suppressed, forever cautious of the camera, ill at ease in the presence of women. As soon as it became common knowledge that he was to marry Lady Diana Spencer, the pressures were suddenly, magically lifted. For the first time in his life he could display pure affection and receive nothing but praise; but after thirty-two years of restraint he was understandably inhibited. Just as Diana occasionally threw dignity to the wind when she openly made fun of her husband, giggled over private jokes and relished being in love, so Charles had to learn to cast off his inbred reticence.

The heir to the throne's choice of marriage partner was never simply a matter of his falling in love. He had said that thirty seemed like 'a good age to marry', probably aware that finding the right girl would be no easy task: 'When I marry I have to be conscious that I am not only choosing a wife, but that one day she will also be Queen' he deliberated, and there was always the distinct possibility that if he did find someone suitable, she, in turn, might not be prepared to contend with all that being Princess of Wales entailed. Interviewed before his marriage to Diana the Prince half-jokingly expressed his amazement that she was prepared to take him on, trying to ignore the fact that she certainly had no idea exactly what she *was* taking on. That early interview in 1981 gave us the earliest glimpse of the couple's differing characters and attitudes. When Diana was asked if she were in love, she instantly retorted with, 'Of course!' almost shocked that such a question need be asked. The Prince mumbled tellingly, 'Whatever "in love" means.'

Did he have doubts as to whether he was in love? Was he simply marrying Diana because he had reached an age at which pressure was being put on him by the Queen to settle down and secure the line of the House of Windsor before it was too late? There are those within the royal circle itself who feel strongly that Diana was required as much to ensure the line of succession as to be Prince Charles' lifetime companion. These are unfair assumptions, despite the Prince's own inference that he did not know whether he was in love or not. It seems almost certain, however, that at the outset Diana was more in love with Charles than he was with her. For a long time prior to the engagement she had been infatuated with the man, and when he eventually asked her to marry him she did not hesitate in her acceptance. Charles did not propose until he was absolutely certain in his mind that she was the right person to be a royal wife: someone lively, energetic and young enough to be moulded into royal duty. Only when he really relaxed into the idea and got to know Diana infinitely better did he realize that he was deeply in love. Had he been asked a year *after* the wedding whether or not he were in love his answer would surely have been definite and unquestioning.

The list of potential brides for Prince Charles in 1958 included Lady Caroline Percy, Lady Georgina Petty-Fitzmaurice, Princess Marie-Christina of the Netherlands, Lady Victoria Percy, and Princess Anne-Marie of Denmark – all daughters of aristocratic families and who happened to be Prince Charles' age. That was when the Prince was only ten and Lady Diana Spencer had not even been conceived. Choosing possible marriage partners for the Queen's children became an amusing pastime for the Press whenever other royal news appeared to be thin on the ground: before her engagement to Mark Phillips, Princess Anne was paired off with Andrew Parker-Bowles, a captain in the Household Cavalry; the Hon. Brian Alexander, a friend of Lord Lichfield's and managing director of Princess Margaret's holiday island of Mustique; Alexander Harper, a polo-playing acquaintance of the Duke of Edinburgh – he escorted the Princess to see the then controversial musical *Hair*; and Olympic gold medallist, Richard Meade, a close personal friend of Princess Anne's but never a possible contender in the marriage stakes. The Princess played cat and mouse with the media, and when she did eventually find her man the Press were the last to know. Anne's and Mark's paths had crossed frequently at equestrian events. Mark had won three times at the Badminton Horse Trials on his horse Great Ovation. When they were guests at the same houseparties, it seemed purely coincidental. They were colleagues and there were family connections since Mark's uncle had married the Duke of Norfolk's sister, and the Duke's eldest daughter, Lady Anne Fitzalan-Howard, was a close friend of the Princess. It was not until Mark was invited much later to spend the New Year with the Royal Family at Sandringham that the speculation began. Even then the Palace denied any attachment practically until the day the engagement was announced. Once Princess Anne was safely married in 1973, all eyes turned to the heir to the throne and unlike Princess Anne's husband, who remains untitled to this day, the wife of Prince Charles would become royal.

The first serious girlfriend that Prince Charles had was a Chilean girl, three years older than himself, Lucia Santa Cruz, who was employed as a research assistant to Lord 'RAB' Butler at Trinity College, Cambridge, where the Prince was studying. The intensity of the friendship became apparent when Lucia was invited as Prince Charles' own personal guest at the Investiture Ceremony at Caenarvon Castle in 1969, but when asked if there was any sign of romance she wittily replied: 'I no longer speak English.' However serious Prince Charles might have been, Lucia, as a Roman Catholic, would not have been a suitable bride. Under the Royal Marriages Act of 1772 all descendants of King George II have to obtain the Sovereign's consent before they can marry. With the Queen as Head of the Church of England it would be acutely embarrassing for her heir to marry a Catholic. It was the first occasion that revealed to Charles how perfect his bride must be. He could never marry simply for love.

A succession of 'possibles' quickly followed, including Princess Anne-Marie of Denmark; Lady Leonora Grosvenor, the Duke of Westminster's sister who later went on to marry the photographer Earl, Patrick Lichfield; and on a visit to Washington in 1971 the

Prince found himself unwittingly pushed by President Nixon and his wife towards their daughter Patricia. In a clear case of matchmaking the Nixons attempted to unite Britain and America by marrying their daughter off to the world's most eligible bachelor – a tremendous coup for America if it had worked, but unfortunately the Prince found the fact that he was left alone with 'Tricia' at every available opportunity lacking in subtlety.

The following July Prince Charles appeared publicly at the Royal Tournament at Earls Court with Lady Jane Wellesley, a direct descendant of the Duke of Wellington – someone with the perfect background as the daughter of the present Duke. For almost two years they saw each other regularly and when he invited her to Sandringham in the New Year of 1974 the speculation mounted. 'I'm fed up with all these rumours,' she finally snapped. 'What do you expect me to say?' The friendship completed its natural course when the Prince spent many months abroad in the Navy.

In 1975 Prince Charles revealed, 'I am looking forward to a few years of falling in love with all sorts of girls,' a remark calculated to keep everyone guessing. Discretion is the key to any royal friendship, be it on a simple social level or of a more intimate nature. One whisper to the Press can sever a royal friendship permanently. Two girlfriends learnt this very quickly to their cost: Jane Ward, a divorcee and therefore already with points against her, said to a journalist, 'We are very fond of each other . . . friends told me the Queen is worried about our relationship. She has nothing to worry about.' The quote made headline news in a national newspaper and her friendship with the Prince ended that day. Likewise, Countess Angelika Lagansky told a reporter that a short stay at Balmoral Castle with the Royal Family had been 'blissful' and that Charles was the 'most wonderful, charming' person she had ever met. 'I cannot say what is in my heart,' she continued when asked if the Prince was in love with her. These remarks instantly killed any relationship that might have developed.

Because of the qualities required in a future Queen, the choice for the Prince was extremely limited. In 1977, Prince Charles contemplated the Grimaldi family and the attractive daughter of Prince Rainier and Princess Grace of Monaco, the then twenty-year-old, olive-skinned Princess Caroline. For the Princess the meeting was seen as something of a joke and she simply played along with it. News of their meeting had somehow been leaked to the Press in advance, and the unfortunate Charles found himself practically engaged to Caroline before they had even met. Under such circumstances no relationship could have any hope.

As if looking deliberately for a Princess, perhaps to form an alignment with a European royal house, the name of the Princess Marie-Astrid of Luxembourg was bandied around for a number of years. The shy Princess appeared to have all the essential qualities, coupled with beauty, and had the overall advantage in that the Queen seemed to favour this contender more than any other. Only one ingredient in this possible love story was absent. Prince Charles felt nothing for the Princess, preferring perhaps an English rose, and so nothing developed even though Marie-Astrid's name continued to dominate the gossip columns.

In Davina Sheffield, Prince Charles, it is said, came closest to finding a marriage partner. Their friendship lasted on and off for some fourteen months from 1975 to 1976 and once more Davina appeared to have all the correct attributes, until September 1976, that is, when her past caught up with her and former boyfriend James Beard sold his story to the *News of the World* of how he had lived with the possible future Queen. Farewell Davina Sheffield, hello one Lady Sarah Spencer . . .

The timing of Prince Charles' meeting with Earl Spencer's eldest daughter, christened Elizabeth Sarah Lavinia, was unfortunate in that it took place during the Prince's twenty-ninth year. In the wake of his comments that thirty seemed to be a good age to marry, whoever the Prince courted at this time was destined to receive unparalleled observation. Despite the inevitable denials, on the sole strength of Prince Charles' much lamented remarks, every newspaper in the country was of the conviction that Sarah Spencer would become the Princess of Wales. Her sixteen-year-old sister, Diana, still a boarder at West Heath School and almost thirteen years younger than Charles was not even considered as a contender.

In the June of Her Majesty's Jubilee Year, Lady Sarah was invited to join the Queen's houseparty at Windsor Castle for Royal Ascot. She was suffering from the slimmer's disease anorexia nervosa, which she recovered from during the subsequent six months after regular visits to a clinic. Because her recovery coincided with the period in which she was seeing the Prince regularly, he has been credited with the cure. Lady Sarah has always claimed that her friendship with the Prince was in no way a contributory factor.

After a skiing trip to Klosters in February 1978, the relationship petered out, not through any misdemeanour on Sarah's part. Quite the contrary, for as we know in retrospect the Spencers proved the ideal family to unite with the Windsors, and Sarah had no secrets lurking in her background. For once it was Prince Charles who was unsuitable, at least in Sarah's eyes. Not only did she abhor the idea of being Princess of Wales, but she stated quite categorically that she was not in love with him. Later she told the portly James Whitaker, doyen of royalwatchers, that she felt Prince Charles had still not met the girl he wanted to marry and at the time it seemed a pertinent statement to make. Only later did it appear so ironic. In November 1977 the Prince had been Lady Sarah's guest at the Spencer seat, Althorp in Northamptonshire, and it was here that the famed meeting between Charles and Diana is supposed to have taken place in a ploughed field, in an area known as Nobottle Wood. If the fortuitous meeting *did* actually occur, the impact was so great that neither of them can remember anything about it. Although Charles might not then have taken any great notice of Lady Sarah's youngest sister, still only a child compared to the Prince, one would imagine that if this were to be Diana's very first encounter with such a familiar figure she would certainly not have forgotten. She was well aware of Sarah's involvement with the Prince. Would a lively sixteen-year-old girl not be curious for a closer look? Would a teenage girl, home only for a short half-term holiday, interested in pop music and fashion, really be plodding through a muddy field on a pheasant shoot? Certainly we cannot believe that so great was the attraction that Charles was to wait until Diana was of a suitable age to make approaches.

At Althorp that weekend, however, the couple obviously did meet. We cannot be expected to believe that Prince Charles spent an entire weekend at the Spencer home without encountering Diana. She had taken a great interest in Sarah's new friend – what sister would not under the circumstances – and Diana even compiled a book of press cuttings it is said each time Sarah's name appeared in the gossip columns. A royal romance in the family was an exciting prospect, and a situation that made Diana jealous. It crossed everyone's mind that if Sarah did marry Charles, then Diana would make an excellent match for Prince Andrew, only a year older than herself. It was the age difference that was to keep the media off the scent for some time. Prince Charles' only recorded comment about the young Diana was that he found her 'an amusing, jolly and attractive sixteen-year-old.'

When Sarah passed out of the Prince's circle he seemed to mature for the first time in his life. Gone was the young man who wanted to fall 'in love with all sorts of girls'. Now the pressure was really on from the Queen for him to settle down. By now Prince Charles had become adept at keeping his girlfriends out of the public eye. While journalists speculated about brewery heiress Sabrina Guinness or Lord Mountbatten's granddaughter, Amanda Knatchbull, the Prince managed to entertain a number of young ladies who escaped notice through his discretion. One such was a Welsh receptionist called Janet Jenkins, who he met in Canada and was able to date on several occasions throughout his visit. On his return to England she was privileged with the telephone number of his suite at Buckingham Palace, and she once visited him at Windsor Castle. They salmon fished together, she joined the crowds anonymously to watch polo matches, and they corresponded when she returned to Montreal. Added to the unnatural conditions imposed on a royal romance, any possible relationship was stifled by the gulf of the Atlantic Ocean between them.

In the autumn of 1979, Lady Diana Spencer with her education complete started work at the Young England Kindergarten, Pimlico, London, looking after a group of small children three afternoons a week. So good did she prove to be at her job that she was quickly invited to look after slightly older children in the mornings as well. These were Diana's most relaxed and carefree days. Financially secure in a flat of her own, with a wide circle of fun-loving contemporaries, and a job that she adored, these are the few short months that Diana now treasures. At almost the same time that Diana began work at Young England, Prince Charles met Anna Wallace.

'Whiplash Wallace' as the fiery tempered blonde became known was introduced to the Prince at a polo match. For someone in Charles' position there were few other places to meet new women socially. Either they were part of the royal circle, friends of friends, or spectators at polo. Friends of the Prince insist that he was smitten with her almost from the start. Six years younger than the Prince, Anna Wallace was the daughter of a wealthy Scottish landowner, and the private secretary of Homayoun Mazandi, Princess Michael of Kent's former employer. An acquaintance of Princess Margaret's, Mazandi has been called the 'Caviar Queen' after the lavish lifestyle the Iranian-born socialite leads, a lifestyle that her less financially secure employees attempt to emulate. Anna Wallace obviously enjoyed the Prince's company; they maintained a relationship for almost a year and it is believed that in May 1980 Prince Charles made his first ever proposal of marriage.

The Queen Mother approved of this attractive girl's Scottish descent, and members of the Royal Household admit that Anna Wallace enjoyed the Prince's company, not because of *who* he was, but for himself alone. Perhaps this was the attraction for Prince Charles that someone wanted him as a man, not as heir to the throne. The last thing Anna Wallace wanted, in fact, was a throne. She could not cope with the royal way of life, the very idea of being a Princess frightened her, and although she did not decline his marriage proposal totally, she did ask for time before giving a decision. Within weeks Anna Wallace lost her opportunity to decline the Prince; the royal machinery for her departure had already been set in motion. News reached the Queen, via the inevitable gossip column, that her son was not Anna's first love – a rumour which happened to be true. Although today the Queen has accepted the fact that the wife of her second son, Prince Andrew, has had lovers in the past, the wife of the heir to the throne must be pure, to echo Lord Mountbatten's words. No matter how besotted Prince Charles was with this girl, he was forced to bow under the weight of convention, unable to marry the person of his choice for the reason he knew only too well. He was not choosing a wife, but a Queen. Words that had dampened every relationship he had ever had.

Anyone who incurs royal displeasure is subtly 'frozen out'.

One icy look from the Queen or the Princess Royal can speak more than volumes. Too upset to confront Anna with the truth, Prince Charles felt that the safest approach was to ignore the problem. At a party to celebrate the Queen Mother's eightieth birthday at Windsor Castle, the Prince left Anna alone at a table while he chatted animatedly to guests as if she were not there. After a time Anna Wallace's patience snapped, and she lashed out her feelings. Most reports insist that she screamed, 'I've never been so badly treated in all my life!' at the Prince himself, but those within earshot reveal that he was not even in the same room when she gave vent to her anger. Tearfully she left the party and was driven home by Lady 'Kanga' Tryon, whom it is said had not given the relationship her blessing.

It would have been better for Miss Wallace if she had taken the not-so-subtle hint to heart, but a few weeks later at a polo ball in Cirencester, given by Lord and Lady Vestey, the Prince spent the entire evening dancing with long standing friend Camilla Parker-Bowles, leaving the girl he had proposed to only weeks before alone again. Furious, once again, Anna Wallace borrowed Lady Vestey's BMW and drove herself back to London, and refused to see the Prince again. One month later she became engaged to the Honourable Johnny Hesketh, farmer brother of Lord Hesketh, whom she later married. Whether or not it was to spite the Prince cannot be certain, but her marriage did not last.

Further, the question has been asked, did the Prince marry Lady Diana Spencer on the rebound? Only a month after Anna Wallace drove out of his life at speed, the Prince met Diana again at Balmoral Castle. Her sister Jane, by this time married to the Queen's Assistant Private Secretary, Robert Fellowes, had just had a baby. As members of the Queen's administrative staff, it was necessary for the Fellowes to accompany the Court to Scotland. With a natural fondness for children, Diana rushed to see her new niece, Laura, at Balmoral. Although the Prince had scarcely considered Diana as even a friend, she had her sights set on this eligible bachelor. The sole purpose of the trip, however, was to visit her sister who had been provided with a small house within close proximity of the Castle.

No-one, not even the Prince and Princess themselves can now say when their courtship began. Balmoral was not the first time they had met that year; Diana had been a member of the royal party at Cowes Week – the annual yachting regatta on the South coast of England – a few weeks earlier, and had been to watch the Prince play polo at Cowdray Park in Sussex. This latter event was probably the most significant move on Diana's part. Why should someone not enamoured with horses, and with even less of a fascination for polo, make the journey to Sussex to watch a game? If it was at Charles' instigation, as many 'authorities' state, it seems uncharacteristically mercenary on his part. If he had been so hurt at the break-up with Anna Wallace, as those around him at the time insist that he was, it is hard to imagine that he would in any way attempt to seek a replacement within a matter of weeks.

In the chronology of the Prince's girlfriends it fits very neatly to have the next relationship following so hot on the heels of the previous one. It is convenient for journalists and authors alike to bring Diana Spencer on to the scene in the immediate wake of Anna Wallace, but Prince Charles is a deeply caring, sympathetic and emotional man; he does nothing impetuously and having taken so long to find a marriage partner in the first place, it seems doubtful that he would have become involved with Diana on the rebound. 'Perhaps he got to the stage where he just didn't care anymore,' says someone on the outer periphery of the royal circle. 'The pressures on him to marry were by then so great, his ego so deflated, that he just gave in and took the next suitable girl that came along.'

Such a notion seriously maligns the Prince's judgment and the truth of the matter is that for some time Prince Charles looked upon Diana only as Sarah Spencer's sister, while Diana viewed him as an attractive man that she would like to know better. In her company the Prince felt that he could relax, only later did his thoughts begin to turn to love.

One of the oldest clichés is 'being in the right place, at the right time' but a true adage in Diana's case. August of 1980 was a fortuitous month for Diana to have chosen for a visit to Balmoral. Prince Charles was depressed and vulnerable after losing the first girl he had ever asked to marry. He desperately needed someone that he could talk to, a shoulder to cry on. Lady Diana Spencer not only provided that shoulder, but her lively personality and ever developing beauty captivated the true blue-blooded male known to have a passion for blondes. The first anniversary of Lord Mountbatten's murder by the IRA was on 27 August. The assassination of Lord Louis had affected Prince Charles more deeply than any other event in his life; it had been a year of silent grieving and the horrors of that day were foremost in his mind twelve months later. Again, Diana's sympathetic nature did much to bring her closer to Charles. They walked together through the hills, fished on the River Dee, and the Prince pointed out his favourite haunts, and revealed some of his fears and aspirations. Most importantly of all these were days of laughter at a time that could have been clouded by tears. 'Sometimes when I'm fishing in the river I'm dying for a pee,' the Prince has said, 'I'm terrified that a photographer will train his lens on me at the wrong moment.' Even as they walked through the heather, enjoying each other's company, the first zoom lens was already focused on Diana. The resulting black and white photograph was uninspiring. With an early intuitive sense that she was being photographed, Diana had turned her back. *Sun* photographer Arthur Edwards took a picture of the girl's back and with Diana wearing a hat over a headscarf, a thigh length anorak, trousers and wellington boots, not an inch of flesh can be seen. The photograph could have been of almost anyone, yet it was enough to start a furore among the Press, who on 8 September 1980, declared **'In Love Again:** Lady Diana is the new girl for Charles', a claim based on no evidence other than that she had been spotted and identified in the hills with the Prince.

On her return to London, Diana unexpectedly received one dozen red roses: in one short summer, romance had really begun. Ahead lay five of the most difficult months that Diana was ever to experience. That she came through this challenge almost unscathed and still smiling, proved her worth as a future member of the Royal Family. Early in September reporters called at Coleherne Court and asked for Lady Diana Spencer in person. The unsuspecting porter innocently gave not only the number of her apartment but her telephone number too. From then on it was a diary of unrelenting pursuit:

16 September 1980: Diana's first taste of the Press at their worst: hoping that a brief period of co-operation would satisfy their voracious appetites, she agreed to be photographed with some of the children from the Young England Kindergarten. Innocently she stood with her back to the sun, unaware that the silhouette of every curve in her body was highlighted through her almost transparent skirt. 'I was so nervous about the whole thing. I don't want to be remembered for not having a petticoat,' she blushed.

17 September 1980: *Daily Mail* gossip columnist, Nigel Dempster, devoted his entire column to the girl he proclaimed as the future Queen, following Harry Arnold's earlier lead in the *Sun*. 'Lady ['Kanga'] Tryon has given her approval,' he declared.

18 September 1980: still embarrassed by the photograph that she would never live down, Diana became angry on finding one desperate photographer attempting to climb through a lavatory window of the Young England Kindergarten. 'All this fuss is disrupting my work with the children,' she said firmly.

After a week of intrusion, Diana literally kept her head down and provided no further comment. She learned to dodge the Press in her Mini Metro, and when a whole month passed with no definite clues, journalists inevitably speculated that the relationship was 'off'.

25 October 1980: the Prince of Wales went steeplechasing at Ludlow. Cameramen trained their lenses on him, hoping for a quote about the now much dubbed 'Lady Di'. Not until he came in second place did a familiar figure begin jumping up and down with excitement, having backed him each way. Diana quickly left in a different car to the Prince.

26 October 1980: Charles and Diana spent their first weekend together since Balmoral, at the home of Charles' old friends, the Parker-Bowles. They occupied their time with dodging reporters.

27 October 1980: Diana's mother attempted to quell the gossip in a statement saying that her daughter and the Prince were nothing more than friends; nobody was convinced.

28 October 1980: Diana was given a guided tour of Highgrove House, the first glimpse of her future home. This increased speculation that Prince Charles had purchased the property as a marital home.

4 November 1980: Princess Margaret gave a party at the Ritz to celebrate her fiftieth birthday. Among the select gathering was

Diana, looking demure in a peach evening gown. It was the first public acknowledgment by the Royal Family that Diana was being included in *private* family events. This would have been worthy of headline news, had Princess Anne not unwittingly captured the leading story herself. Not long before, Princess Anne had discovered that she was expecting her second child and the celebrations at the Ritz seemed like an excellent occasion at which to break the news, which she did at the private dinner before the birthday ball. In the early hours of 5 November the royal party returned to Buckingham Palace in jubilant spirits, which were dampened only a few hours later: with the arrival of the national newspapers at the Palace, came the glaring headlines announcing Princess Anne's pregnancy. It seemed that someone serving the dinner had betrayed the Royal Family to the Press. Having learnt from experience the futility of fighting the media, an official announcement was made from Buckingham Palace immediately, saying that the Princess was expecting a baby the following spring, thus putting paid to any newspaper editor's idea that he had a scoop. It also precluded the need for the Palace Press Office to confirm or deny the story.

It was also, for Diana, yet another important example of the Press's insatiable appetite for royal news, proving that royalty can trust nobody outside their own family and that beyond the Palace walls even the most private conversation, if overheard, is considered to be public information. If she had been unable to cope with such a revelation, especially in the light of the attention that she was already receiving, this was the moment at which Diana would have steered clear of the course that lay ahead. That she continued in spite of everything says much about her strength of character and her obvious love for the Prince.

10 November 1980: the Press wrongly declared that Prince Charles' engagement would be announced on his thirty-second birthday. Diana's step-grandmother, novelist Barbara Cartland, misguidedly 'reveals' her step-granddaughter's love of riding. Well meaning to the last, Miss Cartland simply meant to show that Diana shared the Prince's great passion and thus was obviously royal material.

11 November 1980: the Press are unable to find any suitable quotes from Diana and quote the Queen as allegedly saying 'She

is a delightful girl. Charles could not find a more perfect partner.'
Buckingham Palace refuse to issue a denial.

14 November 1980: Prince Charles' thirty-second birthday and
the much awaited betrothal announcement did not materialize.
The Prince gave no indication that he had seen Diana on his
birthday, even though the couple must have been in contact, said
the papers. What journalists did not realize was that Diana had
been secretly smuggled into Sandringham lying flat in the back of
a Cortina, one of many ploys used throughout their courtship,
reminiscent of Princess Anne and Captain Mark Phillips who
were smuggled past photographers in the back of horseboxes. On
one occasion Princess Anne even met her then husband-to-be in
disguise.

18 November 1980: Diana refused to speak to reporters back
in London, but remained unruffled when she could not open her
car door, and then flooded the engine! She maintained the
tight-lipped smile which was to endear her to so many media men.
'We all adore her,' confessed one hardened hack, who had never
before shown any emotion over his prey. It was a test of Diana's
stamina to appear outwardly unaffected by the coverage, but in
some ways it was her downfall because many journalists fell under
her spell and watched out for her not just to get a story, but also to
see her in the flesh.

21 November 1980: the Queen expressed her fury at a *Sunday
Mirror* revelation a few days earlier claiming, under the heading of
'Love in the Sidings', that Diana had spent the night with Charles
on the Royal Train. The couple had, the story stated, been on the
train on the night of 4 November after Princess Margaret's
birthday party. 'To suggest that the Prince of Wales used the
Royal Train for the sort of thing that is the clear innuendo in the
paper, caused offence . . . and is completely untrue,' stated the
Queen's Press Secretary, Michael Shea, quite categorically.
Editor Robert Edwards refused to retract the story, insisting that
he printed it in good faith. 'I don't even know what the Royal
Train looks like,' insisted Diana. Of all reports that she had read
about herself and the Prince this annoyed her more than any.
'People believe what they read,' she complained.

So angered was her mother, Mrs Shand-Kydd, that she wrote a
forceful letter to *The Times* decrying the behaviour of the media

towards her daughter, declaring that Diana was harassed from 'dawn until dusk'. Although irritated by what her mother termed 'fanciful speculation', Diana was not as frightened at first by the attention as many believe; she actually enjoyed being noticed. She was nineteen, still relatively naïve, and in love. Nothing could detract from the excitement of her romance with the Prince. At home in Coleherne Court she had the support of her flatmates, who could fend off callers, and share in Diana's exuberance. Once she had got used to the attention, Diana even enjoyed playing cat and mouse with the Press. On one occasion she packed up her car with suitcases, a coat and shoes, and then walked around the corner as if going to a nearby shop. She returned three days later, having spent a weekend with Charles in Scotland. Only then did the duped Pressmen realize that Diana was playing them at their own game.

In the Prince's company she had the protection of fast cars, the safety of the Palace walls, and the support of his staff. At Christmas 1980 the world expected Diana to join the Royal Family at Windsor, but she spent the festive period at Althorp with the Spencer family for the final time. It was to be her final non-royal Christmas as a Spencer. The next time she would sing carols she would be Mrs Windsor.

Immediately after Christmas the Royal Family made their annual pilgrimage to Norfolk, to see in the New Year at Sandringham. For royalty it is a second Christmas, decorations stay up until the end of January (disregarding the Twelfth Night tradition), staff on the Norfolk estate receive their gifts from the Queen, and the festivities continue throughout the month in a relaxed atmosphere before the relentless round of engagements begin once again in February. New Year 1981 was memorable, however, for its distinct *lack* of peace and goodwill, as hundreds of reporters and photographers surrounded the house. 'A very happy New Year – and to your editors a particularly nasty one,' grimaced the Prince of Wales, and in an unprecedented outburst (not the last she was to make on Diana's behalf) the Queen let the mask of dignity slip just slightly when shouting to photographers, 'Why don't you go away?' The reason was clear: Diana.

Recovering from an attack of influenza, which had left her feeling 'quite dreadful', Diana did eventually join the Royal

Family at Sandringham despite the siege. This was the ultimate confirmation that she was to become one of the Family. The Sandringham holiday is notoriously a family affair, and one for only the Queen's immediate family at that. The Windsor Castle celebrations are for the entire family, aunts, uncles, cousins, nephews and nieces, whereas the New Year Norfolk retreat is for Her Majesty's children and their partners, her grandchildren, sister and mother. That Diana had been invited as Prince Charles' companion could mean only one thing. Five years later Sarah Ferguson found herself in a similar position, as Prince Andrew's guest. In 1988, Prince Edward, the Queen's only unmarried child was allowed to take along twenty-two-year-old Georgia May, the daughter of a Hampshire yachting companion, leading to instant speculation of an impending engagement. Strangely, on this occasion, it was *exactly* what royal advisers had intended. Prince Edward had in the previous twelve months received so much bad press after resigning from the Royal Marines and spending a year floating around with no obvious role. He had put on a petulant display after organizing the 'Royal It's A Knockout' competition, and had received relentless ridicule on becoming a production assistant for Andrew Lloyd Webber's Really Useful Company. On top of all this, lack of girlfriends led to underground conjecture that Edward might be gay. The introduction of a possible 'girlfriend' to Sandringham at New Year, gave the ever-anxious Press a new, and this time acceptable, subject to bandy around.

By New Year 1981, after much soul searching, Prince Charles knew in his heart that Diana was the girl he wished to marry. He had consulted the Queen and by the end of the Sandringham holiday had her permission to propose. That he intended to ask her to marry him was no surprise to Diana. They had openly discussed marriage for many weeks as the Prince was determined to warn her of the pitfalls that royal life offered. For the most part Diana took no notice of the obstacles that the Prince placed in her way; her sole desire was to marry him, and she was prepared to accept all that such a union entailed.

In mid-January a skiing trip to Klosters, Switzerland, with the Palmer-Tomkinsons provided Prince Charles with a breathing-space which gave him time to finally assess his feelings: whether it was infatuation or love and whether he felt Diana could live with the pressures ahead and support him in his future role. He returned with a clear decision in his mind.

During this time apart Diana confessed that she missed Charles terribly. Perhaps secretly she feared that he might change his mind about her while they were separated, but she busied herself shopping and packing for a winter holiday she had planned to take with her mother in Australia. There seemed no reason to cancel it.

5 February 1981: on his return from Switzerland, Prince Charles invited Diana to dinner in his small three-roomed apartment at Buckingham Palace, on the eve of her departure to New South Wales. It was the night on which Diana was to make the most important decision of her life. She returned home to Coleherne Court bubbling over with excitement, hardly able to contain herself. She was able to share her secret with her flatmates, but had she been sworn to secrecy they would nevertheless have guessed from her mood. Prince Charles had asked her to marry him, and without a moment's hesitation, she had said yes. The two weeks in Australia provided an opportunity to reconsider, but Diana had no doubts.

23 February 1981: Diana officially met her future mother-in-law the Queen to be given the monarch's blessing. The Prince had already met and spoken with a delighted Earl Spencer, who had happily agreed to the union. 'What would I have done if he'd refused?' Charles laughed later. Earl Spencer and Diana's stepmother Countess Spencer, were invited to the Palace that night to meet the Queen and Prince Philip. An embarrassing situation was avoided in that Diana's real mother, Frances Shand-Kydd, was still in Australia so could not possibly be invited.

24 February 1981: the engagement of the Prince of Wales to Lady Diana Spencer was officially announced. This time Earl and Countess Spencer appeared with the crowds *outside* the Palace gates. With coyness and informality Diana showed off her oval sapphire engagement ring from Garrards – the Crown jewellers in London's Regent Street – admitting that she had chosen the most expensive one. Reputed to have set the Prince back £28,000, it felt unnaturally large to her. 'I can't get used to it,' Diana giggled. 'I even scratched my nose because it's so big', quickly adding that she was referring to the size of the ring, not her nose.

Now there was no turning back. In the eyes of the world she had made her choice, and within the time it takes to announce an engagement, Diana Spencer passed from commoner to royalty. She had 154 days left to come to terms with being a Princess. The rest is history. On Wednesday 29 July 1981, Diana gained a husband and became Her Royal Highness for the first time. As Mrs Charles Mountbatten-Windsor, Princess of Wales, she walked down the red carpeted steps of St Paul's Cathedral a member of the Royal Family and in putting her name on the marriage register it was as if she was signing her life away.

The first year of marriage can be a difficult period for any couple. Once the magic of the wedding has worn off, man and wife must learn to live with each other. Marriage to a member of the Royal Family can present many unexpected obstacles, often in the most basic details of everyday life. The first shock often comes on discovering that Prince and Princess will have separate bedrooms. This is perfectly normal for the Royal Family and does not mean that man and wife do not sleep together. The reason is simple. Every morning the Princess will have a maid and a hairdresser help her prepare for the day, possibly one of her dressers will be on hand if there is an official engagement, and the Prince in turn will have a valet. Not only would these five people get in each other's way, but the Princess might object to a valet watching her dress and the Prince would not wish Diana's maid to be present when he put on his clothes. In hotels the less discreet members of staff always look very carefully to see if both beds have been used, and on a tour of Australia in March 1983 it was pointed out that 'Diana's clothes were spread out on her bed in the evening, and were there untouched the following morning. Only one bed had been used . . .' Such unroyal gossip must be extremely daunting to any new member of the Royal Family, finding they have to be on guard even in the privacy of the boudoir for fear of the 'tittle-tattle' that will go on below stairs. When Michael Fagan managed to break into the Queen's bedroom in 1982, much was made of the fact that the Queen was sleeping alone, but she and the Duke of Edinburgh, like any royal couple, have *always* had separate bedrooms and dressing rooms. How they choose to use them remains their own affair.

If there were domestic changes for Diana to get used to, the bachelor Prince of thirty-two years had equally to learn to take his wife into consideration. Apart from periods at University and in the Navy, Prince Charles had spent the majority of his life being waited on hand and foot by a retinue of staff: footmen, under-butlers, equerries, now two valets, housemaids, have always been there to attend every need, from running his bath to polishing his shoes. Although Diana had by no means come from an underpri-vileged family, only a matter of weeks before her marriage she had been ironing her own clothes, buying her own food, washing her own hair. It is difficult to adapt to having people taking over your life when you have previously been in total control. Having finished a meal Diana automatically felt that she ought to clear the table. Although only steps between them socially as Earl's daughter and monarch's son, Charles and Diana were worlds apart in their lifestyles. If Prince Charles wanted a new shirt or tie he asked his valet to arrange it; if Diana wanted something new to wear she preferred to visit Harvey Nichols or Harrods and buy it herself. But as a Princess she no longer carried money . . .

When you own a home, as Diana had the Coleherne Court flat, you feel completely in control. If you are out for the day you know with certainty that nobody will enter your bedroom or sitting room. When you are royal, though you may be master or mistress of the house, staff are always around. When a new footman or underbutler is engaged, the head butler is quite likely to say: 'The Prince and Princess are away today, I will show you their rooms.' I, personally, know of one ex-member of staff who had left royal service in the 1960s, and on visiting an old colleague at Kensington Palace was given a complete guided tour of Charles' and Diana's apartments. With the knowledge that your home is shown off to visitors as an exhibit, and Diana must be aware that members of staff show their friends around in her absence, there must be the feeling that there is never any privacy.

Instead of eating meals that she herself prepares – and although she is modest about her culinary expertise Diana did undertake a cookery course with Elizabeth Russell in Wimbledon, south-west London, and later joined an agency and began providing snacks for cocktail parties – it might at first be fun to simply order any dish of your choice and have it provided by staff but it can become irritating to have people constantly hovering around you as you try to eat. At first Diana was always very conscious of what she said during meals because she knew that she was continually overheard. Although staff sign the Official Secrets Act which prevents them from revealing anything that they have seen or heard in royal service to an outside party, this does not prevent them from talking among themselves. At all costs Diana wanted to prevent someone removing her breakfast tray and returning to the kitchen with the words, 'Well, *she's* in a bad mood this morning . . .'

Prince Charles had grown up understanding how to handle staff, and is no longer conscious of the silent footman bringing his mail or an underbutler pouring his coffee. In many royal households there is a gulf between master and servant. Maids run bath water to exactly the right temperature, which in the case of the late Duke of Gloucester meant using a thermometer, tops are unscrewed from bottles and lotions, soap solution is placed on sponges (the Royal Family do not use face flannels) and the correct amount of toothpaste is squeezed on to the relevant brush. During the reign of Edward VII rows of washbasins were installed, each with a different function – for hands, faces or teeth.

At Althorp Diana had always been used to visiting the kitchen and helping herself to sandwiches; she would sit on the kitchen table and talk to the cook, and even now in her own home she often feels happier among the staff. The Duchess of Kent, formerly Miss Katherine Worsley, encountered identical problems at the time of her marriage exactly twenty years earlier. Her parents were Sir William and Lady Worsley, home was Hovingham House, Yorkshire, and she had been used to some staff being around. But when she married in York Minster in 1961 and subsequently moved to Coppins, Buckinghamshire, staff say that she felt happier with them in the kitchen than 'upstairs' whenever the Duke was away. Like Diana, the Duchess felt conscious that the staff might be watching her, thinking that she behaved wrongly or that she lacked dignity and she worried that they would perhaps talk about her among themselves. 'The old maxim about people being happier in their place is true,' says one now retired member of staff, who appreciated the changes in the Duchess of Kent after Princess Marina had explained how to handle employees.

This was very much the reason why Diana was happy with staff changes, more comfortable with young people with little or no royal experience who had nothing and no-one with whom to compare her. Attitudes towards domestic staff have changed. Gone is the Edwardian atmosphere of the lowly staff, knowing his or her place, and never getting ideas above their station. Only in the Queen's Household does this atmosphere appear to remain. People in service once expected to be ordered about and told what to do; in the enlightened eighties staff prefer to be requested, never demanded to do things.

Although she had known Prince Charles for over a year on an affectionate level, Diana did not really know and understand her husband until they actually lived together. She had been jealous of the Casanova playboy image that had built up around him as a result of his past girlfriends, all beautiful blondes or redheads, but was impressed by the 'action man' character that the Press had created: he had dived, windsurfed and parachuted, been stalking, fishing, shooting, yachting, climbing, golfing, racing and flying, all in addition to the more familiar sporting activities for which he is better known. All this contributed to the image of daredevil Prince.

However, although a courageous man, he had taken part in dangerous activities against his better judgment in order not to disappoint the expectations of his father. He has enjoyed the experiences, but would not have undertaken them without a certain amount of pressure on him to live up to the macho image required. For people in the Prince's position sport can provide a necessary release from the demands of everyday life, which is why he particularly enjoys equestrian sports. His sister, the Princess Royal, has said, 'When I'm approaching a water jump with dozens of photographers waiting for me to fall in, the horse is the only one who doesn't know I'm royal.' Prince Charles rides not only for sport but also because the animals can provide solace. Riding alone can be a form of escapism, and in Princess Anne's words it is refreshing to be with a creature who does not understand or care about royalty.

When Diana married Prince Charles, therefore, she discovered that the daredevil action man did not really exist. One journalist, somewhat unkindly, wrote that Diana had 'kissed a prince only to see him turn into a frog'. What she did find was someone who enjoyed home life and a quiet existence, someone who spends so much of his life being entertained officially, meeting thousands of new people every year, that when he does have time off duty he becomes withdrawn and a loner. In the early days of marriage, the young Princess felt restricted. She would be happy to dance the night away at a club, while her husband was used only to doing a foxtrot or a quickstep at a society ball. Diana enjoyed loud music; Charles appreciated peace and quiet. He liked Beethoven, Bach, Berlioz, Mozart and Verdi and his idea of 'pop' music extended to the Three Degrees and Barbra Streisand, while Diana preferred the Police, Elton John, Tina Turner and Mick Jagger. She publicly claimed that they both enjoyed the opera, but secretly she preferred a rock concert. Very early on Diana realized that she actually had far less in common with Charles than she had imagined. The thoughtful Prince could reflect back to the late 1950s and 60s with ease, days of which Diana could have no conception or interest. His passion for improving inner cities, community ventures, and decrying modern architecture are not social issues about which she feels strongly. Before the wedding she stated publicly that the age gap between them was insignificant. 'I just feel you're only as old as you think you are,' Prince Charles had said, 'Diana will certainly help keep me young.' But the challenge was a difficult one.

Charles' and Diana's courtship had been exhilarating for them both. Meetings had been daring, almost clandestine. They were days when they learned everyday facts about each other, small details which to lovers become endearing. Diana found it fun to piece together an account of Charles' life from his own words as opposed to what she had read in biographies. Here was someone that she *thought* she knew; it came as a revelation to discover that she knew so little. The pre-wedding preparations had kept Diana occupied and invigorated. With the honeymoon over she felt, in her own words, 'like the Princess in the Ivory Tower'.

Looking out on the real world from Kensington Palace, Diana longed to walk through Hyde Park as before, to go to Bond Street without a detective or to visit the cinema alone – she had everything but the liberty she desired. She had been the right bride socially, genealogically and physically for Prince Charles, but was that sufficient in the end? Did she and Charles actually have anything in common?

The Duchess of York is very like her husband, sharing many of his interests, as well as his sense of humour however childish it may occasionally seem to those around them. On a visit to Los Angeles in 1984 Prince Andrew pointed a spray gun at photographers, showering them with white paint and causing hundreds of pounds worth of damage to their cameras and clothes. Compensation claims were sent to Buckingham Palace and paid without question. It was the kind of joke that would have amused Sarah Ferguson who is equally amused by Prince Charles' hobby of collecting old lavatory seats, something we have come to accept in the light of Charles' Goonish sense of humour. Diana is less than enchanted, however, and she, in return, has complained to friends that 'Charles never understands my jokes'.

Charles and Diana have had to 'give and take' much more than many young married couples. He was too mature for his age, she too immature for hers; both have had to learn to be flexible and humour is one area in which Diana has made a very conscious effort to come in line with her husband. Prince Charles has long been a fan of the Australian comedian Barry Humphries and his unique creation, the 'wisteria-rinsed' egocentric Dame Edna Everage, an avant-garde act that Diana did not initially appreciate. Yet in recent years she has accompanied the Prince to a number of 'Dame Edna's' shows and Barry Humphries is a frequent guest of theirs at small dinner parties in Kensington Palace. In the summer of 1987, the Prince of Wales was playing a quiet game of polo on Smith's Lawn, when Barry Humphries arrived in the guise of Dame Edna, wearing a hat in the shape of Windsor Castle. Through a deliberate attempt on her part, Diana has learned to enjoy her husband's taste in comedy to an extent, although The Goons will never appeal – the radio series with Harry Secombe, Spike Milligan, Peter Sellers, and Michael Bentine, was in its heyday before she was even born, and when Charles was at Cambridge doing impressions of his favourite characters, Diana was only seven.

Unlike Charles and Diana, Sarah and Andrew are separated in age by only four months. Soon after they were married the Duchess learned to fly a plane and having acquired her wings, went on to fly helicopters, not just out of one-upmanship – although that is part of Sarah's nature – but also to give her a greater understanding of her husband's work and so provide a common bond. Since leaving the forces, Prince Charles has not had a specific job, though some would disagree: the Queen Mother when confronted by anyone who claimed that Charles had no job, replies curtly, 'He has. He is Prince of Wales.' Unfortunately, as King-in-waiting there is no cut and dried directive. Thus, other than grasping the concept of royal duty and learning the practicalities of official engagements, Diana cannot emulate her sister-in-law by finding out more about her husband's job.

It was not only Diana who had a few illusions shattered on marriage. Prince Charles quickly discovered that the sweet blushing English rose had a will of iron. Diana began to object if her husband appeared to be too much of a 'mummy's boy', and was angered if he attempted to please the Queen in preference to his wife. This was the cause of early friction. The Prince had always followed his mother's guidance and fallen in line with the traditions of the Court, assuming that his wife would 'tag along' wherever possible. But Diana had other ideas. Six months after the wedding they had a blazing row in front of staff at Sandringham when the Prince wanted to join the Queen's shooting party for lunch, and the Princess wanted to spend some time with him alone. So furious was she that she followed him out of the building and chased him in a separate car to continue the 'conversation'. Workers on the Sandringham estate could hardly believe their ears.

Arguments such as this were not uncommon. Always the Prince retained his dignity, while Diana shouted. Always the same subject sparked off the quarrel: the Family. Whether at Balmoral, Sandringham or Windsor, the Queen seemed to have a profound influence on her eldest son. Unlike the Prince, Diana was unable to conceal her moods. She angered the Queen by walking out of a dinner party because she simply could not cope with the demands. This had astonished the Queen's guests and upset

91

Prince Charles. A few weeks later, in March 1982, an argument flared up between Diana and Charles on the way to the Cheltenham Gold Cup race – one of the major horseracing events of the year. At the races she appeared sullen and sulky. The Prince fired questions at her as they stood in the Royal Box, and racegoers watched as the Princess shook her head in answer to each one then looked away. While the race was on she gazed aimlessly, looking everywhere but at the horses. Within hours the staff discovered that the couple were affectionate and apparently none the worse for the friction. Those who had witnessed the pair's less than buoyant mood at Cheltenham saw a different picture in June at Royal Ascot. The Prince and Princess openly cuddled each other in the Royal Box and sat with their arms entwined, almost oblivious to anyone else. The Queen smiled benignly.

The boring truth of Charles' and Diana's marriage to the chagrin of many a newspaper editor is that in seven years they have experienced the same ups and downs as any other married couple, only exacerbated through living in what Princess Margaret once described as 'a goldfish bowl'. In love but perhaps less compatible than most because of their opposite backgrounds, their life together has been happy and unremarkable.

Diana came from an insecure family, having to divide her loyalties between her two parents. With Charles she became part of a tight-knit family, so staunchly loyal that they are like a piece of England itself. Today she has created her *own* family and that is the one thing in her life which she will try desperately to maintain. 'Divorce' is a word that is bandied about by gossip columnists each time Charles and Diana appear to be going through a difficult patch in their relationship. However, it is *not*, never has been and never will be an option. Diana knows that she has an obligation to the Family to whom 'divorce' is an ugly word – it has reared its head too often since divorcee Wallis Simpson changed the course of history when she married Edward VIII, and the marriages of Princess Margaret, Prince Michael of Kent and the Earl of St Andrews have all been tainted by dissolution – but more importantly in Diana's case, even if life with Charles became unbearable she would remain with him for the sake of her children. Never will she allow her sons to suffer in the way that she did as a result of her parents' divorce.

When the state of Charles' and Diana's marriage is discussed, it is invariably sparked off by their apparent separations. When Diana was new to royal duty Charles accompanied her to 'show her the ropes'. Their first major tour of Wales in October 1981 was a resounding success. On a 400-mile tour of their Principality, Diana charmed well-wishers on walkabouts despite the pouring rain. From then onwards the Prince was at her side at a variety of functions from opening the twenty-fifth London Film Festival, to civic luncheons, planting trees in Scotland (when Charles unexpectedly put his arm around her waist and gave her a squeeze) to touring the York Railway Museum. He tried to initiate her in as many aspects of royal life as possible in order to launch her into a round of solo engagements. This came all too soon for her, but nevertheless without a hitch: despite having to make a speech, she opened the Royal Mail Depot in Northampton, later visited St Mary's Church of England Junior School in Tetbury and sat through their school assembly, and more publicly switched on the Christmas lights in London's Regent Street.

Diana having survived the ordeal, it was quickly decided that as the Prince and Princess receive some 4,000 invitations every year between them they could undertake twice as many engagements if they continued to have separate diaries. As soon as they began to live different working lives assumptions were made that their private lives must also be torn apart. The Queen and Duke of Edinburgh likewise share occasional functions, but also attend a great deal alone, which prior to their silver wedding anniversary had constantly led to reports of imminent divorce in all the European papers. In 1972, the year of their twenty-fifth wedding anniversary, the Paris newspaper *France Dimanche* calculated from cuttings that in the previous fourteen years the Queen and Prince Philip's divorce had been reported 116 times! By the year 2006 when Charles and Diana celebrate their own silver wedding anniversary, the number of similar cuttings is bound to be considerably higher.

Unfortunately Diana's informal approach on official engagements can be her downfall, leading to unnecessary comment. Just before Christmas in 1982 Diana visited the studios of Capital Radio. Invited to receive a book entitled *Tales From A Princess* written by fifty young listeners, it was one engagement that she was thrilled to accept as she listened to the radio station both in the car and at home – 'I bath the baby while I listen,' she told disc jockey Roger Scott. But to another member of staff she let slip a much more telling remark. Before Diana's arrival everyone had been requested not to smoke in her presence. One person felt too nervous, however, and was still stubbing out his cigarette as Diana approached. 'Sometimes smoking does help to reduce tension,' she said, then added, 'there are moments in married life when I feel I'm going to have to take it up in a *big* way.' That was the kind of remark she could have said light heartedly to friends but it was not a wise comment to make in a radio studio.

Because of the role they play publicly, the marriage of Charles and Diana is expected to be perfect. It isn't, and nobody could genuinely expect it to be. It is, nevertheless, successful. Following the early, more testing years of their marriage it still works because they have given each other space to breathe. Its strength is proven by the fact that they *can* spend time apart without any damage to their relationship. At the start of their marriage, insecure Diana still harboured jealousies about Anna Wallace, Dale Tryon, and Lady Jane Wellesley. Whenever she waved Charles off from the airport for a solo trip, she made no attempt to hide her tears. Now when it comes to airport scenes she is not only better in control of her feelings, but confident that the Prince will always come back to her.

In 1987 the Prince and Princess seemed to spend an unprecedented amount of time apart. In February Charles stayed on at Klosters after Diana had returned to be with the children and fulfil engagements; in March Charles spent a long weekend in Gstaad with friends, and in early April went to the Kalahari Desert with his mentor, South African writer Sir Laurens Van der Post. In May he went salmon fishing on the River Dee, again without Diana, following a controversial visit to Italy in April when false rumours circulated about his possible entanglement with the Contessa Fiammetta Frescobaldi, an Italian heiress. Finally when Charles spent three days on a remote island in the Scottish Hebrides to experience the life of a crofter like a saga from the Lillian Beckwith novel *The Hills is Lonely*, the Press not only saw it as the total collapse of the Wales' marriage, but in addition branded the heir to the throne mentally unstable, especially in the light of his saying that he talked to plants, a remark that he must have regretted as much as any of Diana's utterances. **'A Loon Again'** ran the punning headlines. With a circulation war between two rival British newspapers *Today* and *The Star* both serializing major articles on the Prince at the same time, and every gossip columnist propounding his or her views, a marital 'crisis' occurred without any help from Charles and Diana.

Still unable to completely ignore newspaper stories about herself, Diana became worried when she and her husband once again became victims of a relentless campaign. 'It's no good simply not reading the papers,' she says, 'I know what they are saying by the way the public react on engagements.' In a television interview with Sir Alastair Burnet she was asked how she felt about all the fabricated stories. 'Well, obviously, you feel very wounded. You think: oh gosh, I don't want to go out and do my engagement this morning, nobody wants to see me, help, panic,' she revealed, adding that she hoped that people did not believe everything that is written in the papers.

One example of how rumours occur was displayed by the French magazine, *Paris Match*. A journalist was convinced that Diana was being disloyal to Charles and above a photograph of her was the headline **'Lady Di Unfaithful?'** On the palm of her left hand, the story claimed, Diana had scribbled a message to a secret lover. With a magnifying glass the words had supposedly been studied to reveal that the Princess had a rendezvous with a Mr Shirley. Readers presumably believed that there was some element of truth, judging by the apparent photographic evidence, yet the words on Diana's hand really said: 'Smile, Daddy'. This story simply added fuel to the fire of the media's obsession at this time.

There is, however, no smoke without fire and although the media's claims throughout 1987 were way off the mark, there *was* a crisis in the Wales household. Contrary to belief, Diana was not the cause but in part the solution. Prince Charles' fortieth birthday, 14 November 1988, marked a milestone in his life. Although 'mid-life crisis' may be too strong an expression to describe the Prince's depression throughout the year approaching this landmark, he has nevertheless become increasingly concerned that his life appears to be slipping by without his having accomplished any great achievement. His mother could well be Queen for another twenty-five years – she would still only be eighty-seven, an age when her own mother was extremely sprightly – and this would mean that King Charles III would be sixty-five, the age of retirement in any other job, before ascending the throne. Sixty-five years of waiting. A deep, serious thinker, Prince Charles found 1987 to be a year of reassessment, a year in which he needed time alone to find himself. Just as Diana had to accept a particular way of life, so her husband wanted to be known for more than just handwaving and handshaking. 'You cannot understand what it's like to have your whole life mapped out for you a year in advance. It's so awful to be programmed. I know what I'll be doing next week, next month, even next year. At times I get so fed up with the whole idea,' said the Prince to a group of journalists in February 1987. An unexpected outburst from a man who has grown up knowing no other life, and most of all an ironic one – something one would expect to come from Diana, never from her husband. Could Diana after all have the edge over a true blue-blooded royal, having at least known freedom and the outside world? Have her experiences outside the gilded cage finally brought home to her Prince what he has missed? Suddenly, after forty royal years, is Prince Charles longing to break free and escape from royal duty? In the Hebridean croft there was no better place to find solace; in the Kalahari Desert there was space, away from people; on his beloved River Dee he could fish unhampered amid the peace of nature, and on the ski slopes at Klosters, amid the snow and *without Diana*, there was freedom from photographers. Even his 'official' visit to Italy to collect an award for sales of his book *The Old Man of Lochnagar* was not included on the list of his engagements submitted to the Press.

Having herself experienced moments of crisis, Diana knew that the best cure for the Prince was to allow him to 'do his own thing'. When from mid-September to mid-October 1987 the Prince was in Scotland away from Diana, the journalists felt that they had the answer to the problems. 'Go to him, Di!' they cried, as if a reunion were necessary. How she must have longed to be in a position to issue a reply, for she knew in her heart that their marriage would survive because they *could* be alone. To the outside world the marriage may seem unstable, only time will reveal that in Charles' and Diana's differences lies their greatest strength.

5

Mother of the King

It is a sad fact of royal life that before Diana could marry the man she loved she had to undergo a gynaecological examination. Had she been found unable to have children she could not have married Prince Charles.

Forty years ago, after a passionate and poignantly public romance, the Shah of Iran married his beautiful wife, Soraya. The glamorous couple were the Charles and Diana of the 1950s. Soraya was nineteen when she married and quickly became recognized as one of the world's most attractive women. As Soraya Esfandiary, the daughter of a Persian diplomat, she was unknown. Almost overnight the fairytale romance captured the imagination of the public, and married to a prince she was transformed into one of the first 'glamorous' royals, only to be paralleled a few years later by Prince Rainier of Monaco's marriage to actress Grace Kelly.

The Shah and Queen Soraya were unquestionably happy in their relationship, although it was very much an arranged marriage: by Iran's law the Shah was not able to choose his own bride, but had eventually to select a suitable person from photographs and a short list drawn up by advisers, almost in the way that Queen Victoria selected marriage partners for her children to link the European Royal Houses together. Although practically strangers when they married, Soraya and the Shah grew to love each other very deeply. Seven years later, still in love, the couple were forced to divorce for one solitary reason: Soraya could not give the Shah an heir. At twenty-six, Queen Soraya departed from Teheran airport supposedly on a short holiday to St Moritz. Smiling and waving, she mounted the steps to the aircraft wearing a truly royal mask that did not betray her inner emotions, and bade a final farewell. Only away from the public's gaze could she break down. She was never again to see the man she loved.

The much told story of Edward VIII and Mrs Simpson, the Duke and Duchess of Windsor, has long been classed as the 'greatest love story of all time', but the tragedy of Soraya must certainly rank very closely. For the Shah, it was his second divorce. Two successful marriages had been sacrificed for the want of an heir. In the principality of Monaco, had Princess Grace not given birth to Prince Albert the outcome could have been similar. Without a male heir the principality of Monaco would have reverted to France.

The constitution of the House of Windsor is such that the first-born male of the monarch is their immediate heir, taking precedence over any females in the line. The Queen had her children in a comfortable order, but had Princess Anne been born before Prince Charles she would have been superseded by him, just as she has now been pushed down the line of succession by her brothers and their children.

If *after* marriage Diana had not been able to have children, it is unlikely that she would have been divorced in favour of a fertile bride, but had she had a medical problem *before* marriage it is certain that she would have gone the way of Charles' former girlfriends. No adviser would allow him to marry in the knowledge that the line of succession would continue through Prince Andrew's children. At that time Prince Andrew was not married; in theory he could have remained single, and if married perhaps childless; it would then have passed down the line to Prince Edward.

The most comfortable and desirable outcome was for Prince Charles to marry and produce a male heir. Diana came up trumps and produced an 'heir and a spare', but from the time of her gynaecological examination she immediately felt the pressure knowing that she had a bounden duty to fulfil. So great was this pressure that she became pregnant as quickly as possible. Charles and Diana married on 29 July 1981 and by the end of September she knew that she was expecting a baby. No one had anticipated that the event would happen so soon; a month before her first wedding anniversary the new wife became a mother, beating the Queen who had given birth to Prince Charles just six days prior to her wedding anniversary by a number of weeks.

Ideally Diana would have preferred to wait. Ten days short of her twenty-first birthday, and with so much to learn about royal duty, she had become a mother while still coming to terms with her role as a wife. Yet she deliberately became pregnant for two reasons. Firstly, so anxious was she to provide an heir that she knew that she would never relax until she had given Charles a son, thereby also winning favour with the Queen. Secondly, less than enchanted with married life, the curtailing of her social life, and the feeling of isolation, she thought that a child would give her a sense of security and provide an object for her attention. A baby would also provide an excuse to stay at home and avoid the public engagements at which she was then still nervous.

Being pregnant held no fears for Diana. She loved children and was excited about the idea of having some of her own. Despite suffering severely with morning sickness, something 'nobody told me about', she had not anticipated the added difficulties of giving birth to a Prince. Because the child would be an heir to the throne and possibly one day King, pressure was on Diana to give birth at Buckingham Palace. There Prince Charles had been born in November 1948 in a temporary delivery room created in the nursery. Even though the then Princess Elizabeth and Duke of Edinburgh lived in Clarence House at that time, it was thought fitting that their first child should be born in a Palace. Princes Andrew and Edward, second and third in line to the throne at the time of their birth, were also born at Buckingham Palace. Ironically, only Princess Anne, who would be pushed continually down the line of succession, was born at Clarence House.

Queen Elizabeth II was born at the home of her maternal grandparents, 17 Bruton Street, London W1, and has now entered the history books as the first monarch to be born in a private house. Ranking third in succession to King George V, the likelihood of the Duke of York acceding to the throne appeared remote. Princess Elizabeth was the first-born child and it seemed probable that her parents, the young Duke and Duchess of York could eventually have a son and heir who would take precedence over her. Also her uncle, the Prince of Wales was heir apparent, free to marry and produce offspring of his own. No one could possibly forsee the path that lay ahead which, as a result of Edward VIII's abdication gave Elizabeth a crown.

With Diana's children there is less uncertainty. In the natural course of events, barring any great tragedy, sooner or later her first-born son will be King William V. For this reason alone there were demands made that Diana's baby be delivered at Buckingham Palace. Here she could stay during the final days of confinement, a delivery room could be created as it had been for the Queen, and when the baby was born it could be kept out of the public eye for as long as possible. Diana had other ideas. In November 1977 Princess Anne set a precedent by becoming the first member of the Royal Family to give birth in a hospital. She did not want the doctors and medical equipment to come to her, preferring instead to go to St Mary's Hospital in Paddington, west London, where all the latest technology was at hand should any complications arise. None did, but it led the way for other royal mothers to follow suit and Diana put her foot down and insisted that she would do the same. If it was good enough for the Queen's grandchildren by Princess Anne, there was no question that it was an unsuitable step for her next grandchild. In Diana's mind, and rightly so, she was concerned for the health of the baby, not the fact that he was royal. No objections could be made to this request. The days of home births are over and the majority of mothers prefer to have their child in hospital so that the baby can be monitored throughout. Much as the Royal Family would have preferred Prince William to have been born at Buckingham Palace, no serious objections to using St Mary's Hospital could be raised.

Although Diana had long decided on a hospital delivery, her concerns for the baby increased in the fourth month of pregnancy when she accidentally tumbled down the main staircase at Sandringham, just managing to catch hold of the banister half-way down to prevent herself from falling further. Prince Charles and members of staff rushed to her aid and the Prince helped his wife upstairs to bed while the doctor was summoned. 'Honestly, I'm alright,' Diana insisted, but she was forced to remain in bed until the doctor had given her a thorough medical examination and pronouced that the baby had been unharmed.

Despite the confirmation, there must have been a nagging doubt for the remaining five months that some harm had resulted from the fall, and members of the Family worried about the effects of delayed shock on Diana. What must have gone through her head as she lay tucked up in the 'Big House' in that January of 1982? She must have reflected back on the events of recent years: how she had once lived anonymously in Park House only a short distance away, now here she was a guest of the Queen, married to a future monarch, while inside her was a slowly-developing new life. Another monarch.

Whether or not Diana knew the sex of her baby before it was born has been the subject of much conjecture. When she worked at the Young England Kindergarten she had often joked that she wanted 'only daughters' because little boys were 'so rough', but her unexpected marital circumstances meant that a boy was necessary. Opening a community centre in Deptford, south London, on her last official engagement before the baby was due, a member of the crowd waiting to see her asked if the baby was a boy or a girl. 'It's a boy,' said Diana, quickly adding, 'I hope.' Speculation increased that she really did know the sex of her child, and certainly she had undergone an ultrasound scan which would have revealed the gender. This was quickly dismissed though by royal gynaecologist, George Pinker, who insisted that the scan was only to monitor growth, not to find out the sex of the baby. Opening a new maternity unit at Newham General Hospital, east London, in March 1986, Diana finally admitted, if unintentional-ly, that she had known the sex of both her children before they were born. So apprehensive was she, that she was determined to know the result as soon as it became available. Earlier reports had suggested that only Prince Charles had known.

Another 'secret' that Diana let slip was the possible birth date for Prince William, although it was intended only as a joke. When Diana visited St Gemma's Hospital in Leeds one of the patients, seventy-four-year-old Edwin Wilson, told her that he shared the same birthday as her father-in-law the Duke of Edinburgh, 10 June. 'It would be alright if the baby is born that day,' he laughed. 'No, it's going to be born on 1 July – *my* birthday,' Diana giggled. It was not intended as a revelation, nor was it the predicted date, merely an off-the-cuff remark to an elderly patient. To her horror the following day's newspapers stated, as fact, that the Princess had disclosed the exact date on which the baby was due. As it happened, Prince William of Wales was born at 9.30 p.m. on Monday 21 June, ten days before Diana's birthday.

From the outset the Prince and Princess of Wales have been progressive as far as royal parents are concerned. Attitudes towards royal pregnancies have altered immeasurably this century. When the Queen Mother, as Duchess of York, was expecting Princess Elizabeth in 1926, nobody other than the immediate members of the family even knew that she was pregnant until after the birth. She simply withdrew from public engagements. The Queen with each of her four children did not undertake any official duties in the final months, and it was forbidden to take photographs of Her Majesty in 'that condition'. Thus, no photographs of the Queen in maternity wear are available. When private photographs of the Queen sitting in bed with the baby Prince Edward were offered for sale there was a national outcry because of the indignity of our sovereign being pictured in a nightdress. Diana has been photographed through practically every stage of her pregnancies. Enjoying the prospect of motherhood she took to wearing maternity coats and dresses long before it was actually necessary. In the run up to Christmas and still only three months pregnant with Prince William she was sporting voluminous coats with hand appliquéd flowers, looking every inch the mother-to-be. Just days before the birth she was photographed at Ascot, obviously suffering some discomfort with one hand supporting the small of her back. A team of doctors and nurses stood by, and no restrictions were placed on photographers. Had the Princess gone into labour during the day, and not at 5.10 a.m. as she did, her mad dash to the hospital would no doubt have been recorded too. 'How would you like to have cameras pointing at your tummy all the time?' she had asked a journalist a few weeks earlier. Fortunately the Prince and Princess were driven to the hospital through the deserted streets of London before dawn.

Unlike previous royal fathers, Prince Charles was present at the birth and had taken a great interest in every aspect of the pregnancy, reading books and even attending a lecture on childbirth. 'He knows more than I do,' Diana joked, and after

103

the birth of Prince Harry she told nurses that her husband could have the next baby instead of her. 'He is so well informed about rearing children,' she told them, 'I'm just going to sit back.'

It is typical of the Prince's character that he should wish to become closely involved in something so important to him. On any routine engagement he has always done his homework thoroughly and has had the best advisers, so it is not surprising that he should be so well informed about children. He sat beside Diana throughout the sixteen-hour labour, mopping her brow, holding her hand and offering words of encouragement. He emerged from the hospital later looking flushed, but excited, announcing that 'it's a very grown-up thing' watching a baby being born. In complete contrast, Prince Philip had played squash while Prince Charles was being born and did not see the Queen or his son until it was all over.

Diana was determined to have a natural childbirth and despite the sparsity of the £100-a-day room in the Lindo Wing of St Mary's Hospital, the gynaecologist, Mr George Pinker, has said that he always tries to make the delivery as close to a home birth as possible. Only at the end, exhausted, was Diana given an anaesthetic to relieve the intensity of the pains. Just as when the Queen Mother gave birth to Princess Elizabeth by Caesarean section and the public were told only that 'a certain line of treatment had been adopted', so the discreet Mr Pinker would only say that the Princess 'did have a bit of pain relief. . . I can't go into details.' Once again, getting away from the mould of past royal mothers, Diana breastfed her children from the very start, something that would have shocked Queen Victoria. When she once saw her daughter, Princess Alice, breastfeeding one of her seven children, she was disgusted and promptly named a cow in the royal dairies 'Princess Alice'.

Only thirty-six hours after being admitted into hospital Diana discharged herself with George Pinker's approval, although the final decision was hers. Normally mothers are kept in the maternity ward for anything from two to ten days, but the Princess was not happy in the small twelve-foot square room, preferring to be home at Kensington Palace. Although nurses are discreet Diana felt constantly that she was being watched because of who she was. At home she could relax, and unlike most mothers she had staff to wait on her hand and foot if necessary. Doctors also believed that an early return home would lessen the chances of postnatal depression.

Diana's departure from hospital after the birth of Prince William in 1982 and that of Prince Harry two years later in September 1984, showed not only her ever-increasing confidence but a marked contrast between 'shy Di' and the glamorous media star that she has since become. After the birth of Prince William Diana appeared briefly with the baby on the hospital steps in a matronly green polka dotted maternity smock with a classic bow at the neck, sensible flat shoes, looking rosy cheeked as the wind blew through the famous 'Lady Diana' hairstyle that had become her trademark. Looking slightly embarrassed she could not wait to get in the car for the drive home. Two years on she emerged through the same doors of the same hospital carrying a new baby and looking a very different woman. Her new longer hairstyle was immaculate in every detail. She was dressed in a *Dynasty*-style red coat, complete with elegant high-heeled matching shoes and brimming with confidence. She looked as if she were on an official visit to a hospital; from her appearance it was almost impossible to believe that she had been through the agonies of childbirth only twenty-two hours before. Instead of keeping the world waiting for the new baby's name, this time the couple were prepared and the name was announced with the news of the birth itself.

On giving birth to Prince Harry, Diana ended thirty-six years of boy/girl births which had been the pattern of Windsor ladies since the Queen gave birth to Prince Charles followed by Princess Anne. Princess Margaret followed suit, so did Princess Alexandra and the Duchess of Kent, the Duchess of Gloucester, and Princess Michael of Kent. Even Princess Anne herself had a boy, Peter, followed by a girl, Zara. The chances of such a phenomenon within one family have been computed at 65,000 to 1. Diana broke the strange tradition and like her predecessor, Queen Alexandra, had two boys in succession.

Although the breaking with that particular tradition was something over which Diana could obviously have no control, there were others that were quite deliberate. First came the delicate question of circumcision, a ritual performed on all male babies in the Royal Family for generations. For four decades this task was performed by the same Jewish physician, Dr Jacob Snowman, who operated on Prince Charles shortly after he was born. Dr Snowman was the Chief Officer of the Jewish Initiation Society and each time he was secretly called to the Palace to carry out his duty the question was raised as to whether the operation should not be performed by a surgeon of the Royal Household rather than a Jewish 'mohel'. Although Dr Snowman is long since deceased, the inevitable question arose as to whether Prince William should be circumcised in the royal tradition. Diana felt the practice barbaric and medically unnecessary, and consequently this ritual was not carried out on either of her sons.

Back in the nursery the young Barbara Barnes replaced the archetypal nanny that had long been employed almost as a governess. She had previously worked for Colin and Lady Anne Tennant, friends of Princess Margaret, and Diana took her on, partly because of her informal approach. She preferred to be called by her Christian name as opposed to Nanny Barnes. She did not wear a uniform, and unlike the sometimes fierce royal nannies of the past, Miss Barnes did not believe in spanking her young charges, claiming that a more loving approach worked better than strict discipline. Those who work for the Prince and Princess have their reservations about this approach, and sadly feel that Barbara became too attached to Prince William, letting him have his own way just a little too often. When Prince Harry came along, Prince William still received most of the attention, something Diana had tried extremely hard to avoid.

As a mother Diana was quite unlike other members of the Royal Family. She was only too aware that she needed a nanny because of the busy life that she herself led, but unlike the Queen who sometimes only saw the children for an hour at bathtime because of her schedule, Diana has always been determined not to become a remote figure. Not only did she want to watch her children grow up and have some influence over their developing characters, she also gained an enormous amount of pleasure from motherhood. Never did she tire of washing, dressing, feeding, and playing with her sons. When she had to be away for a day on official duties she was always anxious to get home and refused to take on evening engagements that would keep her from putting the boys to bed, only accepting invitations that began late in the evening such as a theatre or cinema gala performance. Wherever possible she left dinner engagements to Prince Charles, never enjoying such functions anyway and detesting speechmaking. Although she says that she is never on a diet, she does not like being confronted by large platesful of rich food on any occasion, not only because she is a small eater, but because people always engage her in conversation throughout the meal and it becomes impossible to eat and speak at the same time. She only now attends State Banquets because it is expected of her.

The greatest battle Diana has fought for her sons is an attempt to allow them to live as normal a life as possible within the confines of having the Queen as a grandmother and the future King and Queen as parents. It is a dilemma that Princess Anne faced with her own children and the reason that she has continually fought against Peter and Zara being given titles. Although the Queen is said to have been unhappy at first about two of her grandchildren being commoners, Princess Anne maintains her stand. The Phillips children will never undertake royal duties, and she feels that as plain Master, Mr and Miss they stand a marginally better chance of escaping the limelight for as long as possible. As they grow older and nearer to marital age interest in them will probably grow, but Princess Anne is delaying the evil moment for as long as possible.

For William and Harry there is no possible chance of them ever enjoying the anonymity enjoyed by Peter and Zara Phillips by the very nature of their proximity to the throne. Although the Phillips children are eighth and ninth in the line of succession, they are far enough away to be able to live their own lives and have careers of their own choosing. Before William and Harry were even born their entire future was discussed and tentatively mapped out. Should they go to Gordonstoun like their father? Will they go to Cambridge? Which branch of the Services should they join? Although they are still too young to understand it will come as a shock when they discover that they have so little control over their futures. The day Prince William was born it was pointed out that he would one day become Duke of Cornwall, as soon as Prince Charles becomes King. Peter and Zara Phillips will have to earn their own living, even though their mother is the Queen's only daughter, but for Princes William and Harry the

Duchy of Cornwall and the Civil List will provide an income. When Charles becomes King he will inherit his mother's Civil List allowance, Prince William will inherit the Duchy of Cornwall money, and Prince Harry as the second son of the monarch would, like Prince Andrew now, be entitled to an annual allowance from the Civil List. Few children are born with such cut and dried prospects.

As Prince William became older he became increasingly aware that there was something special about his life, even though his parents tried to keep from him as long as possible the fact that he would one day be King. Although he had to be told before he began school and found out from someone else, he can still have no possible conception of what it means, other than that he *is* different. Over the past years varying reports of William's arrogance filtered through and those who came into contact with him remarked on his precocious nature, something which could have been avoided. It is an unfortunate trait that was never allowed to develop in Prince Charles at that age because, many of the older members of the Household feel, he had a much stricter upbringing and learned the meaning of respect at a very early age. Prince Charles was upset when his son was cheeky to staff or misbehaved, but despite his conscientious reading does not always know how to handle the situation. Likewise, Diana can never find it in her heart to be really angry with her children if they misbehave; she cuddles them if they have been told off by their nanny, and bribes them with sweets and biscuits if they will not do what she wants. For too long she allowed Prince William his own way, and it is only since the departure of Barbara Barnes that he has begun to grow into a better-mannered child. Diana found it difficult to draw a line between protecting her children from the pressures of the world outside that would one day intrude upon their lives too greatly, and instilling standards that would help them cope when the realization did dawn. In many ways, it seems, she over-compensated with too much love. Because she had come from a broken home and had suffered an unhappy childhood, she tried to make sure that William and Harry experienced a loving and secure home life. Separated from them because of royal duty, she offered only love and not discipline when they were together.

Ideally Diana would have liked to have taken a few years 'off work' and spent the time entirely bringing up her children. Had she married a member of the aristocracy, this would have been possible, but she married someone royal and as a result she was forced to continue with her duties. Each time she and the Prince had to go away on an official tour she worried that her sons would forget her. With the approach of their 1983 tour of Australia Diana fought to take Prince William with her, anxious not to miss his first steps, his first words, and determined not to be apart from his for so long. In July 1982, after Diana's first public engagement since giving birth, the Wales' Australian tour was announced: **'Baby Prince Must Stay At Home'** said the headlines, 'He must stay because Prince Charles and his son are not allowed to travel on the same plane . . .' It was the start of a five-month battle, for Diana was determined not to be parted from her son. 'If William doesn't go, I don't go,' she eventually threatened, knowing that seven weeks is a long time in a young baby's development. The Queen as a young mother was often parted from her children for months on end. In 1953 she embarked on a tour of the Commonwealth in the knowledge that she would not see her children for six months. When they did meet up later on board the Royal Yacht *Britannia*, the Queen said of Prince Charles and Princess Anne: 'They were terribly polite. I don't think they knew who we were.' The first time that the Queen ever heard Prince Charles read was over the telephone. Even though royal tours are now much shorter, Diana was adamant about not missing out on her baby's development. Eventually Buckingham Palace announced that Prince William would be travelling to Australia after all. He would not tour with the Prince and Princess, they revealed, but would remain with Barbara Barnes at Woomarga-ma in eastern Australia. Charles and Diana flew to see him at approximately three-day intervals, making Diana's first major tour even more physically exhausting than it might have been.

Although she had won the first round by becoming the first member of the Royal Family ever to take their baby on a foreign tour, ultimately she was forced to concede. Diana had to admit that having William with them abroad had not been 100 per cent successful and when they left for a three-week tour of Canada on 14 June of the same year, Prince William stayed at home and

Diana had to miss her son's first birthday. No matter how hard she fought against royal dictates, somehow she invariably lost out in the end. Or so it seemed. The reluctant royal, however, nearly always continues to fight back. In October 1983 Charles and Diana had a tour of Italy on their schedule which once again meant leaving William behind. Was it mere coincidence that she became pregnant for a second time and the tour had to be postponed?

When the Queen had young children she always placed duty before her family. Charles and Anne were, at five and three, the same age as William and Harry are now, when Her Majesty left them for six months to undertake her Commonwealth tour in 1953. When they later suffered childhood illnesses there would often be a period of isolation for the children if there was ever a risk of the Queen catching their germs. In total contrast Diana's children have always taken precedence over her working life, and far from receiving criticism her concern has won her praise. Even though she could leave her sons in the safe hands of a nanny through the night, she will invariably spend the night in the nursery if either William or Harry are unwell.

Sunday 8 May 1988, was a relaxing day for the Wales family. The Queen and the Duke of Edinburgh were still on their Bicentennial tour of Australia, and Diana took Harry and William to Windsor to watch Prince Charles play polo on Smith's Lawn before he set off for a sketching holiday in Italy. That evening Diana and the young Princes were driven to Kensington Palace in preparation for school the following day, unaware of the drama that the next twenty-four hours were to bring. During the night Prince Harry developed severe stomach pains. Anxiously Diana had a doctor summoned and a call was put through to the kindergarten to say that the Prince was unwell. A hernia was diagnosed, and that same evening the Prince was admitted to Great Ormond Street Hospital in London for a minor operation. Hospital staff were given no warning of who their patient was.

Normally hernia patients are kept in overnight and are operated on the following morning, but within a short time of being admitted Prince Harry was given a general anaesthetic by Dr Edward Sumner before the forty-minute operation was carried out by consultant Mr Patrick Duffy with 'complete success'.

Diana was given a room at the hospital but remained at her son's bedside for most of the night, keeping in touch with Prince Charles by telephone. At midday on Tuesday the Princess drove back to Kensington Palace with her son and although relieved it was obvious that she had not slept. Returning to her engagements the following day to open the new Leisure Pool at Sheringham in Norfolk and visit a hospital in Norwich, she revealed that she had not slept for two nights and having fulfilled her duties she could not wait to get home to Kensington Palace. For Diana, being a mother will always take priority over her position as Princess.

Ahead of Diana lie a number of battles. One will certainly be that of the young Princes' education, with which she has so far had her own way. She ruled out any suggestion that a governess might be employed to teach the children at home. She had a governess until she was six, Prince Charles until he was eight, and they both experienced a difficult transition when eventually they had to mix with other children at school. At the earliest opportunity both William and Harry were sent to Mrs Jane Mynors' discreet kindergarten in Notting Hill Gate, London, less than five minutes' drive from Kensington Palace; William in September 1985, and Harry two years later in September 1987. On entering his fifth year, Prince William progressed to Wetherby School, even closer to Kensington Palace, that the Kent children already attended. Prince Harry will follow in 1989. This early education has proved acceptable, but the fight will come for Diana when suggestions are made about boarding schools for her sons. Already advisers feel that the Princes should go to a boarding preparatory school at the age of eight. Even if Diana wins the battle to keep them at home, she is certain to lose the fight, and will have to give in when it comes to sending the boys to boarding school at thirteen. By that time (1995 for Prince William) Diana may well have more children at home and might then be less concerned about the absence of her two eldest sons. Sending them away, however, will be an event to which she will be forced to concede in the knowledge that it will be best for her sons to experience a 'normal' education with children of their own ages. If she is still the doting mother, she might well try and arrange for them to be weekday boarders only, in the same way that Princess Anne's son Peter is away from home from Monday to Friday, but returns home each weekend so that the Phillips can be together as a family. Wherever possible Princess Anne avoids engagements on Saturdays and Sundays that might keep her away from home.

'Compromise' is the key word for Diana when it comes to bringing up children. She is keen that she and Prince Charles will have the final say in the Princes' future, but when it comes to further education and 'careers', higher authorities within the Royal Family may well insist on making decisions if it is felt that Charles and Diana have made the wrong ones. On 22 December 1965, a typical conference was held at Buckingham Palace to discuss what was to be the next stage in Prince Charles' future. The select gathering included the then Prime Minister, the Archbishop of Canterbury, Earl Mountbatten, the Chairman of the Committee of University Vice Chancellors, the Duke of Edinburgh and the Queen. It was Earl Mountbatten who came up with the programme that was finally accepted – Trinity College, Cambridge, like his grandfather, the Royal Naval College at Dartmouth like his father, and then into the Royal Navy. The heir to the throne's future was thus settled by a committee, not just by his parents, and the same will happen at various junctures in Prince William's life. When a member of the Royal Family rebels and does not follow the course laid out for them, horror is expressed at dissension in the regal ranks. This was apparent when Prince Edward chose of his own accord to resign from the Royal Marines in 1987, resulting in a rift with the Duke of Edinburgh who is their Captain General.

To have her sons' lives mapped out at an early age is upsetting to Diana, who continually insists that they must be brought up as ordinary children, but can her wishes be seriously carried out? Possibly Prince Harry as the second-born son can remain further in the background, but is it really possible to treat Prince William as anything other than a future King? Already it seems that the young boy is confused. As he began to grow older and more inquisitive it became impossible to shield from him any longer the fact that he is royal. He and Harry now join the Family on the balcony at Buckingham Palace at major royal events, such as Trooping the Colour. As he gazes down at the thousands of people crowding down outside the Palace railings, he must know with what Prince Charles once called a 'ghastly inexorable' sense that he is different. He may not know why, he cannot know why, but it is a truth that cannot be stifled.

Prince William's behaviour at Balmoral in the summer of 1987 shocked members of the Royal Highland Fusiliers when he announced that he would one day be King. 'Come on soldier boys, you're useless,' the five-year-old shouted at the horrified guards. From the cute chubby-faced 'mini tornado' whose mischievous antics charmed the public, overnight William established the image of a precocious, uncontrollable spoilt brat. Obviously he had been told the truth, but it can have meant nothing. To William and Harry the Queen is 'granny', and as they chase her around the private apartments at Buckingham Palace, often on her hands and knees, she is nothing more than that. They have no concept of her official role. When her children were asked, 'What is it like to have the Queen as a mother?' they could only ever reply that she was their mother first and foremost; she also happened to be Queen. The same can be said for the young Princes of Wales. To them, Charles and Diana are simply 'Papa and Mummy'.

The saddest image of Prince William was seen on the day he left Mrs Mynors' kindergarten for the last time. His classmates asked him which school he was going to next. 'I don't know. I'm not allowed to know because of security,' he said. Even at the age of three Prince William was met at the steps of an aircraft bound for Aberdeen, Scotland, on the first stage of a journey to Balmoral Castle. As he had been taught to he shook the hand of Group Captain Jeremy Jones, who was to pilot the craft. It was an early display of protocol, and a rehearsal for someone who will spend a lifetime shaking hands. At three he understood how to shake hands, but he did not know why he was not allowed to fly in the same plane as his mother, father and brother. The lonely boy mounted the aircraft steps with just Barbara Barnes in attendance.

For Prince Harry the pressures are fewer as the second-born son; a position which was described by King George V as 'either a burden or a blessing depending upon your luck'. In reality second-born *can* imply second best to a royal heir, as the interest always appears to centre on the elder brother or sister.

Invariably this situation turns the second-born into a rebel: Princess Margaret always felt overshadowed by her sister,

Elizabeth; so did Princess Anne by her brother Charles. Anne was livid when her brother was allowed to attend their mother's Coronation while she, as a three-year-old, had to remain at the Palace. At such a young age the Coronation itself meant nothing to her, but she had a strong sense that she was not wanted. She remembers vividly the feeling 'of being left out of something . . .' the sisterly fury of being left behind. She was left to play with a group of cousins 'for whom I couldn't have cared less.'

As a mother Diana tried very hard to avoid the possibility of Prince William becoming jealous of Prince Harry. In a normal family the first child *does* need to be coaxed into accepting a new brother or sister who suddenly takes up a large slice of the attention, but their family is in no sense normal. The attention will always be on William, and it could be that Prince Harry required a great deal more care to avoid an inferiority complex. One criticism of Barbara Barnes was that she appeared outwardly more affectionate to William than Harry. The over-confident William has already held his timid brother out of a window at Windsor Castle by his ankles, and when they travel by car it is the quieter, more withdrawn Harry who is travel sick. One blessing for Prince Harry though is that there will not be the sense of 'inescapable destiny' that Prince Charles has said he feels and that Prince William will feel too. Harry will also have the freedom to marry a bride of his own choosing. Prince Andrew, for example, as a second son was allowed to marry Sarah Ferguson who freely admitted to previous relationships, while Prince Charles was only able to marry a girl with 'no past'. If he so wishes, Prince Harry could easily opt out of royal duty and pursue a career. For the future King William this option does not exist.

One blot on the horizon which must be considered, however, is the way that many second-born sons have by a strange hand of Fate eventually become monarchs. The Queen's grandfather, King George V, was a second-born son, and became heir to the throne when his elder brother Prince Albert ('Eddie') died very suddenly at the age of twenty-eight after influenza caused a fatal inflammation of the lungs. The Queen's own father, King George VI, was not expected to inherit a crown but no one could have anticipated that his brother would abdicate. Neither King had contemplated their future, nor had they any training to be

In 1972 the Queen gathered twenty-one members of her immediate family together for this formal photograph by Patrick Lichfield, an exercise which has not been repeated since *(Camera Press)*

Diana makes her first appearance on the famous Buckingham Palace balcony in June 1981, still not officially a royal *(The Photo Source)*

One of the Family . . . ?

While Diana still seems slightly ill-at-ease in the presence of the more senior royals such as Princess Anne, Princess Margaret, the Queen and the Queen Mother, she certainly enjoys a good natter with younger members of the Family, like sister-in-law Fergie and Lady Sarah Armstrong-Jones *(Syndication International, The Photo Source, Camera Press)*

Above: A new generation of Windsors; Diana breaks with tradition by taking Prince William to Australia in 1983 *(Anwar Hussein)*

Opposite: Diana displays the much coveted Family Order bearing the Queen's portrait . . . ultimate acceptance? *(Camera Press)*

Right: A characteristically informal shot of Charles and Diana with the young Princes. Diana is far more interested in her thumb-sucking son, Harry, than in the camera *(Syndication International)*

A sense of belonging; Diana smiles affectionately at her father, Earl Spencer *(The Photo Source)*

Diana with her father and step-mother, Raine watch proudly as the Princess makes a speech to mark the opening of the Spencer Wing at Northampton Hospital *(The Photo Source)*

Diana's elder sister, Sarah, once tipped to be Princess of Wales *(Anwar Hussein)*

Diana's maternal grandmother, Ruth, Lady Fermoy, a member of the royal circle before Diana entered it *(Anwar Hussein)*

A nostalgic return to West Heath school for its most famous pupil. Other past students include Anne Beckwith-Smith (centre) and Diana's sisters Jane and Sarah (far right) *(Press Association)*

Two former non-royals find it hard to accept that royal grief cannot be kept from the public eye as they return home from Switzerland with the body of Major Hugh Lindsay in March 1988 *(Syndication International)*

monarch. George VI said that he had never seen a state paper in his life until he reluctantly accepted Edward VIII's unwanted crown.

Obviously Diana cannot bring herself to think that her second son may one day be King, it would mean untimely deaths for both her husband and her eldest child. We cannot foresee great tragedies, but history teaches us that Prince Harry could, in theory, become Henry IX; both Henry VIII and Charles I came to the throne only through the early demise of their elder brothers. As sensible parents, Charles and Diana will see that Harry is given a specific role in life to avoid the second-son syndrome, but if Diana has her own way it will be a role of Harry's choice. Nevertheless, just as William is trained from birth for sovereignty, so Harry should learn to be an understudy.

The burden of responsibility will come to William and Harry all too soon and for as long as possible Diana will allow her sons to be children, young boys rather than Princes. The need for a nanny is inevitable and the current holder of the post is forty-one-year-old Ruth Wallace who for five years looked after Prince and Princess Michael of Kent's children, Frederick and Gabriella, at Kensington Palace. Looking like Julie Andrews in *Mary Poppins*, she pushes Prince Harry through Hyde Park in a pushchair anonymously, and she becomes equally unobtrusive back at the Palace whenever Diana is free to take charge of the children herself. Although it is nanny 'Roof', as she is called, who wakes the boys up in the morning at 7.30, washes, dresses them and gives them breakfast at the pine nursery table in the mornings as Charles and Diana are usually preparing for a day of engagements, they never go to school without seeing their parents first and Diana will often drive them to school herself. On their return at 3.30 in the afternoon, Ruth Wallace will supervise their play if Diana is not around, but as soon as she returns to the Palace Diana immediately goes to see William and Harry. She frequently visits Sainsbury's supermarket herself to buy food for their tea, and whenever possible both she and Prince Charles bath the children, put them to bed and read bedtime stories.

During weekends, back at Highgrove, the Princes are able to spend more time with their parents, but in London if official duties keep Diana away she ensures that they are constantly occupied and stimulated. There are the Fellowes children to play with (her sister Jane's), and more recently Diana has encouraged the Princes to take responsibility for pets. Each of them now has a rabbit, and there is a Jack Russell terrier called 'Tigger', who is leading the future reigning family away from corgis. As lovers of music, Charles and Diana have also encouraged their sons to play the piano and Prince William is taken to St John's Wood in London each Wednesday for a music class in a church hall at £50 a term. Taught by the noted promoter of children's concerts, Anne Rachlin, the appropriately called 'Fun with Music' class could lead to the Prince one day performing publicly.

Having two healthy sons has been a constant source of pleasure to both the Prince and Princess of Wales, and fatherhood has certainly lost Prince Charles his former crusty bachelor image. Before marriage to Diana few could have envisaged the Prince changing nappies and bathing babies – parental skills at which he is now quite adept. So relieved was Prince Charles to have a son and heir that when Diana gave birth to Prince William he gave her a £100,000 necklace in the shape of a loveheart for her birthday, a contrast to the £2,000 watch he had given her as a birthday present in the previous year. One year later he gave her another necklace, this time in gold, with a medallion that bore an inscription in his own handwriting. On it was just one word: William.

It is just one more irritating fact about Diana's position that for the next twenty years journalists will always be on the lookout for signs that indicate further pregnancies. When she fainted at the Expo '86 exhibition one British national newspaper ran a front page headline not only stating that she was expecting a baby but even giving the date on which it was due. The couple's harassed Press Secretary, then Victor Chapman, had to issue a firm and positive denial. A year later on an official visit to Spain in February 1987 Diana stated quite deliberately at a Press reception 'I'm too busy to have any babies for at least a year,' in an effort to prevent any more rumours from starting up. When, after the year had passed, in February 1988 news of the Duchess of York's impending 'happy event' was announced, those close to Diana knew that with four years having passed since her last pregnancy she would soon get broody and that not many months would pass before an announcement would come heralding Diana's third child. 'I'd love to have lots of daughters, it would be so much fun dressing them up,' she once confided. It is a prospect that has royal fashion designers waiting with bated breath.

6

One of the Family?

'If she can't endure an ordinary family dinner I simply don't know how she is going to cope at banquets,' complained the Queen to Prince Charles, not so privately, after Diana had appeared bored throughout an evening meal at Balmoral shortly after their return from honeymoon. Throughout dinner the Princess had toyed with her food and made little conversation with anyone other than her husband. The Queen refused to dismiss Diana's behaviour as nerves. Having been a guest at Balmoral and Sandringham long before their marriage it seemed impossible that she might now be intimidated by the august collection of Prince Charles' immediate family. Although the Queen's observations that her daughter-in-law could not apparently cope with a family dinner were astute, it came as a surprise to Her Majesty to discover that Diana sparkled at her first State Banquet, in March 1982, given in honour of the Sultan of Oman.

Meeting important dignitaries, dressing up for a glittering banquet and making smalltalk with celebrities, presented no particular fears for Diana. It was the private Family occasions that caused greater anguish. At a State Banquet or reception there was an opportunity to speak with dozens of different people, often terribly nervous individuals who the Princess could make feel confident. On an official visit she was accompanied by the trusted Anne Beckwith-Smith or an equally competent lady-in-waiting, but at a small lunch or dinner with the Windsors, Diana felt an absolute outsider. Not witty enough for Princess Margaret, not horsey enough for Princess Anne, too remote from the Queen and the Queen Mother, there were few members of the Family with whom she felt really comfortable. It was a problem that Prince Charles found difficult to appreciate.

Diana's own family life had done little to help integrate her into the Royal Family. Although she was close to her sisters and younger brother, the atmosphere at home in Park House was not always happy. Certainly the relationship between her parents, then Viscount and Viscountess Althorp, was strained as their twelve-year-old marriage began to founder when Diana was only six. For the three preceding years it had been heading towards rocky ground and despite attempts to hide this, it was impossible for their children not to sense the friction between the feuding Frances and Johnny.

In many ways Frances Spencer was discontent with her way of life, and more importantly the prospect of her future. As Frances Ruth Burke Roche, the younger daughter of the late Baron Fermoy and Ruth, Lady Fermoy, she had married Edward John Althorp in Westminster Abbey on 1 June 1954. It had been the society wedding of the year. Like Diana, Frances became pregnant within the first year of marriage, their eldest daughter Sarah being born nine months after the wedding. Eventually, they moved into Park House on the Sandringham estate which had been Frances' childhood home, and where Diana would be born in 1961. Johnny, as Viscount Althorp was heir to the title of Earl Spencer and would eventually become eighth Earl on his father's death, inheriting Althorp House, the estate in Northamptonshire, and all that it entailed. This meant that the first years of marriage were a time of waiting, in the knowledge that 'greater things' were one day to come with the inheritance, but in the meantime Johnny had to find a role for himself.

Not only was Frances discontent with the job that her husband found as a farmer, which meant that she spent a great deal of time alone and had a very limited social life, she did not relish the idea of becoming Countess Spencer in the future or moving to Althorp. After a rift with his father, Johnny did not visit Althorp House and it held no pleasant memories for the couple. A kindred spirit to Diana, Frances enjoyed socializing, loved the theatre and adored watching tennis, she liked buying clothes in London, but preferred a quiet life without hankering after a title. Today she is able to divide her time comfortably between her houses on the remote Scottish island of Seil, in London and Australia, providing her with both variety and anonymity. Her daughter has the former, but never the latter; unlike Diana, Frances was eventually able to escape from a situation that she found intolerable.

At a dinner party in 1967 Frances met Peter Shand-Kydd, wallpaper heir and sheep farmer (from whom she is now separated). Although both were married with several children, there was an instant rapport between them, Frances admiring what has been called the 'gypsy' characteristics of Peter, who was so different to Johnny Spencer: Johnny had resigned himself to his future, but when Peter Shand-Kydd inherited his father's firm, he rejected it and began a new venture in New South Wales. Frances admired this independent spirit who did not give in to the apparently inevitable, and a short time after their meeting, Frances and Peter fell in love. Eventually she left Johnny, prepared to put up with the 'scarlet woman' tag with which she would be branded in the late 1960s. To Viscount Althorp the departure of his wife was not foreseen so apparently involved in his work was he. For Diana, her mother left home literally overnight and at only six years old, the separating of her mother and father was emotionally traumatic, leaving a permanent scar. For some months the Spencer children's nanny took them to visit their mother in Cadogan Place, London, which had become her home, but they always returned to Park House. It was confusing for Diana when Frances returned home for Christmas in 1967 for the sake of the children, but it was the last one that they would all spend together. 'Is mummy home for good now?' Diana asked that December, but nobody could answer. When Frances re-turned to London in the New Year, so emotionally distressed by the ordeal of the previous year was Diana's father that he put a stop to the children's visits to their mother. A few days later Diana was sent to school for the first time and her governess, Ally, departed. Ally (Gertrude Allen) had taught Frances as a child and it was with her that she felt her loyalties lay. Rather than employ another governess, Johnny took Diana to Silfield School in nearby King's Lynn; her secure years at Park House had ended with a vengeance.

In 1967 Frances began a petition for divorce on the grounds of cruelty on the part of her husband. Johnny immediately counter-acted this by citing her adultery with Peter Shand-Kydd as the reason, and as the former Mrs Shand-Kydd was also using adultery to sue for divorce, the ensuing proceedings turned into an ugly and public court case, including a widely reported custody case. In the 1960s mothers were almost certain to win custody of their children, and perhaps Frances was advised to suggest cruelty by her lawyers to help secure her three daughters and young son. After a lengthy battle it was Johnny who was granted custody. The consolation for Diana was that although she had lost her mother, she could still remain in the house in which she had grown up. Security was of paramount importance for her.

Even today when staying at Sandringham, Diana will some-times sneak off alone for a nostalgic look at Park House. Since 1987, it has belonged to the Leonard Cheshire Foundation who turned it into a £1.5 million hotel for the disabled, officially opened by the Queen (who had donated the property) on 31 July of that year. The room in which Diana was born has become a guest bedroom with a double bed, while her former nursery has been converted into two single bedrooms. Shortly before its conversion Diana took Prince Charles on a tour of the then deserted house. She rediscovered a window of a former cloakroom that had been turned into their telephone room and had over 500 telephone numbers written on the white frame, many in her own handwriting. The whole window including the original frosted glass was later sent to the Princess at Kensington Palace as a keepsake. Among the numbers were the hairdresser that Diana used, the doctor, fishmonger, laundry, chimney sweep, her schools and, to those in the know, the telephone number of Sandringham House is discernible. A plate from her nursery door depicting Enid Blyton's lovable Brer Rabbit, and an architrave on which Diana's height when she was fourteen had been marked for posterity are kept on permanent display in the hotel to remind guests that a future Queen 'once lived here'.

Immediately after the divorce, in the full knowledge and realization that her parents' separation was irrevocable, Diana became something of a rebel. With unfortunate timing, her favourite cat Marmalade died when Diana seemed in the greatest state of confusion. Nannies who were hired to replace Gertrude Allen had difficulty controlling the girl. One was locked in the lavatory by Diana; another had her clothes thrown up on to a roof. They found her always deliberately getting into mischief, from sliding down the banisters to running away from home. Psychologists suggest that these obvious changes in Diana's character were simply cries for help, a desperate craving for attention. At school she always dedicated her paintings and drawings to 'Mummy *and* Daddy', unable to think of them separately and refusing to discuss her parents' divorce, as if it had not taken place. She continued to see both her mother and father after the divorce, but became withdrawn and solitary.

Of all the Spencer children, Diana seemed to be the one most affected by the divorce. Possibly her sisters Sarah and Jane were old enough to understand and her brother just too young to worry; but Diana was at an impressionable age and suffered as a result. When she was nine years old a new nanny was employed, Mrs Mary Clarke, who had a stabilizing effect following a succession of intimidated predecessors. For some reason Diana accepted Mrs Clarke and became less demanding. In deep reverie one day, Diana spoke about her future. 'I want to fall in love and get married and have lots of children,' she said, 'but I'll never marry unless I really love someone.' Conscious that her parents' love was not strong enough to survive, Diana had no intention of repeating their mistakes, which is why today she is always irritated and deeply upset by any media suggestion that she and her husband might part. It will never happen, not least because Prince Charles would without question gain custody of the children she loves so dearly. Unlike Frances Shand-Kydd, Diana would not give up her children for anything.

Losing her own natural mother was bad enough, but Diana found it almost as difficult when at the age of thirteen she gained a stepmother. Not that Johnny and the then Lady Dartmouth married at that time – they did not wed until 1976 – but effectively the woman who had initially only written the text to a book of photographs that Johnny was compiling called *What Is Our Heritage?* also took over the 'author', his home and children. 'Acid Raine' (as she was wickedly dubbed by the Spencer girls), née Raine McCorquodale, was the daughter of romantic novelist Barbara Cartland. Miss Cartland, the advocate of virginity and eternal undying love, ironically married twice, divorcing Raine's father, Alexander, and Raine herself divorced her husband of twenty-seven years, the Earl of Dartmouth, to eventually marry

Johnny. By the time they eventually married, Johnny had inherited the title of Earl Spencer following his father's demise in 1975.

Raine, now Countess Spencer, has been credited with reconciling Johnny with his father, bringing them together after a long estrangement. A born fighter, Raine is a former member of Westminster City Council, chairing the Greater London Council's Historic Buildings Board and the Covent Garden Development Committee. It was at a heritage committee meeting that she first met Johnny Spencer, a fortuitous meeting that was eventually to save his life, for when he suffered a massive brain haemorrhage in 1978 it was Raine who brought him back to life. Diana hated her because she kept Johnny's children from his bedside, but the Spencers must always be grateful that Raine stayed at his side for four solid months willing him to live. So strong is her character that even God, it seemed, dare not cross her. A former colleague of Raine's during her political career gave a classic quote when he said that she has 'an iron hand in an iron glove which is so beautifully wrought that people don't realize even the glove is made of iron until it hits them'. As Johnny lay senseless in a coma, Raine shouted at him, telling him he must not die. If determination alone could keep someone alive, nobody in the hospital would have died, but eventually it was one drug that ensured Earl Spencer's survival. 'I'm a survivor and people forget that at their peril,' Raine has said since. 'Nobody destroys me, and nobody was going to destroy Johnny so long as I could sit by his bed, though some of his family tried to stop me.' She had heard of a drug called Aslocillin in Germany that might be the answer to her prayers. Although not available in Britain, she had some brought over and persuaded doctors to use it. Miraculously it worked and while the desperate Raine was loudly playing a recording of her husband's favourite opera, he opened his eyes for the first time in sixteen weeks, starting on the road to recovery.

Although Raine Spencer was instrumental in saving Johnny's life, it did not bring her any closer to Diana, who had resented her intrusion from the very first day. Diana had refused to attend her father's second marriage and she would not credit the woman who had become the story-book 'wicked stepmother' with his recovery. 'I could have saved his life ten times over . . . it wouldn't have changed anything,' Raine has said bitterly.

What Diana resented most of all was the fact that Raine seemed to take over control of Althorp and her father. First it seemed that she had lost her mother to Peter Shand-Kydd and now her father appeared to have been taken over by Raine. There has never been any love lost between Diana and her stepmother. Raine referred to her stepdaughter as 'pigeon toes' and once declared that Diana was boring. 'How can you have an intelligent conversation with someone who doesn't have a single 'O' level?' she is reputed to have asked.

Although Diana is close to her two sisters, Sarah and Jane, she feels a greater affinity to her brother, Charles. Only three years separates them, and when their mother left home it was Diana who took on the maternal role towards baby Charles. Guests of Earl Spencer in the early 1970s were amazed to find eleven-year-old Diana so affectionate and protective towards her young brother at an age when most children are usually fighting like cat and dog. She used to enjoy dressing him up, almost as if he were a doll, and this was her earliest training for motherhood.

In recent years, Diana and brother Charles have found themselves in similar positions, both inheritors with a huge burden eventually to fall upon them. Although Johnny Spencer had four children, his son is considered the most important from the point of view that he is heir to the estate. His importance is stressed by the fact that when he was born the Queen became one of his godparents; a role she did not take on for any of the Spencer daughters. It also seems not insignificant that the Spencer marriage went into a decline as soon as Frances had produced an heir. In less than nine years they had five children. One son, John, lived for just ten hours. Eighteen months later Diana was born, and it seemed imperative to keep the Spencer family going so that the couple would continue having children until the birth of a son. Did Frances, like Diana, feel the demand for an heir so great that it became a burden? Having finally produced a male and secured the line, maybe Frances began to feel that she had served her purpose. Fortunately, in Diana's case, she produced two sons very quickly and her 'duty' was over. Any child that they have in the future will be because she and Prince Charles want another baby, not because they feel they have to. Yes, Diana wanted children, but she may not have got pregnant so quickly given the choice, and had she given birth only to girls the pressure would still be there and like her mother she might have begun to feel like a production line.

Charles Althorp knows that like his royal namesake, the pressure will be on him to marry and have a son himself, to continue the Spencer tradition. He, possibly better than Prince Charles, knows how his sister feels about her position. He has witnessed the loss of freedom and he too has suffered at the hands of the Press for no other reason than that he is the Princess of Wales' brother, and like Diana he has occasionally rebelled, Although he has inherited money, he has always worked for a living and will be the first Earl Spencer to have worked as a supermarket quality control checker and a messenger boy. Like Prince Edward, he has leanings towards the arts world and, having already played a small part in a film, he now works for NBC in the United States as a reporter. With the Atlantic Ocean between them, Diana now sees far less of the one member of her family to whom she is closest in spirit.

The Spencer family are strangely divided by both distance and attitude. Diana's real mother is either at the opposite end of Britain or on the other side of the world (she has dined at Kensington Palace less than half a dozen times in seven years); her stepmother provides a barrier between Diana and her father; for some time, it is said, there was a coolness between the Princess and her elder sister Sarah because one had married the other's ex-boyfriend (ironically, Lady Sarah Spencer is now married to Neil McCorquodale, one of Raine's relatives), and brother Charles lives and works in America. Only sister Jane remains physically and emotionally close as a member of Queen Elizabeth's court.

From such an unsettled background, would Diana have preferred to have married into a 'normal' stable family where rank and heritage were of no importance? Although a tight-knit family, joined together by a single bond of status, the Royal Family are an enigma. Although they present a united front, and on formal occasions turn out in force, they seldom get together socially, despite the fact that many branches of the family live very close together. The Princess Royal and Captain Mark Phillips live at

Gatcombe Park, between the village of Minchinhampton and the small Gloucestershire town of Tetbury. Just four miles along the road, on the other side of Tetbury, is Doughton where Highgrove House, the Prince and Princess of Wales' country home is located. Although the two houses are but a short distance apart, the two families do not visit each other's homes. They are more likely to meet at one of the Queen's residences than they are to see each other socially. Just a few miles further north is Bisley, where the small classical style villa Nether Lypiatt Manor, the home of Prince and Princess Michael of Kent, can be found and again there has never been a gathering of these Gloucestershire royals.

In London, at Kensington Palace, many groups of royal relatives live quite literally as neighbours. When they are all in residence there could well be fourteen members of the Family sleeping under one roof: Princess Margaret, the Prince and Princess of Wales and their two children, Prince and Princess Michael of Kent and their two children, and the Duke and Duchess of Gloucester with their three offspring. Yet they all remain self-contained. It is not, however, unknown for members of staff from one family to call upon the household of another to borrow a kitchen implement, and on one occasion some bacon!

Formality is the keynote in royal life. If asked, private secretaries insist that heavily filled engagement diaries prevent unscheduled social visiting as such, but do not deny that should Diana wish, for example, to visit Princess Margaret or Princess Michael, etiquette requires that an invitation be issued. If the Queen were to visit her son and daughter-in-law for afternoon tea, she could not simply drive, or be driven, the five-minute journey from Buckingham Palace unannounced, on the spur of the moment. It would have to be formally arranged: for example, a call would be put through from Buckingham Palace at the exact moment that Her Majesty had driven out of the forecourt so that the Kensington Palace butler could open the door to coincide with the Queen's arrival. The door must be open as the monarch approaches. Non-royal guests would have to ring the bell.

WINDSOR CASTLE
CHRISTMAS 1987
GUEST LIST

Queen Elizabeth the Queen Mother	235 York Tower
The Prince & Princess of Wales	52/55 Queen's Tower
The Prince William & the Prince Henry	127 Queen's Tower
The Princess Anne, Mrs Marks Phillips and Captain Mark Phillips	240 Lancaster Tower
Master Peter & Miss Zara Phillips	324 Augusta Tower and 331 York Tower (lady-in-waiting's Rooms)
The Duke & Duchess of York	124 Queen's Tower
The Princess Margaret Countess of Snowdon	251 Lancaster Tower (Blue Rooms)
Viscount Linley	248 Lancaster Tower (Blue Rooms)
Lady Sarah Armstrong-Jones	352 Edward III Tower (Chintz Rooms)
Princess Alice Duchess of Gloucester	312 Queen's Tower (Shelter Rooms)
The Duke and Duchess of Gloucester	219 August Tower
Earl of Ulster	229 Augusta Tower
Lady Davina and Lady Rose Windsor	231 Augusta Tower
The Duke and Duchess of Kent	257 Edward III Tower
Earl of St Andrews	176 Edward III Tower
Lady Helen Windsor	151 York Tower
Lord Nicholas Windsor	162 Lancaster Tower (Maids of Honour)
Prince and Princess Michael of Kent	178 Edward III Tower
Lord Frederick and Lady Gabriella Windsor	163 Lancaster Tower (sitting room) 164 Lancaster Tower (bedroom) 153 York Tower (bedroom)
Princess Alexandra, the Hon Mrs Angus Ogilvy and the Hon Angus Ogilvy	343 Lancaster Tower (Ministers' Rooms)
Mr James Ogilvy	173 Edward III Tower

Christmas is one of the rare occasions when almost the entire Royal Family are together. The Queen's guest list reads like that of the world's most exclusive hotel. For Diana such family occasions have proved to be extremely daunting, especially her very first Christmas as a member of the Family. She knew from past experience that it is the Queen who is the matriarch today, and it is under her roof that the whole clan gather. Whenever reporters and journalists have attempted to find photographs of the whole Royal Family together, it has proved impossible. Only at weddings, funerals, and the Christmas Day Church Service are they seen together publicly. Even at christenings, only the immediate branch of the Family usually attends. In 1972 Patrick, Fifth Earl of Lichfield and cousin of the Queen, gathered together twenty-one members of the Royal Family for an informal photograph to commemorate the Queen's and the Duke of Edinburgh's Silver Wedding Anniversary, an exercise which has not yet been repeated. Diana was only eleven at the time and, had she seen that picture then, she could not in her wildest dreams have visualized herself as ever being part of that élite group; now that she is on the inside she must contemplate her acceptance. For us it is hard to remember a time when we did not have the Princess of Wales; if one sees photographs of the Royal Family from just a decade ago one instinctively looks for Diana. For the Princess it is a different story.

To Diana, her mother-in-law will never be a close member of the family. She will always first and foremost be The Queen. Because Her Majesty presides so strongly over her relatives, it is impossible not to fall in with tradition. The Queen enjoys a number of pursuits, from horse breeding to pigeon racing, and cannot understand when her pleasures are not shared. The uncompromising standards that are imposed on what are often the most private and informal occasions are difficult for an outsider to comprehend. For example, to any other family the traditional present giving at Christmas would be a very intimate, relaxed affair, but for the Royal Family the rituals and protocol that dominate the rest of the year continue. Not even at Christmas, not even in private, can tradition and etiquette be cast aside.

In the Red Drawing-Room at Windsor Castle approximately

two dozen members of the Family gather at tea-time on Christmas Eve, the day and the time when the Royal Family open their gifts. Beforehand, extravagantly wrapped packages will have been placed on a long white table, each bearing a very formal label written by a member of staff. 'To Her Royal Highness the Princess of Wales from Her Majesty the Queen' will say one, and it will be handed to Diana by a uniformed footman. Two footmen and three underbutlers are employed on this day to pass round the royal parcels. Even Prince William and Prince Harry will receive some of their gifts in this way – only some, however, because it is not a practice that Diana endorses, preferring to see her children tear open the wrapping paper excitedly on Christmas morning. 'Actually I used to feel very embarrassed about handing out Christmas presents like that,' says one ex-underbutler who had previously taken part in the royal ritual. 'All the Queen does is sit and open her gifts as they are handed to her by a member of staff.'

When King Charles and Queen Diana preside over the court, informality is bound to creep in. Possibly the inevitable relaxing of standards has affected Diana's relationship with the Queen. Her Majesty knows that occasionally her practices are mocked by her daughter-in-law. Diana can understand that the Queen has to be seen to be dignified in public, that she must wear the majestic mask for officialdom, but at the same time expects the image to be dropped behind closed doors. What Diana, as a non-royal, is only just beginning to see is that the Windsors are not acting out a soap opera. Being royal is a way of life and the Queen knows of no other; she accepts all that she does without question. She does not just act at being Queen Elizabeth II. Unlike her children, the Queen has never even been to school; she always had private tutors. She has never been able to go shopping, or anywhere for that matter, without a great deal of pomp, ceremony and high security. Even during the war when she joined the Auxiliary Territorial Service (ATS) as Second Subaltern Elizabeth Alexandra Mary Windsor No. 230873, she was chaffeur-driven to Camberley, Surrey, each day and back to Windsor Castle at night. Even at a simple family lunch at Balmoral the Queen will be the last to arrive at the table because of protocol. People with whom she is in contact daily have to bow or curtsey on meeting, members of her own family included. It is social graces like these that have maintained the magic and the mystery of the monarchy. Elizabeth II has a very special aura that has developed not because she acts the part of Queen so well but because she has become the Queen with every fibre of her being.

In this vast shadow stands Diana, who feels that she might not live up to expectations. She has publicly expressed her admiration for Princess Anne ('she crams into a day what I could never achieve'), but how does she feel about her mother-in-law? 'Basically I think that Diana is very much in awe of the Queen,' says one member of the royal circle, 'just a tiny bit afraid.' If she is afraid, it is not so much fear of the woman, but fear of what Her Majesty represents. In the Queen's presence she can never relax; she feels that she must always be on her guard, conscious that she is being watched and assessed. Nervousness in the monarch's presence can make Diana either giggly, resulting in a picture of immaturity, or very withdrawn, implying that she is sullen. Neither now are true.

Despite reports to the contrary, Diana does not discuss problems with the Queen, constantly finding her too remote. Not only is there a thirty-five-year age gap between the Princess and the Queen, they also are divided by attitude. The Queen's overriding passion is horses. Her greatest ambition is still to win the Derby. Although Diana attends horsey events to support the Family, she could happily live without them. It is impossible to imagine Diana seated at a computer, when she and Charles are resident at Buckingham Palace, working out the breeding pro- gramme for the Hampton Court stud, or learning by heart the ancestry of every horse in the Royal Mews. The Queen can look at any of her horses and discuss at length its character, temperament and abilities and will also know its parentage and track record. Not only does Diana neither possess nor desire such equestrian knowledge, she also has no interest in the Queen's other love – dogs. Corgis are synonymous with the Royal Family. The Queen, Queen Mother and the Princess Royal, all own dogs of the breed that they have made peculiarly their own. As a child Diana had guinea pigs and kittens, and looked after small animals that were kept in Pets' Corner when she was at Riddlesworth School, Norfolk. They were considered to be therapeutic in view of her homelife, but rather than caring for them as pets, Diana is remembered for having 'mothered' the animals. This form of fostering was a typical feature of her growing-up, but with baby brother Charles also to look after, and eventually children at the dancing school where she taught for a time, followed by the Young England Kindergarten and now her own sons, Diana has always placed people before pets. We have all seen photographs of our monarch with corgis on her lap, dressed in tweeds with labradors jumping around her, but we will not see Diana in similar poses; no Emanuel dress or Jan Van Velden coat will ever be seen covered in dog hairs. Soon after their marriage, the bachelor Prince Charles' faithful golden labrador companion, Harvey, was banished to Sandringham because, the story goes, he became too badly behaved and, in Stephen Barry's own words, 'relieved himself on some of the best carpets in the country'. It seems hard to believe that any dog belonging to royalty should be improperly trained and is it mere coincidence that Harvey has been replaced by a much smaller dog in the shape of a Jack Russell terrier, and that it appears to be Prince Charles who has to look after it?

Early suggestions that Diana's fashion style would have a marked influence on the Queen's wardrobe have proved to be fruitless speculation. The Queen has declared that she should look 'reassuringly the same' and she never lets us down. Although Diana's fashion revolution has done much to boost Britain in the glamour market – much to the Queen's delight – love of clothes is not something the Queen shares. To her clothes must be functional, practical and made to last. She once sent a twelve-year-old dress back to the designer to have a stained panel replaced. Fortunately the dressmaker had kept some of the material, but 'it was not an expensive dress in the first place,' he insists. Diana has denied reports that she is a 'shopaholic' and defends her buying of clothes by pointing out that she had nothing to wear when she joined the Royal Family and has had to build her wardrobe up. Nevertheless, we are unlikely to see her wearing something from a decade ago and she obviously enjoys wearing clothes that are fashionable and eyecatching. In the next twenty years the Queen might adopt the policy of the Queen Mother who has settled on one particular style and only wears variations of that theme. Author Alan Hamilton said of the Queen Mother that she is recognizable even from the back (*The Royal Handbook* 1985) and wickedly dubbed her the 'royal lampshade'. Although Diana admittedly stands out in any crowd, she never warrants the criticism of predictability. The Queen's style of dressing is quite deliberate. She learned very early on that if you wear anything too outrageous you can really only wear it once; any more than that and it will become instantly recognizable. When designers have tried to make her a little more fashionable she has sometimes played along with their ideas, if only to prove them wrong. Occasionally Her Majesty will intentionally wear an outfit that people recognize to counter any criticism that too much money is wasted on clothes. For her Silver Jubilee Day celebrations in 1977 she wore a rose pink outfit that she had worn in July 1976 to open the Olympic Games in Canada. The two events could not have been more public.

In 1953 Norman Hartnell designed a dramatic evening dress for the Queen, stunning in its simplicity – a full-length, strapless gown in black and white – which she wore for a charity show given by top stars of stage and screen. The twenty-seven-year-old Queen's outfit created such a sensation that within twenty-four hours copies were in all the London stores and she could never wear it again. Creating an impact in the fashion world never has been one of the Queen's ambitions. Not only does it prove financially unviable, but since 1981 she has been determined not to be considered as an 'also ran' to Diana. If Her Majesty had decided to update her wardrobe to shake off the 'dowdy' tag, it would only have been seen by the media as an undignified attempt to compete with her daughter-in-law. Our shrewd monarch made no attempt to take part in the fashion game, yet when Diana caused such an impact with the now famous black low-cut taffeta dress for her first formal engagement on 9 March 1981, at the Goldsmiths' Hall in London, inspring the headlines **'See Nipples and Di'** the Queen must have smiled secretly to herself in the knowledge that she had worn a practically identical dress thirty years earlier, provoking an equal amount of comment. Nothing is new.

The Queen's attitude towards her daughter-in-law is debatable. Even those rare people who are taken into the sovereign's confidence cannot be really sure. There are three attitudes which the Queen could take towards Diana: one is total indifference, an unlikely reaction considering that she is married to her eldest son and heir and will one day be Queen Consort; another is that she could be greatly relieved that Diana has stepped into the spotlight and taken away some of the media pressure that was once centred on herself, but those with a deeper understanding of Elizabeth II are sure that she feels a certain amount of resentment at being pushed into second place by someone so young and inexperienced.

A popular myth is that royal ladies dislike the constant media attention that they receive, but in fact the number of column inches devoted to them in the daily national papers is always carefully studied: not only by the lady concerned but also by the Queen herself. It is said that royal engagements are carefully spread out geographically so that when a member of the Family attends a function they know with all certainty that no other royal person will be in the vicinity. When Diana attended her first Festival of Remembrance at the Royal Albert Hall on 7 November 1981, the Queen looked disconcerted when her son's wife received the loudest cheer. 'I'd better get out of the way,' she said in a rare comment to cameramen, stepping back so that they could get better pictures of the Princess of Wales.

The attention Diana receives today was for half a century directed at the Queen. The British public took an extraordinary interest in Princess Elizabeth from the moment of her birth and crowds gathered daily outside her parents' home at 145 Piccadilly. It was reported that open-topped buses, then still common on London's streets, were seen to tilt sideways as they passed the house with passengers all congregating to one side trying to see in through the nursery window. When her nurse Clara Knight, known as 'Alla', wheeled her through Hyde Park the pram was surrounded by people desperate to get a look at the baby. In the end 'Alla' was forced to wheel the Princess around the park-like gardens at the rear of Buckingham Palace instead.

At the age of three Princess Elizabeth was featured on the cover of *Time* magazine in America, wearing a yellow dress. 'P'incess Lilybet [sic] she has the babe fashion for yellow' said the cover, and soon every mother was foresaking blues and pinks for their offspring. The public seemed obsessed with the child, she appeared on everything from chocolate boxes to china plates, hospital wards were named after her, and even a piece of Antarctica became Princess Elizabeth Land. The interest was phenomenal considering that she was then the equivalent of the current Duke and Duchess of York's child, she was not heir to the throne and nobody even contemplated that she might one day be Queen. The public obsession was encouraged throughout 1936 to divert media attention away from the Abdication crisis, even to the extent of inviting journalists to inspect the Princess' nursery at a time when such intrusions were unheard of. Naturally as Elizabeth's status grew on her father's accession to heir-presumptive, so fascination with every aspect of her life increased in accordance. With her wedding, the Coronation, four pregnancies and the Jubilee, Her Majesty managed to remain at the top of the media tree. Weddings gave other members of the Family transient glory only. It is Diana alone who has posed a threat. Unfortunately for Diana, the Press adulation has been beyond her control and if there is even the slightest jealousy from some quarters of the Family, there is nothing she can do about it.

If the Queen did not give Diana the warmest of welcomes it is hardly surprising: few mothers completely accept their daughters-in-law. The reception from Princess Margaret, however, has been positively icy. The Queen's sister enjoys witty, flamboyant company, people with an acid sense of humour and who are daringly exciting. She likes plenty of laughter and gossip, but her circle must never forget her position, and even close friends have learned to call her 'Ma'am'. Diana may be the jewel in the crown, as far as the media are concerned, but her facets have not impressed Princess Margaret. So close to the throne that it was once mooted that she might rule the country jointly with her sister Elizabeth, Princess Margaret is not too pleased at being pushed down to tenth in the line of succession by her sister's children and grandchildren, and she will continue to diminish in importance through the likes of Diana. Bored by the Princess of Wales, the Queen's sister has also criticized Diana's voice, an accent which has been called 'BBC Newsreader' rather than 'Queen's English'. When Princess Margaret watched the play *Crown Matrimonial* by Royce Ryton in which actors perform the events leading to the Abdication, she criticized those portraying members of her family: 'The accent is all wrong,' she said. 'We do not speak like that.'

Diana's relatively low rating in the eyes of Princess Margaret was proven by her absence at the christenings of both Prince William and Prince Harry. She had no official engagements on the day Prince Harry was christened, and was on holiday in Italy for Prince William's, choosing not to interrupt the vacation. 'I don't think it is essential to be at the christening of your nephew's children,' a member of the Princess' staff said in her defence. Others saw it as a deliberate snub on Princess Margaret's part: as the Queen's sister and 'Charlie's Aunt' she could have been selected as a godmother. She was not, and so stayed away.

Princess Anne, Charles' only sister, was not chosen as a godparent either, and although she attended Prince William's baptism, she opted for a pheasant shoot instead of going to Prince Harry's. Her non-appearance became the cause of much comment. 'She wasn't chosen as a godmother for Harry. Had our child been a girl, the possibility was there, but Harry arrived so we went to a man,' said Diana feebly to Sir Alastair Burnet in a television interview. An unconvincing excuse, considering that Prince Harry had Lady Sarah Armstrong-Jones, Lady Vestey (wife of the meat baron Lord 'Spam' Vestey, a polo-playing friend of Prince Charles) and Mrs William Bartholomew (Diana's former flatmate, née Carolyn Pride) as godparents. It did not seem an unreasonable suggestion that Princess Anne might have been included among them.

However, although not selected, it came as no great disappointment to the down-to-earth Princess Royal. Not a great lover of family occasions, she simply preferred to be in the country with friends. Her so-called 'snub' gave the Press a field day and, in an attempt to create a real-life soap opera out of the Windsors, they invented a rift between the two Princesses. 'That was one of their better fairy stories,' Anne told television chatshow host Terry Wogan in a subsequent interview. Sensationalists preferred to interpret the affair as a fit of pique on Anne's part: 'She was deeply hurt and disappointed,' one not so close friend mumbled. Knowing full well that *anything* she said would be misinterpreted, Princess Anne felt that it was preferable to say nothing, but privately revealed that any royal rift between herself and Diana was pure 'media mythology'. As an aside to Terry Wogan she said, almost under her breath, 'We probably weren't missed anyway,' realizing that her only function would have been to swell the already large ranks of royals.

Much has been penned about the relationship of the two Princesses, and while both would admit that they are not bosom buddies, neither are they enemies. The Queen tried desperately to make them put on a united front, making sure that they were seen laughing together as they left church on Christmas Day, 1984, but the situation was not helped when Princess Anne had a row with her brother, within earshot of many, about Diana. She was heard to call the Prince a 'wimp' and his wife a 'brainless woman'. What had begun to irritate Princess Anne was that she undertakes over 500 engagements a year, visits the poorest countries in the world to see the sick and dying, and has been heaped with praises for her worthwhile work, but the Press frequently give Princess Anne one small paragraph, while one new dress of Diana's can make front-page news. Anne feels that royal reporting has reached a 'frivolous level'. She works hard to justify her Civil List income, and like her brother Charles, tries desperately to give something back to society in return for the privileges of her birth.

In both character and values Anne and Diana are poles apart and there are few bonds to draw them together. Peter and Zara Phillips have always been impeccably well behaved, and their mother does not approve of some of Prince William's antics, or the fact that he has gone unpunished when naughty. The difference between the children was highlighted in front of millions during the wedding of Prince Andrew to Sarah Ferguson in 1986. Zara Phillips was a bridesmaid and her brother Peter was a pageboy, along with Prince William. The Phillips children were commended on their dignity and excellent manners, while four-year-old Prince William fidgeted throughout, scratched, put out his tongue, and scarcely for one moment could Diana take her eyes off him. Princess Anne in complete contrast scarcely looked at her children; she knew that they would not be a problem. Although it was probably untrue that she had 'put the fear of God into them first' as one journalist suggested, Princess Anne has been a strict disciplinarian and it has paid dividends.

Princess Anne, like her mother, does not share Diana's fashion sense and although it took her a long time to find clothes that suited her, whenever she has been a success she knows that it is through her own doing and not, as in Diana's case, through a team of fashion designers and advisers. When she swept into the Grosvenor House Hotel for the 1985 BAFTA Awards in a *Dynasty*-style outfit and red streaks in her hair, she stole the show and won herself a standing ovation. In the early 1980s Diana was credited with reviving hats. This must have peeved Princess Anne who, barely out of her teens, became known as the 'Duchess of Luton' (Luton, Bedfordshire, being the hub of the British millinery trade) for the boost she gave to the hat industry with her 'cheeky' hats.

As with the Queen, Diana feels intimidated by Princess Anne and her forthright approach. Had the age gap been less than eleven years they might have been closer, had it been greater Princess Anne could have perhaps adopted the role of a guiding aunt and mentor, just as the late Princess Royal (Princess Mary) did with younger members of the Royal Family. As it is, the gulf between them is vast but as with Princess Margaret, it is Diana who has unintentionally created it. She could not help being beautiful or stylish. It is not her fault that she does not share their hobbies or interests. She cannot, to any significant extent, control the interest in her that has so obviously left the Queen's sister and daughter in the shadows. In the year of Charles' and Diana's marriage Princess Anne and Princess Margaret both attended the State Opening of Parliament because the Princess of Wales would be present for the first time.

It cannot be mere coincidence either that Princess Anne finally decided in 1987 to accept the title of Princess Royal. This title is given to the eldest daughter of the monarch, usually at a time when she has achieved great public esteem. The title has been vacant since 1965, and Princess Anne could in theory have had it at any time. Speculation as to when this would happen increased at the times of Anne's eighteenth and twenty-first birthdays, her wedding, and at the time of most New Year and Birthday Honours Lists ever since. Continually she declined the honour, even though the Queen was very keen for her daughter to accept it. In 1981 Lady Diana Spencer became Princess of Wales, taking precedence over Princess Anne; five years later, another commoner, Sarah Ferguson, became Duchess of York. Suddenly two new additions to the Family had gained more significant titles than the Queen's own daughter who, under different laws of succession, could be much closer to the throne. So, less than a year after her younger brother, Andrew, became Duke of York, Anne finally agreed to become The Princess Royal, twenty-one years later than anticipated.

With other female members of the Family Diana has encountered fewer problems. The Duchess of Kent and the Duchess of Gloucester were both commoners before their marriages, Katherine Worsley and Birgitte Van Deurs respectively, and so have been able to sympathize with the Princess and her position. The Queen's cousin, Princess Alexandra has been equally sympathetic to Diana, but they seldom meet other than at equestrian events, such as Royal Ascot, or when both are guests of Her Majesty at Windsor.

Likewise, the male members of the Family have accepted Diana without question. At one time the Press considered Prince Andrew as a possible husband for Diana, and they now have a very good relationship. Equally, the Duke of Edinburgh feels able to tease his daughter-in-law in a fatherly way.

The closest relationship that Diana has within the Family, however, is with Princess Margaret's daughter, Lady Sarah Armstrong-Jones, who has been described as the 'least royal of the royals'. At twenty-four she is close to Diana in age, neither are academically brilliant although Lady Sarah has one 'A' level in art, they enjoy the same music, and have both been through the traumas of their parents' divorces. Lady Sarah was also chief bridesmaid at Charles' and Diana's wedding, keeping the younger bridesmaids in order, but always laughs off any suggestion that she should marry Viscount Althorp.

The attraction for Diana is that Lady Sarah is not 100 per cent royal – her mother and aunt are, but her father is not; Sarah will never be a princess or a duchess and it is improbable that she will opt for a life of royal duty. If she did she would qualify for a Civil List income, but she prefers to earn her own living, like her brother Viscount Linley. Currently pursuing her artistic talents, she is studying at the Royal Academy School. Preferring London life to the country gave her an instant bond with Diana, who sees

Lady Sarah as the one link between the Royal Family and the outside world. She is in a position that Diana envies, being able to travel on buses and the London underground, or cycle through the streets of London unrecognized and unrestricted by security. She is always there on royal occasions, but can cross the divide into 'real life' whenever she wants. Lady Sarah, until the arrival of the Duchess of York, was also Diana's saving grace at Balmoral in the summer, providing a companion with whom she could go shopping or for a drive. She is one of the few members of the Family who does not intimidate the Princess.

The Royal Family is an institution revelling in its glorious past, averse to the inevitable changes that prevent it from becoming an anachronism. New blood can only penetrate slowly; too great a surge can result in rejection. In less than a decade the Princess of Wales has made an indelible mark on the minds of the public who now see her at the heart of the Family, but from the inside she is still barely past the periphery. It takes some two decades for total acceptance, sometimes even longer. Katherine Worsley married the Duke of Kent in 1961. Only when they celebrated their twenty-fifth wedding anniversary did she somehow cease to be 'young Katie', the newcomer.

The lifeblood of the Royal Family is its continuity, and it is here that Diana has made her mark: through her and from her has come the Royal Family of the future. In the next century it will be she who waves from the centre of the balcony; at the Trooping of the Colour and the Cenotaph ceremony it will be her husband, King Charles III, who leads the events; by the year 2000 it may be her twenty-one-year-old son, William, who will receive the coronet and mantle of Prince of Wales. Within a relatively short space of time in the long history of the monarchy, the wheel of time will move on. The Royal Family will become *her* family.

Like an outsider who takes a position of seniority in an old established family business, Diana has a long initiation period still to undergo to dispel resentments, fears and rejections. In her annual Christmas broadcast, the Queen always stresses the importance of family life and it is a sense that all her children have. The Princess Royal has said that as a child she used to fight with her brothers, like 'cat and dog' with Prince Charles, 'but', she adds, 'the family was always there, the feeling of being in a family, and we are stronger for it, I think. And the family is still there.' Whatever Diana lacked in her own family life, she will eventually come to find the strength and security she has always craved behind the Palace walls, as one of the Family.

❧ 7 ❧

Ambassadress of Fashion

Diana glanced down as Prince Charles signed yet another visitors' book on their six-day visit to Germany in the winter of 1987. Her black and white checked suit by Alistair Blair had been topped by a large-brimmed Spanish style hat, which momentarily hid her face as she glanced down at the page she herself was about to sign. Briefly she looked up and the peace was shattered as a barrage of cameras clicked and flash guns sprayed out their blinding white light. Their German host looked horrified, believing some tragedy to have happened which he had somehow failed to witness. 'I raised my head,' Diana explained reassuringly. She has come to accept that one smile, one single look, is all that photographers crave, but it can be disconcerting to anyone who has not previously encountered Diana's magic.

Since the advent of cameras royalty either posed officially, or were photographed doing something specific. Diana can simply be watching tennis at Wimbledon or stepping out of a car, and – click! – a saleable picture is produced. On a recent trip to Florida in advance of a royal visit, the Wales' Assistant Private Secretary, Rupert Fairfax told social columnist Kathryn Robinette of the *Palm Beach Post* that Prince Charles looked much better in the flesh than in photographs, whereas Diana photographed well. This could be misconstrued as indiscreet, but it was not intended as such. The Hon. Mr Fairfax meant quite simply that Diana is photogenic. Ninety-eight out of every hundred pictures taken of her are publishable. An exclusive can earn the lucky photographer in excess of £50,000. It has now become an adage that writers make contacts, photographers make money.

Out of sixty issues of a monthly magazine *Royalty*, Diana was featured on the cover forty-four times. This has little to do with the fact that she is Princess of Wales; it is due entirely to the way she looks. Royal ladies in the past have to a certain extent introduced their own style, be it good or bad. The Queen Mother after the dim dark days of the war dressed as she felt befitted a Queen. The crinolines, furs, feathers and sequins were often outrageously over the top, but they came to be what the public expected. Even now she dresses for dinner each evening, even if she is dining alone at Clarence House. The Queen again has a distinctive style, but what no female member of the Family has ever done until now is to take the world of fashion by storm. Diana's influence on what women wear today cannot be underestimated. Paris no longer has the monopoly on the catwalk. The French and Americans now buy clothes from Britain, which ten years ago was unheard of, and it is the Princess of Wales alone who deserves the credit.

Prince Charles has commented that one of the first things he noticed about his future wife was her 'marvellous sense of style', something with which a person is born. But it often takes time to develop that style and the Princess was no exception. Prior to her engagement in 1981, she still had plump adolescent cheeks, she frequently wore jeans and sweaters, and she never wore a hat. For her first official photograph with Prince Charles she wore a blue silk suit that had been bought 'off the peg' from Harrods. Slightly matronly, this hastily chosen outfit was selected to please the Queen, who watched discreetly as Diana received her first real taste of life in front of the cameras. She felt that she ought to wear a smart suit in keeping with the royal image, but it was not necessarily through choice.

One month later for her official photograph with her future mother-in-law, after the Privy Council had announced their approval of the engagement, she once again chose a classic suit, this time navy, with a sailor collar, and shoes in which the Queen herself would have felt comfortable. Inside the dowdy chrysalis was a butterfly waiting to burst out, and fashion editors who instantly spotted Diana's potential drooled in anticipation of top designers being let loose on her. A fashion revolution was just around the corner.

Diana's transformation from plump adolescent, through fairy-tale Princess, to sophisticated beauty is now history. One woman who must have bitten her tongue many times is the late Fashion Editor of *The Times*, Prudence Glynn, who in an article for the *International Herald Tribune* hailed Lady Diana as 'a fashion disaster in her own right' and described the sensational black strapless dress that Diana wore for her début at the Goldsmiths' Hall in 1981 as making her look as 'if she were sitting in a hip bath'. Many disagreed with these unprophetic comments and it was not long before Diana had pushed herself to the top of the World's Best Dressed lists. If Diana did receive criticism for her lack of dignity and non-royal behaviour, not one member of the Royal Family can condemn the interest she has brought them in one massive public relations exercise. What *has* received condemnation though is that the Princess has become an unpaid fashion model, promoting Britain's designers but discrediting the character and status of the Family.

In 1981 the Princess of Wales made a significant and fundamental change to the Royal Family's image through her wardrobe, and the timing can be recorded precisely: at 10.56 a.m. on 29 July 1981 the then Lady Diana Spencer stepped from her glass coach on to the steps of St Paul's Cathedral wearing the dress which so many had waited to see. David and Elizabeth Emanuel, the designers, dashed up to straighten the hem and rearrange the skirt, which had emerged creased and crumpled from the carriage – in thirty seconds a whole new relationship had been displayed between royalty and couturier. If in the past Her Majesty the Queen had stepped from her carriage at the State Opening of Parliament and Norman Hartnell had rushed forward to fiddle with her hem, people would have died of shock. Once at a cocktail party, *as a guest* Hardy Amies revealed that it was the first time he had entered Buckingham Palace by 'the front door' – until then he had always used the tradesmen's entrance in Buckingham Palace Road. In a few fleeting moments Diana had lifted the dress designer from the role of someone almost anonymously providing a discreet service for royalty to forming an essential part of her team. Like equerry or private secretary, designers have become courtier and confidante, equal on a social level rather than tradesmen honoured to supply the Royal Family.

In the past we were only vaguely aware of the people who dressed royalty and those who were privileged with designing garments did so in fear and trepidation. The late Norman Hartnell always said that he was terribly nervous whenever he went to the Palace with his designs for the Queen and the raising of one royal eyebrow could signify that he had made a mistake. Unlike the Queen, who tends to stick almost completely to two designers, one for day wear and one for evening, Diana has built up a whole team of British designers. Invariably they are young, often completely unknown until her patronage, and instead of remaining in the background, young designers have often been put on the map and almost have a licence to cash in on their famous client. Most take great delight in fielding off journalists and announcing that they cannot talk about the Princess, but . . . and then they let slip the smallest titbit, the tiniest detail that cannot possibly offend their most important customer while nevertheless ensuring that the world at large knows whose wardrobe they are responsible for. Discretion no longer means total silence, it is a licence to talk without giving too much away.

When Norman Hartnell designed the Queen's Coronation Dress he remained completely silent about the final choice. Within the intricate design, incorporating the national flowers of the Commonwealth, he subtly wove in a four-leafed clover, and even the Queen who saw the dress being made and wore it on her big day did not know that this 'lucky charm' had been added. The designers of Diana's wedding dress, David and Elizabeth Emanuel, cashed in just a little too publicly for the Palace's liking. The couple became instantly recognizable, appeared on chat shows, talked ever so discreetly about the Princess, but in thus promoting themselves fell from favour for several years. Becoming a household name through royal patronage is not acceptable to the regal clients.

Diana has tended to steer clear of the tried and trusted royal designers, other than favourite milliner John Boyd, opting instead for younger, more adventurous people like Arabella Pollen, Jasper Conran, Victor Edelstein, Bruce Oldfield, Donald Campbell, and Jan Van Velden. Nearer to her own age they have, perhaps, a better grasp of what would suit the Princess and at the same time be fashionable. Those who design for the Queen are content to produce classic styles, which they defend by saying that Her Majesty is not a pop star, she is not a seventeen-year-old model, and the word 'fashionable' is not on their list of credentials. Diana is a Princess of the eighties and has drawn the very fine line between fashion and royal dignity, confident that the two can be combined.

Where Diana differs from other royal ladies is that the public now expect her always to wear something stunning. When she embarks on a tour of Italy or Australia, fashion editors immediately begin speculating as to whether or not the future Queen will dazzle them with her wardrobe. If she wears anything that has been seen before, reporters leap upon it, and her hosts feel slighted because they obviously did not warrant anything new. If, on the other hand, she suddenly wears a number of new outfits, there is criticism that she wastes too much money on clothes. As one who now points the fashion world in the right direction, she is never so overtly fashionable that her clothes will quickly date. Any that do appear outmoded are returned to the original designer for alteration; they are not totally discarded.

The criticism from the Royal Family is that the world has become so obsessed with Diana's wardrobe, that the work she undertakes for charity and worthwhile organizations seems to take second place. Before 1981 if we saw a newspaper report of a royal engagement it stated precisely what the person concerned was doing, be it visiting a hospice or opening a new factory. Today, with Diana, the one point that predominates is the name of the designer who created the outfit that the Princess is wearing. Whether she is visiting people dying from AIDS or premature babies, it is her clothes that will invariably be given priority in any report. This 'frivolous interest' is sometimes frowned upon by the Queen, and it is a media preoccupation that has extended now to other members of the Family. We know, for example, that Lady Sarah Armstrong-Jones occasionally frequents Oxfam and charity shops; the Princess Royal favours Gilly Jacques and Gina Fratini, and that the Duchess of York wears clothes by Lindka Cierach, Yves St Laurent, Edina Ronay and Zandra Rhodes. The question many royal advisers ask is, should we really know such details and has the emphasis not become too much clothes-orientated?

Having said that, however, clothes create visual impact. What the Royal Family wear is an integral part of what they do. They

145

are not merely functional and practical, but are symbols, displayed down the ages. When the Queen opens Parliament each November she is vested with the visual symbols of her role. She has to be seen to be Queen, thus she adopts the glittering Imperial State Crown, and the crimson velvet Robe of State, its eighteen foot long train edged with ermine. With long white silk dress, heavily embroidered, and diamonds glittering at her throat she embodies everything that is majesty. She becomes every child's image of what the Queen should look like. For ceremonies such as the Order of the Garter, or the Thistle, Her Majesty adopts the robes of chivalry, the long black mantle bedecked with orders, the white-plumed black velvet Tudor hat, emblems of continuity. When appropriate, full evening dress, family orders and tiara, are worn as a uniform of position. Because such emblems are impractical for the day-to-day duties of royalty, they have been modified down to equally recognizable styles. The inevitable hat for royal ladies is symbolic of far more than mere head covering or protection from the sun. It characterizes formality. While one would not expect to know the names of the makers of royal regalia, that the ceremonial robes were supplied by Ede and Ravenscroft, or the white gloves by Cornelia James, it seems equally unnecessary to know exactly who supplies the day dresses and suits that have become the working uniform of royalty.

The change that Diana has introduced is the subtle move in importance from interest in *clothes* to *fashion*. It is no longer the garments that the Princess wears that are of consequence, but the mode. It is a fine but significant distinction. This in itself is no bad thing, but the Princess and the Duchess should never reduce themselves to being mere clothes horses or mannequins at the expense of their dignity. If the fashion world chooses to follow Diana's lead, then all well and good. That she has become an ambassadress of fashion is a credit to her style and dress sense, but what courtiers fear is that she may deliberately set out to start a trend, be it a return to the mini-skirt or butterfly tights, which would only cheapen her official position as Princess of Wales.

To become a leader of fashion was never Diana's intention. It is a position thrust upon her rather than a self-adopted mantle. Like her mother, Frances Shand-Kydd, she has always appreciated good clothes and the earliest designers she used were

146

recommendations from her mother. That they happened to be British initially was pure coincidence, although as Princess of Wales the onus is on her always to back Britain. The Italian couturiers would welcome an opportunity to dress this most perfect of figures, but know that it will never be allowed. Diana occasionally wears clothes in private by American designers, but feels that she can only publicly be seen to support her own country. Once Charles has become King, she may feel that she can legitimately branch out into Commonwealth designers, or those from the territories over which he will rule, but this is not thought diplomatic at present.

On joining the Royal Family Diana discovered that she needed to change her whole style of dressing altogether. As a public figure she could not continue to wear the casual clothes that had dominated her wardrobe before. She felt comfortable in trousers, her eyecatching 'Black Sheep' sweater from the 'Warm and Wonderful' company became an instant favourite with the public in the pre-wedding months, but her wardrobe lacked the suits and dresses which were going to become such an essential part of her life.

Diana rejected royal designers and did not accept advice from aides at the Palace, turning instead to her sister Jane, who had been an editorial assistant on the magazine *Vogue* before her marriage. She immediately put Diana in touch with a team of fashion consultants – editor Beatrix Miller, senior fashion editor Anne Harvey, consultant Grace Coddington, and beauty editor, Felicity Clarke – who, between them, took the new Princess in hand: they darkened her eyelashes, lightened her hair, introduced her to top make-up artist Barbara Daly (who then did the wedding day make-up) and above all were able to advise from a professional viewpoint what would suit Diana's figure. Invaluable though this advice was, Diana is not completely taken over by consultants and knows exactly what she wants. At the end of the day it is she who has always made the final decisions.

Even today she is still learning and enjoys nothing more than watching a fashion show often spending a great deal of time talking to the models after the show to learn new tips. 'I'd like to be one of you, I do so envy your job,' she told a group of professional fashion models in 1986, 'I'd love to have been with

147

you there, with all the clothes flying about. I know it's chaos, but it must be great fun.' She then added, 'I found it hard to sit still while I was watching, you've got a wonderful job.'

She spent so long asking questions about make-up, whether they used gel to style their hair, and an all important question about hairspray, that Prince Charles eventually had to break up the conversation. 'We do have other commitments,' he said, unable to appreciate how much his wife was enjoying the girl-talk. Ever conscious about the environment (paper and glass are kept for recycling at Kensington Palace) in February 1988 Prince Charles publicly condemned the use of aerosols in the home, urging industry to find hairspray alternatives that would not damage the earth's ozone layer. When Diana went hours later to open a new school in Watford, all eyes were on her to see if her hair would 'flop' now that aerosols had been banished from Kensington Palace. Her hair looked immaculate and remained in place despite a very heavy wind. Her hairdresser, Richard Dalton revealed the secret – he did spray her hair, but with a pump, not a harmful aerosol.

The wind, Diana has admitted, is her enemy and it is not only her hair that needs to be held firmly in place. One early lesson that she learned was that a sudden gust of wind can damage one's dignity on an engagement. When Diana arrived in Bath in May 1985 for a visit to the Royal National Institute for the Deaf, her pleated pink dress by Victor Edelstein nearly took off under the breeze created by the helicopter's rotors and she found it almost impossible to keep the skirt down as she shook hands with the waiting reception committee. Only once has this happened to the Queen, on a tour of the Gulf States in 1979, when the desert wind revealed too much of the royal petticoat. From her mother-in-law Diana learned a tip – to have lead sewn into the hems to weight them. Although there are many female members of the Royal Family with decades of experience behind them, it was basically left to Diana to make mistakes and learn from trial and error. The list of requirements is always the same: nothing too short – people will see up your skirt if you bend over or walk down steps; nothing too tight that will restrict getting out of cars; nothing too flimsy that the light can shine through; no hat that hides the face or will blow away; and *always* wear comfortable shoes, because one fundamental requirement of royal duty is that you have to be on your feet for long periods of time. Observers have also noticed that for many engagements Diana does not wear a coat, except in winter. Here, again, experience has taught her that if you wear a coat there may well be problems: taking it off and putting it on in front of a crowd can be embarrassing and undignified and having taken it off, it either has to be put away somewhere, which can be a security risk, or it has to be held by the lady-in-waiting. Unless it is a function at which a coat can be kept on throughout, Diana chooses not to wear one preferring to opt for suits or matching jackets for warmth.

Dressing the part is one aspect of royal life that Diana enjoys, and it is an area in which she is confident that she has the edge over every other member of the Family. Designers love working on her clothes because of her figure which makes her 'a dream to dress'. At 5'10" she has the height to carry off chic styles, at 8½ stone and a size 10 she has a model physique, and being married to one of the country's richest men she has a choice of designers that many women envy. When she walks into a room Diana knows that every woman present will be scrutinizing her hair, her make-up, her shoes, her dress, her jewellery, and as a perfectionist she tries to obtain a total look and also enjoys an element of surprise. On a visit to Australia in 1985 she foresook the traditional tiara and instead used a diamond and emerald choker, a gift from the Queen, as a headband. The Art Deco style necklace had caused much gossip when she first wore it in 1981, for knowing that it had come from the Royal Family's collection of jewels, everyone wondered if it might be one of the famous 'Alexandra Emeralds' supposedly given to Wallis Simpson by Edward VIII in 1936. Not only had the famous emeralds failed to materialize on the death of the Duchess of Windsor in 1986, but a careful study of royal photographs would have revealed Queen Mary wearing the very same choker as late as 1948. It was then inherited by the Queen five years later, but chokers are not Her Majesty's style and it has never been worn by her.

It is jewellery more than clothes that will eventually set Diana apart as Queen when she and Charles receive the inheritance of the crown. As Lady Diana Spencer she had few jewels other than her sapphire and diamond engagement ring. For her actual wedding she had to borrow the Spencer family tiara (which she has on permanent loan as the only member of the family who will ever now need to wear it), and for her honeymoon a three-strand pearl drop pendant choker, which her siser Sarah wore for the ceremony. Her only valued piece of jewellery was a gold 'D', a gift from schoolfriends at West Heath, which she wore on a chain around her neck. When she posed for the official photograph taken by Lord Snowdon for the 'Royal Wedding' programme and order of ceremony, she borrowed a diamond necklace and earrings from Collingwoods the London jewellers.

Within a few years this lack of gems had been more than remedied. At a government ball in Bonn at the end of 1987 she dazzled guests, quite literally, wearing a necklace, bracelet and earrings worth in excess of half a million pounds as an accompaniment to the Spencer tiara – gifts from the Sultan of Oman. Exactly a week earlier she had brought gasps of amazement at a gala for Birthright, one of her patronages, when she wore an Elizabethan style gown, complete with ruff, as a backdrop to a crucifix, encrusted with amethysts on a string of large pearls, a gift from Prince Charles. As a wedding gift the Queen gave her a tiara of her own, a diamond bow-knot tiara with suspended pearls which had once belonged to Queen Mary, and the Queen Mother gave her a sapphire brooch, this being Diana's favourite stone. When the Prince wanted to have a necklace designed for her she appropriately, and tactfully, chose the Prince of Wales' feathers as an emblem and had it made up of diamonds and sapphires, a piece by Lexi Dick that is destined to be worn by all future Princesses of Wales. Sapphires came too from the Crown Prince of Saudi Arabia as a wedding gift and more gifts came from the King and Queen of Tonga, the Emir of Qatar, the President of the Seychelles, Sheikha Fatima Bint Mubarak al-Nayiyan of the United Arab Emirates, the Crown Prince and Princess of Jordan, and General Kenan Evren of the Turkish Republic: chokers, necklaces, a watch, rings and bracelets totalling well over a million pounds. In 1984 Prince Charles visited Southern Africa, where in Botswana he was given a single perfect diamond for his wife, which has now been set into a ring. What is surprising is that so few of Diana's jewels have actually come from the British Royal Family who have a vast stock from Queen Victoria, Queen

Alexandra and Queen Mary that are scarcely, if ever, worn. Possibly they feel that Diana should not receive too much, too soon.

As Princess of Wales Diana does have the honour of being able to borrow from the Queen's jewel pool, a vast collection of gems that have been left to the Crown as opposed to Her Majesty's personal jewels, but she chooses not to do so. Unlike many royal ladies of the past and present, Diana is never ostentatious with jewellery and often appears not only at daytime engagements but in the evening with nothing other than earrings or a simple pearl necklace, giving greater emphasis to the clothes she is wearing. For the Queen, on the other hand, evening gowns are often a mere backdrop for the glittering array of necklaces and brooches that she always wears. Out of the hundreds of outfits that Diana wears in any given year she rarely ever wears a brooch. When she does it is usually functional rather than decorative, to keep a sash in place. She only ever wears a tiara when it is officially required, claiming that they press into her head and give her a headache, and her short hairstyle makes attachment difficult.

The greatest treasures in Diana's collection are the small, often inexpensive items, that have been gifts from family and friends. Her favourite is a charm bracelet to which Prince Charles adds a trinket on each important occasion, and some members of the Family raised their hands in horror on the discovery that the future Queen sometimes wears fake jewels! It is ironic that someone who has millions of pounds worth of diamonds at her fingertips, is equally content wearing costume copies. It is probably a subconscious attempt to cling on to the girl in the street image, the 'ordinary' person that she so often longs to be.

Although Diana enjoys wearing new clothes, selecting outfits for an overseas tour, or planning the day-to-day engagements can be a lengthy process and certainly less fun. When she first began public engagements her wardrobe was limited and had to be built up. Newspaper reports that she had bought 200 outfits in the first year were not as wildly inaccurate as was later suggested, but the estimated cost of £2,000 per dress in 1981 was wide of the mark. It is a fabrication that angers the Princess, and even as recently as Ascot in 1987 fashion 'experts' were declaring that one dress alone had cost £10,000. The truth is that Diana has a set budget for clothes and it cannot be overstepped. Because she uses so many different designers, the number of clothes in her official wardrobe does seem to be vast, but keen royal watchers note than many dresses go back to the designer and are re-styled. First seen on the 1983 tour of Australia, for example, was a pink and gold dress made by Catherine Walker of the Chelsea Design Company. The full-skirted evening dress was distinctively loose, with frills and flounces around the neck, three-quarter length full sleeves and matching frilled cuffs. So full was the dress that it could easily have been worn as maternity wear, although Diana was not pregnant at the time. Three-and-a-half years later the same dress reappeared when the Princess attended a gala concert at London's Guildhall, but now it had long leg of mutton sleeves, a high plain neck, large shoulder pads and a dropped waist slimline skirt. Not only had the character of the dress become sleeker and more sophisticated, but so had Diana. In 1983 she looked under her fringe surrounded by the girlishly feminine flounces; in 1986 her eyes brimmed with confidence and the revamped dress matched her mood.

Many of her clothes have been similarly restyled. The entire wardrobe made for her Middle Eastern tour was made longer than she would normally wear so as not to offend her hosts, but all were deliberately chosen so that they could easily be shortened and worn again in Britain. Another pink dress for day wear, also by the Chelsea Design Company, when it had served its usefulness with a full skirt, suddenly reappeared with a dropped waist and pleats from mid-thigh. By having dresses cleverly redesigned an enormous amount of money is saved, and many outfits cost far less than the public are led to believe. Invariably she receives a large discount, and designers are happy that she is wearing their creations. Her patronage alone does more good than thousands of pounds worth of advertising. Many designers have reached superstar status through dressing the Princess of Wales: Bruce Oldfield and Jasper Conran, David and Elizabeth Emanuel are now household names.

One of Diana's favourite designers has remained the most discreet, does not seek publicity openly and refuses categorically to talk about her most famous client. She has been rewarded with very close friendship and now also designs for the Duchess of

York. Catherine Walker's shop is as discreet as its owner, hidden among houses and almost lost behind two large potted trees, in a fashionable Chelsea street. French-born, Catherine Walker moved to England at the time of her marriage to an English solicitor, who died tragically of a heart attack at the age of thirty-two. Not formally trained in fashion she made her own clothes, and so decided to make her living creating clothes for children. It was a case of starting small and working her way up. Through sheer hard work and dedication this shy, dark-haired woman, the same height as the Princess, is now considered to be one of Britain's foremost designers. Anne Harvey of *Vogue* who was one of the early advisers to the Princess admits that she herself wears 'almost nothing else. I wear her tailored things because they are so superbly made.'

A close study of Diana's wardrobe reveals that she wears Catherine Walker's designs over and over again, and has selected them for some of her most important engagements. The black lace creation that she wore to meet the Pope, the Elizabethan dress with which she wore the amesthyst and diamond cross, the unusual suit with gold frogging and the puffball skirts, and four outfits on the 1988 Bicentennial Australian tour are just some of Catherine's creations. The cost of the various garments also gives some indication of the amount Diana spends on clothes: Tailored suits start from £395, almost double for a pure wool suit; cocktail dresses at £450, evening dresses at £800 and a more lavish ballgown from £900 upwards. Each design is exclusive and material is only purchased in limited quantities. The prices are considered to be average, and nowhere near the speculated £10,000.

Although there are constant additions to the Princess' wardrobe, there are far fewer per annum than in the very first year of engagements when she began with very little, but because she did have to buy so much in 1981 that reputation has been difficult to shed. New and striking garments make the magazines and front pages, but there are numerous local engagements around the country each month at which Diana can wear the same outfits again and again and get away with it. Only on major public appearances is something special called for.

Before any foreign tour, speculation begins in advance as to what the trendsetter will wear. Months before the 1985 visit to Italy, fashion editors began to discuss what the Princess might wear and whether or not she could beat the Italians at their own game. 'She has been recycling her old clothes recently, a sure sign that she is saving *all* her new clothes for the tour,' wrote freelance Royal reporter, Margaret Holder. Other writers announced that £100,000 had been spent on clothes for the sixteen-day visit. So angry did such fanciful comments make Diana that she actually left some outfits that had been specially made for the tour behind. Almost every day she wore a dress that had been seen before, including some Catherine Walker redesigns. 'Unwise,' muttered some critics, 'she should have shown the Italians that she can compete in the fashion race,' but quite deliberately Diana decided to avoid playing the game. Milan has been as productive as Paris in controlling what women wear, and she knew that if too much emphasis were placed on her wardrobe, it would dominate the tour. She did not go to Italy to promote clothing, she and the Prince were there as representatives of the Queen and therefore it would have been unwise to reduce the visit to the level of a fashion parade. When Diana did wear new outfits they received an unprecedented amount of criticism, perhaps because initial expectations had been too high. A white suit with a black bow-tie was ridiculed as making the Princess 'look like a waiter', unfortunately it seemed to take on any shape other than Diana's. A cobalt blue evening dress with a dropped skirt and a dark blue velvet bodice with electric blue stars by Jacques Azagury was condemned as looking like a Christmas tree. A burgundy striped dress that bunched at the waist was described as a 'riot of over-detailed disorder' and the accompanying saucer-shaped hat was only one of a number of millinery creations that came under attack, others being an Italian fez, which seemed not to be appreciated, and a large green upturned brimmed hat like an oversized version of one of the Queen Mother's has never been worn since. The accompanying green coat by the Emanuels, which seemed to be two sizes too large, received some of the worst comments, the kindest of which came from the Americans who declared that it was 'a horseblanket'. It was probably the least successful tour fashionwise that the Princess had encountered. Voted the overall winner was a white suit with navy pinstripes worn with a small sailor hat that reappeared at a memorial service two months later in St Paul's, Cathedral, London, at which the Queen unveiled the South Atlantic Campaign Memorial.

One great change for Diana came when she discovered that buying clothes as she had done before her wedding ceased to be a pleasure. After the engagement, and occasionally even now, she would rush into Harvey Nichols in Knightsbridge accompanied only by a detective. Staff were given strict instructions that they were not to react if they saw her, if she asked for anything they were to get it and show it to her without asking any questions and at the first available opportunity they were to have a senior member of staff come to the floor to accompany the Princess personally. Because this drew attention to the fact that she was there, Diana often tried to escape the accompanying entourage. Although she has visited all her designers in their place of work, relishing poking about the racks and rails and looking into the workroom, she has reluctantly learned to accept the fact that it is easier for designers to come to her, than vice versa.

In her pastel green dressing-room at Kensington Palace, almost twice as long as it is wide with landscape prints on the walls and a white kidney shaped dressing-table and full-length mirrors, the Princess is fitted for each new garment. Most of the clothes begin life with one particular engagement or tour in mind, and the official diary is the starting point. If there is a long tour of Australia or America she will go through her wardrobe with her dressers to see which clothes she can wear again, while consulting detailed records which show exactly when and where she has worn them previously. Although she is happy to be seen wearing something that has appeared publicly before, it would not ever be considered wise to wear the same thing in the same place. A yellow silk evening dress by Murray Arbeid that caused such an impact at a banquet in Canberra, might not have quite the same effect if she were to wear it there on a subsequent visit. So once suitable garments from the existing collection have been chosen, the engagement diary will be studied to see where new additions are required. Designers of Diana's choice will then be contacted by lady-in-waiting Anne Beckwith-Smith, occasionally with a very detailed brief, but more frequently with a request simply for ideas for 'a formal evening dress' or 'a smart day suit'.

Unlike some members of the Family who settle for a particular designer for evening wear, another for cocktail dresses, and so on, Diana tends to traverse the entire spectrum. Thus David and Elizabeth Emanuel might be brought in to make the extravagant ballgowns that have become their forté, but equally, they might produce a stylish coat or day dress. A shimmering silver evening dress by Bruce Oldfield has been seen at many events, but he has also created some plain well cut suits. For the Queen Mother's eighty-third birthday Diana wore a slim-fitting soft grey two-piece suit in complete contrast to the eyecatching dresses that Oldfield had previously designed.

Once they know the Princess' requirements, a designer will submit thirty to forty sketches along with samples of material. When Diana has had an opportunity to study them, the designer will then be invited along for what usually turns out to be a very informal meeting on the sitting-room floor, surrounded by illustrations and swatches of material. Of the designs possibly one will eventually be made up, sometimes five or more, but the end result will be very much the Princess' choice. She has learned to know what suits her, she will make constructive comments about adjustments to the design and she will make the final decisions on cloth and colour. Sometimes she will have an idea in her mind that can result in sketches being drawn on the spot. The final choices will then be made up in the designer's workroom where there will be a dummy with the Princess' exact measurements. Designers are always extremely secretive about which model belongs to the Princess, just as nobody is allowed near her wax likeness at Madame Tussauds with a tape measure. As they have models of many of their top clients, such as Joan Collins, Bianca Jagger or the Duchess of Kent, each is only identifiable by a letter or number. Only the designer will know that a specific letter on a dummy's chest or a certain number refer to the Princess of Wales.

In the Kensington Palace dressing-room designers will arrive with perhaps four or five semi-completed garments for Diana to try. They now have it down to a fine art and mostly they need little alteration other than adjustments to the hem or a tightening of the bodice. A fitting will now take less than an hour to complete. One much used designer says, 'Her shape has changed enormously since I've been dressing her. As she has matured so her bone structure has altered. She has a smaller bust than she used to have, she stands straighter and has become much more elegant.'

Now that Diana is experienced in royal duties she has learned what designs are and are not suitable for certain occasions: backless evening dresses have proved embarrassing as hosts lead the Princess along a reception committee and feel that they should not touch her bare flesh; evening dresses for the theatre have sometimes had large buttons down the back which can be uncomfortable; once she wore a long pearl necklace hanging elegantly between her shoulder blades, but discovered that she could not lean back in a seat without some discomfort.

David Sassoon, who made Diana's 'going away' suit for after the wedding says that the Princess has 'her finger on the pulse of contemporary fashion . . . she will take elements of new trends and interpret them.' She is prepared to experiment and has the advantage as a fashion leader that she can to an extent wear what she likes without conforming.

One concession she does not make to comfort is with shoes, which she has a passion for with pairs to match every outfit. Because new shoes take time to wear in, many members of the Family have a number of tried and trusted pairs that match many outfits. On a tour of Australia in 1986 headlines shrieked **'Has the Queen only got one pair of shoes?'** but the Queen chose comfort at the expense of glamour. The Princess Royal has been criticized for being in a 'sixties time warp' with footwear, but admits that she hates spending money on shoes more than anything. Waiting for the King and Queen of Spain to arrive on a state visit to Britain observers saw that Diana was suffering obvious discomfort from her flimsy sandals. 'Where are my other shoes?' she mouthed to her lady-in-waiting, who was concentrating on the proceedings in hand. Eventually she caught the eye of Colonel Sir John Miller, the Crown Equerry. 'Ask her where my other shoes are,' the Princess whispered and after much discussion the lady-in-waiting realized that the shoes were in the car and it would be impossible to get them without drawing great attention. Diana had to suffer and as soon as she climbed into the carriage for the journey to Windsor Castle she hastily, but discreetly, removed the offending footwear.

In the early days Diana was conscious that with high heels she became taller than her husband and so adopted 'flatties' which became one of her first fashion innovations. For the sake of elegance she now wears a slight heel, invariably wearing two-tone court shoes to match her outfits. The size 7½ double A fitting are mostly custom made by Charles Jourdan, and Manolo Blahnik in Chelsea, at just under £100 a pair, and boots from Hobbs in South Molton Street. Although the initial outlay appeared expensive they are classic designs and having built up a wide range of colours Diana's stock can now be used with a whole gamut of outfits. A detailed study of photographs reveal that two obvious favourites that have complemented numerous outfits are a pair of white court shoes with a black toe and heel, and a pair of black patent leather shoes, both by Charles Jourdan. Other shoes are often recoloured to match a particular dress, the dye being matched exactly. Diana's interest in shoes has extended into Prince Charles' wardrobe, and he now wears ready-made slip-ons and fashionable evening pumps that would never have appeared in his bachelor days.

Part of her fashion initiation into the Royal Family was the need to wear a hat, an item that had not previously appeared in her wardrobe unless she was attending a friend's wedding. Tentatively at first, but with increasing confidence, she sported colourful feathery creations, at first designed by tried and trusted milliners (who also happened to supply Diana's mother) and later by her own discoveries. John Boyd is a favourite among all royal ladies, and Diana is no exception. He created some of the first hats that she wore and continues to create much of her headgear today. At first she would visit his showroom and pick hats without a moment's hesitation. 'I want that one!' she would giggle, and the design was immediately withdrawn from public sale so that it would be exclusive to her. Sometimes John Boyd cringed at the way she wore his work, often too far back on her head, or at a different angle to his original intention, but he quickly learned to forgive her. Many milliners dislike the way members of the Royal Family wear upturned brims and off-the-face styles, but when Diana is walking past a crowd who have waited hours to see her she knows what disappointment there would be if her face were obscured by the hat. She has, however, worn styles sporting small net veils with great success and these flattering creations are said to be Prince Charles' favourites, perhaps because they remind him of his grandmother!

Most of Diana's hats are now made specifically rather than simply taken from the block. The starting point is a sketch of the outfit with which Diana will wear the hat, which will be sent together with samples of material. Ninety per cent of the Princess' hats are made in the identical material to that of her jacket or dress. If the dress is patterned, one colour will be chosen to produce a complementary plain hat to offset it. Sometimes a patterned skirt will inspire a patterned hat. Once John Boyd knows the style of outfit and the function for which the Princess intends to wear it, he will send basic shapes to Kensington Palace, not completed hats, but moulds which will later be covered with fabric once Diana has settled on a design. Occasionally she might have three or four different hats to match one particular outfit, so that it can be worn several times and yet appear different on each occasion.

Another milliner, Viv Knowland, points out that there are sometimes problems. Certain fabrics that make up dresses are not always suitable for covering a hat – silk, for example, is particularly difficult – in which case lengthy discussions will ensue as to a possible alternative but complementary fabric. Occasionally, if there is a problem, Diana prefers to visit the showroom personally for ideas of ready-made hats. She may then select something in coloured straw or a plain white hat that can be teamed with a whole range of clothes. Freddie Fox is another much favoured royal designer, making many hats for the Queen and the Princess Royal. All milliners know that their royal clients demand more than just a stylish hat. Warm climates can make soft hats go limp, too wide a brim can not only have obvious disadvantages in the wind, but can all too quickly be squashed out of shape by leaning back in an aircraft seat.

Although Catherine Walker makes many of Diana's hats to match her own designs, Diana does tend, in common with other royals, to stick with the familiar milliners. When designer Jacques Reiss suggested that he make a hat to match the outfit the Princess Royal wore for the Duke and Duchess of York's wedding, Anne replied with typical bluntness, 'Cobblers!' and remained faithful to John Boyd who has created hats for her since she was seventeen. Diana equally will have Mr Boyd produce a hat to match the dress of another designer. It is noticeable that Diana is now beginning to find a style in hats. The feathered creations have now been replaced by less fussy, larger brimmed hats worn at a flattering angle instead of the close fitting kind. At Ascot, 1987, the Princess and the Duchess of York displayed humour in their styles by wearing identical hats with different coloured brims, not the first occasion on which there have been similarities: on one of Sarah's early engagements, a public trip to Prince Andrew's ship when he docked in London, she appeared wearing a boldly checked black and white coat that Diana had worn a year earlier. Journalists wrongly assumed that Diana had given Sarah some of her cast-offs, but just a few weeks later at Balmoral she went to church, sitting next to the Queen in the car on the way, with the coat returned.

Fortunately, for all of us, Diana still finds clothes 'fun' and for as long as this is so she will continue to spring her occasional surprises: at the end of April 1988 she arrived for a fund-raising greyhound meeting at Wembley in aid of the London City Ballet, wearing pencil slim trousers, a man's style evening jacket, complete with wing-collared shirt and a black bow-tie, with an emerald green double-breasted man's waistcoat (bought on a shopping expedition for Prince Charles at a favourite haunt in the King's Road). The whole outfit was completely masculine and yet the stylish Princess looked totally elegant and feminine.

A casual find, such as that of the emerald waistcoat on a shopping expedition, is not an unusual occurrence. She could so easily buy all her clothes without setting foot outside Kensington Palace, but she still relishes shopping. It is one of the few remaining activities that enable her to feel 'normal', just as long as she ignores the armed detective who is forever on her tail, who will himself pay for any purchases. Diana no longer carries money. Her official wardrobe is paid for by the Privy Purse, but personal clothes are paid for with an American Express Gold Card, charged to Prince Charles' account. The detective will stand guard outside the fitting room if she tries any garment on. A great deal of her private wardrobe is bought 'off the peg' in this way, and although the pressures may be on her to buy British for the public, in private she chooses her own labels.

160

Diana's increasing self-assurance is demonstrated by the development of her wardrobe. In 1981 she was demure and girlish in behaviour and style. Everyone loved her romantic frills and crisp virginal pleats. Two years later at the Hilton Hotel in Melbourne a new Diana emerged for the first time. She stepped out on to the dance floor in a figure-hugging white silk gown, shimmering with silver beads emphasizing every female curve. Her left shoulder was bare. Her longer, fuller hairstyle was immaculate. The dress by Hachi proved irrefutably that the prim lace and delicate ruffles were a thing of the past. Australians, who had until then criticized her style as 'too conventional', agreed beyond doubt that the Princess of Wales oozed something that had never before been associated with royalty. Sex appeal. In one sweeping visual statement she had pushed the Royal Family firmly into the fashion scene. From now onwards all have an additional role to fulfil.

✳ 8 ✳

Royal Duty

'The Queen of England used to be my cleaning lady,' is something that very few people will ever be able to boast, but when Prince Charles eventually inherits the throne, theatrical producer Lucinda Craig Harvey will have this ultimate line in one-upmanship.

From the age of seventeen until just before her engagement Diana was a temporary cleaner, employed first by a London agency, Solve Your Problems in 1978, and later by her elder sister Sarah, and Lucinda who then shared a flat with her. As a weekly 'char' Daina would dust, polish and vacuum and was in her element being left to get on with the work alone. It is a skeleton in the Princess' closet that the present Queen would no doubt prefer to have kept locked away, but Diana is amused by the revelation. Meeting Lucinda at the launch of a foundation for young leukaemia sufferers in January 1988, Diana was quick to remind her former employer of her once humble role. It is typical of her that she enjoys introducing a note of informality into her work today. A few weeks earlier Diana paid an official visit to the Whitehall Theatre in London to see a charity performance of Oscar Wilde's *The Importance of Being Ernest*, again in aid of leukemia and a theatrical venture of Lucinda's; the Princess amused the cast by taking hold of *the* handbag, held by Dame Hilda Bracket, playing Lady Bracknell, and examining it closely. The image of a royal fashion leader holding a ghastly giant handbag was an hilarious sight, but secretly Diana must have longed to take the prop home to do a parody of her mother-in-law.

Outwardly Diana may sometimes appear too frivolous for the serious position that she holds, but it is her way of making her role easier, the duties less of a chore. Prince Charles was made aware of his duties as a member of the Royal Family from the youngest possible age. He became a respecter of position, he had to bow to his great-grandmother Queen Mary whenever they met, and his earliest training was geared specifically to the work he would eventually undertake. From her aristocratic background with no greater expectations placed upon her other than that she would marry well and have lots of children, Diana was ill-prepared for the 'career' that is now hers. Many pour scorn on her lack of formal qualifications, but no degree or doctorate could possibly have equipped her for royal duty.

On leaving West Heath School finding work was necessary only to occupy her time, it was never meant to provide her income. She knew that on 1 July 1979, she would inherit a considerable sum from her maternal great-grandmother, Frances Work, a former Lady Fermoy, on her eighteenth birthday. With this certain knowledge, there was little incentive to train for a serious career. Her only great interest was children and so in April 1978 she went to Headley in Hampshire to look after the baby daughter of Major Jeremy Whitaker and his wife Philippa, old friends of the Spencers through Philippa's brothers. For three months Diana acted the role of a paid *au pair*, helping out in all aspects of the home and living as part of the family group in their delightfully named home 'The Land of Nod'.

That summer she returned to London and decided to join a couple of agencies undertaking work as a baby-sitter for a company called Knightsbridge Nannies, through which she looked after the child of an American couple, Patrick and Mary Robinson, and began domestic work for Solve Your Problems. These were unsettled days for Diana; not only was this the beginning of her father's long illness, but still scarcely out of school she had no real purpose in life, no specific goal at which to aim. With no pressure upon her to work and no actual incentive, she seemed to move from job to job, never really remaining anywhere for longer than three months. These were the years that saw her flitting around, too restless to keep still and too fragile for someone to take hold of.

In September 1978 she began a three-month cookery course with Elizabeth Russell in Wimbledon, south-west London, travelling each day by underground to the school where she achieved expert culinary skills, inspired by her then flatmate Laura Greig who was herself taking a Cordon Bleu cookery course. When interviewed with Prince Charles before their marriage she revealed that throughout their courtship he had never tasted her cooking. The opportunity to prepare the Prince dinner did not arise, he was never a guest at Coleherne Court because of the secrecy in which their relationship had then to be conducted, and as his future wife, cookery was not a skill that Diana would ever require. Although she enjoyed housework, she now never has to lift a duster or plug in a vacuum cleaner. Some people would consider this to be a great advantage, but just very occasionally Diana rebels against having everything done for her, which is why she has gone through phases of obsessive tidiness out of a desperate need to do something constructive.

On completion of the cookery course that Christmas Diana joined yet another employment agency, Lumleys, this time specializing in catering. Her career in this field was short but varied, ranging from waitressing at Slim Jim's, a London restaurant, to providing delicate canapés for cocktail parties. In January 1979 Diana turned to dancing. Having always wanted to be a ballet dancer she had won an end of term dancing competition prize at West Heath and one of the judges had been Madame Betty Vacani. The Vacani school has long been a favourite for royal children, and Betty's aunt Marguerite had taught the Queen, Princess Margaret and Prince Charles to dance when they were children. It was to Madame Vacani that Diana now turned. She had no recollection of Lady Diana Spencer, but agreed to take her on as a student teacher to tutor very young children in basic steps. Spending five mornings a week with two dozen children under the age of three at first seemed an idyllic proposition to Diana, but she soon found herself overwhelmed by the boisterous babies, and dancing to the most simplistic nursery rhymes became very tiresome. She did, nevertheless, enjoy the ballet classes with older children and proved that she had the necessary skills to progress further. She was not suitable to be a performer, but Betty Vacani insisted that with hard work Diana could become a ballet teacher, perhaps embracing the saying: 'Those who can, do. Those who can't, teach.' Unfortunately

Diana lacked the will-power to persevere, and after a now typical three-month period she left the Vacani School at the end of March without giving notice. She was too embarrassed to tell her employer, who had given her the chance she had originally requested, that she no longer wished to continue. From then onwards she absorbed herself in the solitary occupation of cleaning her sister's flat, which she continued to do even after joining the Young England Kindergarten in the autumn of 1979. This was to be the longest time she would hold a single job working there until she married the man she loved and unsuspectingly gained a career for life.

Opening a new £30 million shopping centre in St Albans, Hertfordshire, in April 1988, Diana let slip a revealing comment about her position as Princess. Pet shop manageress, Judy Stratton was talking openly about her work. 'It must be very difficult doing what you do,' she said to the Princess, 'I know there are days when I don't feel like smiling and being pleasant. Do you often feel the same?' Diana shrugged her shoulders, and said 'It's not all it's cracked up to be.' 'It must be awful to have to be perfect all the time,' Mrs Stratton continued. 'You are so right,' agreed the Princess without a moment's hesitation.

When she first became aware that she would be Princess of Wales, she saw her role as simply being there to support her husband. He would do the work while she remained in the background, like a royal vicar's wife. Before he proposed marriage, Prince Charles took great pains to explain that in marrying him Diana would become part of the Family and all that it entailed. 'With the Prince beside me, I can't go wrong,' she had said on the day of her engagement, unaware, or unwilling to accept, that one day she would have to face the public alone. When she did have to make the break and begin the round of solo engagements she was an unqualified success because of her obvious lack of experience. Launching a ship, for example, is a particularly royal task that no amount of training can prepare you for. The brief is simple. You make a speech, release a handle that smashes a bottle of champagne against the bow, and miraculously the vessel glides down the slipway into the water. Easy. For her first ever launching Diana began small with a Liverpool canal

165

boat. She dashed the champagne bottle against the boat and it immediately bounced back at her, refusing to break. Three times she tried and each time the bottle simply bounced and the Princess was left blushing on the quayside until Prince Charles came to her rescue. The launcher's nightmare had come true for Diana on her very first experience, the memory of which haunts her on each successive ship launch. Only one other major hitch can occur and that is if the launching mechanism fails and the ship does not move into the water. When launching HMS *Cornwall* at Yarrow shipbuilders in Glasgow, exactly that happened. Calmly, if unregally, Diana leant over and pushed on the ship with all her might to wild applause!

When Princess Anne was asked if she ever gave the Princess of Wales any advice she said that you can do little but recount your own experience 'if it helps', but a novice very quickly learns that no amount of reminiscing from other members of the Family can take the place of personal knowledge. A measure of Diana's growing confidence was displayed when she launched the mammoth liner *Royal Princess*, the most expensive of its kind ever built. The choice of the Princess of Wales was popular for the launch and was ranked alongside previous royal ships of equal grandeur. In 1934 Queen Mary launched her namesake, then the most luxurious liner of its kind; four years later Queen Elizabeth gave her name to an elegant cruiseship, followed in 1967 by her daughter's launch of *Queen Elizabeth 2* (known affectionately as QE2, the second liner named *Queen Elizabeth* and not, as many believe, a ship called 'Queen Elizabeth the Second' after Her Majesty). The *Royal Princess* weighing 45,000 tons and built at a cost of £130 million, is equally prestigious.

No chances were taken with this launch and the previous evening the ship's crew undertook numerous tests with the mechanism that would smash the champagne bottle. Empty bottle after empty bottle was shattered against the gleaming white steel bow, and when Diana came to use the £62 magnum of Krug, she was unaware that it had been unceremoniously weakened with glass cutters. She relaxed with a look of unashamed relief as the bottle smashed and the ship slid graciously into the water. Dressed in brilliant scarlet with a nautical hat, the Princess not only stood out in the crowds on the fog shrouded pier at Southampton, but also as a confident performer. She met many of the 500-strong crew, asking engaging questions, taking a strong interest in all that she saw and with girlish delight blasted the foghorn on the bridge. She dined at the Captain's table on appropriately named 'Chicken Breasts Princess Diana', created in her honour, and as a lasting reminder of that day a large portait of her hangs in the Princess Court, the central foyer of the ship that all passengers enter. It was a memorable day for all concerned, the Princess departed with gifts of a gold necklace and bracelet, a silver sculpture of a seagull, a silver bowl and two teddy bears for the Princes. 'I cannot get over how kind you have all been to me today,' she said, 'I have been showered with beautiful presents . . . from now onwards I shall have a special interest in wherever *Royal Princess* sails, and I am sure she will prove a great asset to P & O and Britain.'

Of royal duty Diana has said, 'It's seventy per cent sheer slog and thirty per cent fantastic,' and what she was beginning to discover once she had found her feet was that the 'fantastic' parts were nearly always at her solo engagements. It became increasingly apparent to her that wherever she went people *wanted* to see her. One handshake, one smile, one word, were such simple actions on her part, yet the people that she met treasured these fleeting seconds for a lifetime. On visits, such as the *Royal Princess* launching, she receives the warmest of welcomes, an abundance of gifts, and if she does make the tiniest of errors people, if they notice, do not care. On solo engagements she can have an amusing journey with plenty of laughter from her accompanying lady-in-waiting, nearly always Anne Beckwith-Smith on any major function, and has learned to relax. The duties that she enjoys far less are those that she undertakes with other members of the Royal Family.

At any public event at which the Queen or any senior member of the Family is present, Diana is instantly reserved in her demeanour. Even if it is a short drive from Crathie Church to Balmoral Castle, one mile along the Braemar Road sitting beside the Queen, Diana looks uncomfortable. For the 1985 film première of *A Passage to India* the Princess accompanied the Queen Mother and the Princess Royal, who have eighty years experience of royal functions between them, and she felt conscious that she was in competition. Would the questions she asked the long line-up of celebrities be as intelligent as Princess Anne's? Would she appear as regal as the Queen Mother? If she unwittingly made a mistake would it be more apparent next to the real professionals? There was a very long reception committee, but Diana reached the end immediately after the Queen Mother and stood waiting for some considerable time for Prince Charles, Princess Anne and Captain Mark Phillips to join them, her cheeks glowing. Only when she had spoken to people she had met before, such as the actor Nigel Havers, did Diana show any sign of relaxation. Princess Anne was in a particularly buoyant mood and had obviously set out to prove that she was an equal match for her sister-in-law in the fashion stakes. She wore a Princess of Wales style four-strand pearl choker complete with Diana's favourite stone, a large sapphire, plus a large sapphire brooch that had been a gift from the Queen and a copy of the one given to Queen Victoria by Prince Albert and worn on her wedding day. Dressed in a fashionable grey moiré silk evening dress with large puffed sleeves, Princess Anne for once pushed Diana in a jade green off-the-shoulder creation in the shade. Was it significant that this was in the same month that Princess Anne dazzled everyone at the BAFTA Award ceremony with dashing red streaks in her hair and a *Dynasty* style Jacques Reiss gown in dramatic pink? Obviously enjoying this new found sport Princess Anne jauntily accepted a posy of cream flowers as Diana looked on silently. 'They've given us all the same,' grinned Princess Anne, noticing that Diana and the Queen Mother had identical bouquets, 'They obviously didn't know what colours we were going to wear.' Diana smiled bashfully.

Observing Diana on a solo engagement one sees a total contrast. On Thursday 11 February 1988, as Patron of the British Lung Foundation, she visited the Faculty of Medicine of the University of Southampton at the Princess Anne Hospital and Southampton General Hospital to see research projects and open a new laboratory. Looking suntanned from her recent Australian tour and wearing a dramatic yellow and black checked coat designed by the German company Escada, Diana appeared radiant and self-assured. As with all her patronages and presidencies, the Princess has only accepted them from organizations in which she has a genuine interest, and here she toured a special baby care unit where some babies, many weighing under one pound at birth, spend their first critical days; their lungs are underdeveloped and breathing is their greatest difficulty. Diana asked about the research being undertaken that is helping minimize risks, and looked shocked when she heard that oxygen itself can seriously damage the babies' lungs. She met and spoke to mothers with sick babies and, aware of the dangers, she said as she has done so many times how thankful she is that her children are strong and healthy.

At Southampton General Hospital she went on a walkabout among two hundred Hampshire children aged between seven and eight, invited to be there because they were all taking part in a year long research project, funded by the British Lung Foundation, into asthma and other respiratory problems. Many children carried brightly coloured gas filled balloons and Diana was in her element chatting to them animatedly. After opening the new research laboratories she walked along the corridor to where twenty-four-year-old Simon Trangmar was exercising on a treadmill machine, fighting asthma with fitness. A keen anti-smoker, whose father has long suffered with breathing problems, Diana was eager to listen to information but she seemed hesitant when invited to try the treadmill out for herself. Abandoning her clutch bag she laughed, 'My skirt's too tight,' but wearing high boots to protect her from the cold February wind, she managed to retain her dignity as she climbed on to the machine which had been deliberately set at a very slow walking pace. Had she been asked to get on to a treadmill a few years earlier she would have immediately refused, and if it had been part of her programme she would have done it blushing like a beetroot. On this day she climbed on confidently and when one of the doctors made a flippant remark to the gathering photographers she turned to him, still treading, and said, 'I'll make the jokes, OK!'

Outside again, carrying a bouquet of pink and white roses, she gathered more flowers from the research project children. Most were handed expertly to the lady-in-waiting who placed them directly into the open boot of the royal car. A final relaxed wave, and Diana climbed into the car for the return journey to London, leaving behind dozens of gas filled balloons on the ceiling as the only visible reminder of her visit, but a much longer lasting memory in the interest and compassion she had shown.

On occasions such as this Diana is in control. Not only will she have done her homework, but she is familiar now with enough of each of her organizations' work to talk knowledgeably on the subject and to learn from each successive visit. If she visits one research project now, she is able to compare it with visits to others around the country and can monitor progress. Her patronages have all been selected after much consideration in areas where the Princess feels that she can bring some benefit. In the first few months of her royal life 150 organizations approached her to be their patron. She selected five: the Royal School for the Blind; the Malcolm Sargeant Cancer Fund for Children; the Pre-School Playgroups Association; the Welsh National Opera (as Princess of Wales); and the Albany, a community centre in the East End of London. Over the years she has slowly built that number up to twenty-five patronages in Britain and eight overseas, plus three joint patronages with Prince Charles, and four presidencies. None have been selected without thought, and she has deliberately not taken on too many so that each can have a share of her time as her patronages and general appointments form the basis for every working year.

A look through the Princess' patronages (See Appendix II page 209) provides an insight into her areas of interest and concern. A large proportion, as would be expected, are connected with children – in her first interview she described her job as a 'challenge' and her interests as 'children', but quickly added 'They will broaden. I'm only twenty' – but it would be wrong to classify her only as 'The Children's Princess'. In her work for adult organizations she has taken a considerable interest in the blind, deaf, disabled, the aged and infirm, cancer sufferers, and people suffering from nervous disorders. Along with many members of the Royal Family she has also expressed a growing concern for AIDS.

Where possible she has attempted to set examples for others to follow. It is early days for her yet, but with increasing maturity she could well follow Princess Anne's lead and become a figurehead for particular causes. As Patron of the National Rubella Council she became fully aware of the importance of vaccination against specific diseases and illnesses and although inoculation against

German measles is common practice, she set an example by having both Prince William and Prince Harry vaccinated against whooping cough at a time when many mothers feared the possible side-effects. By making it known publicly that she had done this and that children were more at risk from whooping cough itself than from the vaccine, many children throughout Britain were vaccinated who might not otherwise have been.

One function of the Royal Family, Prince Charles believes, is to put something back into society in gratitude for the privileges that their birthright has afforded them. Diana has frequently expressed publicly her thankfulness that her own children are healthy and that during pregnancy, other than unpleasant morning sickness and severe backache she experienced no difficulties. Although she has joked, 'If men had to have babies they would only have one each,' she genuinely knows that she has been lucky. The charity Birthright of which Diana is Patron is the first to raise funds solely for research into all aspects of pregnancy, raising money for scanners and ultrasound equipment that can monitor the progress of the unborn child. Birthright is the vital financial link with the Royal College of Obstetricians and Gynaecologists, of which the Princess is an Honorary Member. Diana has been Patron of Birthright since 1984, and her position was officially announced on the day she opened the Harris Birthright Centre, an advanced scanning unit, at King's College Hospital in London. Each year since then she has attended numerous fund-raising events. Sometimes the nature of these engagements has been questioned by cynics. The Princess may visit mother and baby care units, maternity hospitals and clinics, which appear to be worthwhile events. But when the Princess' engagement diary appears frequently to contain lunches, galas, film performances, and theatrical productions, is not her attendance at them in the name of Birthright's Patron just a little tenuous? Although senior royal courtiers would raise their hands in horror, the work of the Royal Family goes hand-in-white-glove with commercialism. The proceeds from a theatrical performance at which the Princess of Wales is present in sheer monetary terms can swell the coffers of a charity more than a national appeal. At the end of the day it is the proceeds from what is after all a 'fund-raising event' that is the important consideration. Unfortunately, the Princess feels, some of these events can only cater for a very élitist sector and it seems ironic that often so many men and women who give their time tirelessly to charity cannot afford to attend fund-raising events.

On the eve of Derby Day in June 1987 a gala performance of Massenet's opera *Manon* was held at Covent Garden, London, in aid of the National Society for the Prevention of Cruelty to Children and was followed by a ball in the Jubilee Hall, Covent Garden, which Princess Margaret attended as President. Tickets for the opera and ball cost £750 for one or £1,000 for two. It is a method of raising a considerable amount of money, but it is out of the price range of the average person in the street for one evening's entertainment. A week later, Diana attended a 'special perform-ance' of Verdi's *Requiem* in the Royal Albert Hall. The most expensive tickets were £50, the lowest were £10, a much more realistic and accessible price, which the Princess prefers. Although some members of the Royal Family have learned to live with this aspect of their work because of the money raised for good causes, they are only too aware that such fund-raising occasions provide a showcase for people to see and be seen.

Watching the Princess of Wales at work, I have seen people arriving at a royal film première on a warm September evening wearing fur coats that would protect them in the Arctic, leaving their arrival as late as possible just to be seen in the presence of royalty. I have seen Diana walk along a reception commit-tee of dignitaries when opening a new building, only to be told by staff that scarcely one in the line had any real right to be there. 'They're the ones who've done the hard work,' they will say, pointing to eager faced men and women on tiptoe at the back of the crowd. The Royal Family accept this 'fault' in society because, and *only* because, they know that a worthwhile cause will be pounds richer at the end of the day. But it is for this reason that Prince Charles will sometimes break off from his expected schedule and say, 'I want to meet the man who sweeps the floor,' and he is always keen to meet enterprising young people who have created their own employment, using their own skills, putting something back into society in more than monetary terms. Equally unscheduled, the Princess of Wales will occasionally request at the last minute that she visit a Help the Aged home, or a hospice for the dying. Practically unannounced and without months of preparation, she knows that she will receive a much more realistic view. It is an attempt to prove also that she is not just an empty-headed fashion plate. A few hours bringing comfort to the dying, helping an old man select a horse for a bet, or learning to 'speak' the sign language for the deaf, leave her emotionally drained but feeling that she has achieved something worthwhile.

Ultimately she will find the real job satisfaction through her patronages, that no other royal duty can provide. Sitting at the State Opening of Parliament, making small talk at a State Banquet or a garden party, sometimes bores her rigid. Like any woman of her age she enjoys putting on the glamour for an evening, 'I enjoy wearing bright colours,' she says, and of course she has fun at a good film première or dance spectacular, but she is fully aware that it is all part of the frivolous side of the job. Here she comes into line with the Royal Family in wanting to achieve something, and be seen as a responsible person. What she hates is the inevitable protocol, and the pressure. Only when she can accept engagements because she wants to, and not because she has to, do we see Diana at her best.

Coming from a broken home was an instrumental factor in Diana's acceptance of the Dr Barnardo's Presidency. Founded in 1866, Dr Barnardo's is a child care society, providing special services for children in need. It has the image of providing homes for orphans, but today its role is just as much helping families whose children might be taken into care before they reach a crisis point. They run residential homes, special schools, units and foster homes. Their most famous 'son' is one of Diana's favoured dress designers, Bruce Oldfield, and her first fund-raising event for the charity was a ball he organized in March 1985, which with the presence of its new President raised £108,000. Princess Margaret had been Dr Barnardo's President for over thirty years, but she passed it over to Diana who, being of a younger age, perhaps fitted the image better. Possibly after three decades in the role Princess Margaret felt that the Princess of Wales might now be a greater asset to them. In 1987 alone Diana visited a Dr Barnardo's Community Day Centre in London, one of their schools in Berkshire, attended a centenary concert in Cardiff, Wales, a school of printing in Hertford, a Young People's Centre in Bristol, a Centre and a Barnardo's shop in Birmingham, a Centre in Mid Glamorgan, and opened a school in Bromley, Kent, all wearing her Presidential hat.

In March 1985 Diana became the first Patron of Help the Aged in its twenty-five year history and made her maiden speech to launch their Silver Jubilee Year. Once again she took time over making her decision to accept the role, having visited the Help the Aged offices some six months earlier to discover more about their work, and whether or not she could be of any practical help. One fear is of being nothing more than a name at the top of an organization's notepaper. Princess Anne has described the word 'Patron' as a very non-descript position, preferring the more straightforward 'President'. The Princess of Wales is less concerned about the vagueness of a title if she can fulfil a useful purpose. One point that won her over with this, as with so many of her other patronages, was that it enabled her to keep in touch with reality and ordinary people. Also she saw that Help the Aged was not only dealing with the sick and the infirm, but also with those able-bodied men and women who through their years had outlived their family and friends and now suffered from loneliness and insecurity. Two conditions with which Diana, though years younger, could personally identify. Often loneliness has nothing to do with lack of people; it is possible to feel isolated in a crowd and she understood this only too well.

Just as Diana's patronage gives a charity publicity, so she enjoys being able to make the work of one of 'her' charities known to a wider field. In 1985 I spent a whole day at the Help the Aged headquarters and discovered that many elderly people suffer unnecessary hardship simply because they are not aware of their rights. They sometimes shun any kind of supplementary benefit, looking upon it as charity rather than something owing to them. They do not like to reveal how little or how much they have, thinking back to the old means test and fear that they will lose their homes. Often as much work is required to educate people as to provide practical help. Help the Aged have a vast stock of books and leaflets simply explaining how the quality of life can be improved by people accepting the financial help to which they are entitled. Diana has also launched an information bus that travels around Britain giving details of the charity's aid and of a 'Lifeline

Unit' – a special telephone with an emergency button. She has also opened day centres where the elderly can find warmth, companionship, food, and facilities such as a hairdresser and chiropodist. 'We have a duty to ensure they are seen as valued and important members of our society,' says the Princess of the elderly people she meets.

Unlike with any other job, Diana cannot complain of lack of variety in royal duty. Her days do not always involve meeting the sick and frail by any means. In 1985 she proved that she does not object to dressing-down when she flew to the Forties Charlie oil rig, 110 miles off the East Coast of Scotland. Although admitting that she is scared of heights, she landed by helicopter on the rig in the middle of the North Sea wearing a fluorescent orange jacket, warm yellow knitted gloves, trousers and a bright yellow plastic safety helmet. 'I am a bit of a chicken,' she said breathlessly, 'I don't like looking down at the water.' She remained on the rig for nearly three hours, climbing up narrow ladders and captivating the 150 workers with her charm and off-the-cuff comments. An example of her growing confidence in smalltalk.

Making conversation with strangers is an important pre-requisite for anyone beginning royal engagements, and something the 'shy Di' found difficult in the early years. The Queen and the Duke of Edinburgh have a set of stock questions, ranging from 'Do you live here?' to 'How long have you worked here?' The Princess Royal asks very direct questions, totally relevant to the occasion. I was once walking a few paces behind her at a film première at the Cannon Cinema in the Haymarket, London. She asked one member of the line-up exactly how the film had come about. 'It's based on the book,' said the unsuspecting man. 'What do you mean it's based on the book?' she asked quizzically, 'That doesn't tell me anything. Does it follow the book exactly, is it just loosely based on the story, is it . . .' The probing came from a genuine interest. The Prince of Wales is less demanding in his approach, but he attempts to begin a conversation rather than fielding off one-word answers, and he is always full of praise and encourage-ment whatever the situation. 'Well done. You're doing a marvel-lous job,' is his most frequent phrase, and he has practised the art of walking away just a few paces and then turning back with a quip that makes a person feel that the Prince is really interested in what he has been told. The Princess of Wales falls somewhere in between.

Diana does not resort to bland questions and carefully avoids 'Yes/No' responses. One much repeated example is that of the Queen Mother who once asked a student from Phoenix, 'I believe Arizona is very hot?' 'Yes, Ma'am.' 'And sometimes it is very cold?' 'Yes, Ma'am.' The Queen Mother smiled and walked away. A situation to be avoided at all costs and one that can be resolved by a carefully worded open-ended question. Diana has also learned from her father-in-law that smalltalk can get you into trouble. Sitting next to a Brazilian general at dinner one evening, the Duke asked him how he had come by all his medals. 'For the war,' said the General. 'I didn't know that Brazil was in the war that long,' Prince Philip sniffed. 'At least, Sir, I did not get them for marrying my wife,' came the crushing response. Prince Philip not infrequently adds a touch of sarcasm to his smalltalk too.

'How was your flight, Sir?' asked a host as the Duke stepped from a plane. 'Have you ever been in an aircraft?' asked the Duke. 'Yes, Sir.' 'Well, it was like that.'

From these examples, and others like them, Diana has learned a great deal, and her smalltalk is noted for being much more personal than that of the rest of the Family. If people have been waiting in the wind or rain her first words will nearly always be, 'You must be so cold, thank you for waiting so long,' which has the immediate effect of endearing her to people. Visiting RAF Wittering in Cambridgeshire to review her first guard of honour as Honorary Air Force Commodore she was shown the cockpit of a Harrier Jet. 'Is she temperamental like a woman?' came the Princess' unexpected question to Flight Lieutenant Steve Fox.

Sometimes her light-hearted comments are taken too seriously. Told to mind her head when walking around Florence she said, 'It doesn't matter, there's nothing in it.' In 1981 when she had visited James Lock and Co to be fitted for a riding hat, she was told that she needed a size 7½, quite large for a woman. 'My head may be large, but there's not much in it,' she said, and when invited to play Trivial Pursuit by a fourteen-year-old patient at Tadworth Court Hospital in Surrey for chronically sick, handicapped and terminally ill children, she declined saying, 'No thanks. I'm as thick as a plank.'

Such remarks are quite deliberately calculated and not as off-the-cuff as they might at first appear. By putting herself down she immediately makes people feel at ease. Those who are in awe of her relax with a smile. The not-so-thick Princess also knows that such remarks lower expectations of her from the Royal Family. Princess Anne once called her sister-in-law 'a brainless woman', but Diana must secretly enjoy the attention she receives through her slightly helpless image. People are gentler and more considerate because of it. 'She has put the feminist movement back thirty years,' grumbled one left-wing councillor, keen to promote sex equality and destroy the very image that Diana attempts to promote.

Sometimes Diana is just *too* down to earth for the Royal Family: 'The trouble with being a Princess is that it is so hard to have a pee,' she told people after her 1983 visit to Melbourne where she had to be taken nine floors to the toilet for reasons of security. 'I was crossing and recrossing my legs all the way up in the lift,' she revealed. Hardened royal aides remember the time on a state visit to Brazil in 1968 when at an official lunch in Rio the Queen desperately needed to visit the bathroom. She had a discreet word with her lady-in-waiting, at that time Lady Rose Baring, who made equally discreet enquiries about which room had been set aside for Her Majesty's exclusive use, and it was decided that she would be able to disappear during coffee with it being too obvious. As the Queen was about to sneak out, Prince Philip noticed. 'Where are you going?' he asked. 'It's very late, we're not going to get to our next appointment on time.' 'Let's go then,' replied the Queen, and off she went to unveil a plaque as planned. Such personal self-control is expected of Diana, and at the very least Palace officials do not expect the future Queen to discuss such intimate details at a reception, but it is occasionally the element of shock amid the stuffiness of court that Diana so enjoys. On a visit to York she asked a young boy if he had taken the day off school just to see her. 'Yes,' he grinned. 'How naughty!' she scolded, as if he were one of her own children, and the people loved her for it.

Often the very deliberateness of Diana's smalltalk on walkabout becomes apparent only when it is reported in the Press. From the comments she has made and the emphasis laid upon them, you know with certainty that she meant them either to be overheard by reporters or repeated by the crowd. She knows only too well that only minutes after she has spoken to someone on a walkabout a journalist will be there demanding to know what the Princess said. If she has been angered by current media reports, walk-abouts provide a subtle vehicle for dispelling rumours. After the birth of Prince William in 1982 Princess Michael of Kent said at an award ceremony, 'Prince William is absolutely adorable. He has little tufts of red hair all over his head,' adding, 'I thought you all knew that,' when people expressed surprise at the revelation. Two days later on a tour of Wales Diana made every effort to dispel the rumours and the then media obsession with her son's red hair. 'He hasn't got red hair – he's fair,' she told a group in Aberdovey, Gwynedd. On a walkabout at Pentre she said, 'He's got masses of beautiful blond hair,' a phrase she repeated in Rhydyronnen, and just in case the Press had not got the message she pointed to a child in the crowd with fair hair saying loudly, 'He's got the same colour hair as my William.' She knew that her point would be driven home, even if her approach was less than subtle. Just to cock-a-snook at royal officialdom she told by-standers equally loudly that her son 'keeps widdling all over me,' only too happy to satisfy the public's appetite for details of Prince William, her favourite subject. Princess Michael of Kent was later forced to admit that she had only seen a colour photograph of the baby 'taken in a reddish light'. If there are rumours about her marriage, or extravagant expenses on clothes, the Princess of Wales departs from expected royal protocol and puts her comments forward. When American fashion critic Richard Blackwell voted her the world's worst-dressed woman in January 1983, saying 'Shy Di has invaded Queen Victoria's attic,' her immediate response just a few weeks later in Australia was to stun the fashion world with the slinkiest, sexiest dress she had ever worn.

The task of organizing the Princess of Wales' official life is an onerous one. Each year she receives over two thousand invitations which have to be reduced down by ninety per cent. In 1987 she undertook 180 engagements in the UK and carried out

Progress of a Princess: the plain
schoolgirl and the shy 'Lady Di' *(above
left and right)* are transformed into a
stylish beauty who can now confidently
wear more than a million pounds worth
of jewellery at one time

After the birth of Prince William in 1982, Diana leaves St Mary's Hospital, Paddington, looking flushed and frumpish *(Camera Press)*

Two years later the Princess emerges from the same hospital looking immaculate and stylish with her second son, Harry *(Camera Press)*

Diana, glamorous and relaxed, with Prince Harry, the most recent addition to her *own* family, after his christening at Windsor Castle, 1984 *(Camera Press)*

The Prince and Princess of Wales involve themselves as much as possible in the day-to-day lives of their children: *(left)* taking Prince William to Wetherby and *(below)* accompanying Prince Harry on his first day at nursery school *(Photographers International and the Photo Source)*

Diana receives a ticking off for sitting on Charles' cherished Aston Martin sports car at Smiths Lawn, Windsor – the sort of scene on which the Press always capitalize *(Syndication International)*

Despite rumours the Prince and Princess' marriage is based on solid foundations *(Anwar Hussein)*

Alexandra, Princess of Wales *(inset)*, was into her sixties when this untouched photograph was taken. Diana, the ninth Princess of Wales, is destined to attain the dignity and respect of her predecessor, as one of the Family *(The Photo Source)*

eighty-six engagements abroad (that is eighty-six in seventeen days, which is roughly five engagements a day on overseas trips, as opposed to just one or two a day in the UK). Her diary is less crowded than that of the Queen's or the Princess Royal's, with two- or three-day breaks, sometimes more between each engagement so that she can spend time with the children. That is not to say that she works only on days that are officially recorded. As Patron of Help the Aged she visited a number of day centres on the spur of the moment during the freezing winter of 1987, having deposited Prince William at a new school that same morning. Her official engagement diary that month had just four entries (see Appendix IV, page 214); unofficial visits rarely come to the public notice, but these Diana enjoys because of the obvious lack of pomp and circumstance. Giving me a particular list of the Princess' engagements for one month, her Assistant Private Secretary and chief lady-in-waiting said, 'I fear this list will not be complete . . .' knowing full well that Diana would be paying visits not officially recorded.

Tentative planning of the engagement diary begins six months in advance, at two half-yearly meetings in July and December. Co-ordinating the final selection is done with the skill of a military manoeuvre. It is perhaps no coincidence that the Private Secretaries in the past were chosen for their military background, and had previously served in one of the forces. Only in recent years have people with administrative experience taken their place, but the skills are still required; strategies are involved in the planning. Invitations arrive daily, but it is easier to deal with them in two concentrated sessions. The task of planning was described by royal biographer Harold Nicolson as 'a nightmare' and few would disagree. Although the Private Secretary is responsible for the Prince's and Princess' public life, what is ironically described as their 'private life' often requires an equal amount of administration. If Diana and the children are visiting Althorp in Northamptonshire, attending a polo match on Smith's lawn or simply returning to Highgrove, she cannot depart without a certain amount of advance planning. The mantle of royalty can never be cast aside. Even in private the Prince and Princess of Wales need constant security protection and communications have to be arranged for even the shortest visit to friends so that they can be contacted should an emergency arise. Charles and Diana can never simply escape for the weekend without taking precautionary measures. Should they at any time be uncontactable the worst possible disaster might occur. If something tragic were to happen to the Queen, the Prince and Princess of Wales would suddenly become monarch and Queen Consort. Should such a thing happen, and the unexpected can so easily occur, it would be equally tragic if Charles and Diana were not kept constantly in touch with the Palace. As every detail of their lives is monitored by the media, so the Wales' Private Secretary and the Buckingham Palace Press Office must be constantly on the ball with proceedings, always ready with an answer and where possible always one step ahead of every newspaper editor. Are the Prince and Princess of Wales to divorce? Is Diana pregnant? Has the Princess quarrelled with the Queen? These are the kind of questions that have to be fielded off daily from newpaper and magazine reporters around the world.

At the six-monthly planning meetings the Princess, often accompanied by the Prince, will sit at the long table of the dining-room at Kensington Palace with her Private Secretary, Sir John Riddell, Assistant Private Secretary, Rupert Fairfax, and additional Private Secretary and chief lady-in-waiting Anne Beckwith-Smith, to consider carefully future engagements. Diana will sit with the large forbidding diary in front of her and listen to the suggestions for invitations she should accept, that will have been sorted out before she even sees them.

Diana sees every letter that is personally addressed to her, but seldom is there time to read them all in detail. With her consent Sir John will always categorize each days' correspondence and send it to various departments. Some, for example, might be questions that can be dealt with by the Press Office at Buckingham Palace, others could be from children, which a lady-in-waiting will answer. Occasionally letters will be sent direct to a particular charity to deal with, or a Government department if they can deal with the matter more suitably.

On a day-to-day basis applications constantly flood in for the granting of dedications of books or music (these are always declined), requests for photographic or portrait sittings (only accepted after very careful consideration). Diana's first official portrait, by Bryan Organ, was slashed in the National Portrait Gallery in August 1981 and since then Diana has been reluctant to sit for painters. She has agreed to portraits for her various charities and regiments, and after her wedding gave four sittings wearing her wedding dress to artist Susan Ryder. Her most famous portrait is permanently housed at Cardiff City Hall, Wales. After five sittings, artist John Merton portrayed the Princess from three different angles in one picture, following the style of the famous Van Dyck portrait of Charles I, which has also been used in a portrait of Elizabeth II. In 1987 Diana refused to endorse a painting by Canadian artist Andre Durand, portraying her touching the hand of an AIDS victim. The controversial painting was said to 'demonstrate the healing power of Royals' and the Princess objected strongly to being portrayed as a saint-like figure.

Once all invitations and requests have been carefully vetted, the possibilities will be put to Diana at the planning meetings. She will note which are worthwhile causes to consider especially those invitations from charities that she patronizes. She will take into account those that she has visited in recent months which perhaps do not need a return visit quite so soon, and always some events will catch her eye that she will feel need researching further before she can accept. The hardest part for all members of the Royal Family is fitting together the jigsaw of dates. If several invitations come from one specific region or town an attempt might be made to combine a number of visits on one day. For example, with invitations at the end of 1987 to launch the Brigg Regeneration Project in South Humberside, open a new terminal building at Humberside International Airport, a new factory in Brigg, and a new Enterprise Centre in Grimsby, it was possible to fit four separate engagements into one day and this was planned for 29 March 1988.

Centenaries and anniversaries are always borne in mind when compiling the engagement diary as these present a perfect reason for royal patronage. 1987, for example, was the 900th anniversary of the death of William the Conqueror, providing an excellent opportunity for the Prince and Princess of Wales to visit Bayeux and see the famous tapestry depicting the Battle of Hastings. The same year was also the Golden Jubilee of the Cornwall Federation of Young Farmers' Clubs, the 650th anniversary of the Duchy of Cornwall and the 25th anniversary of the founding of the Elizabeth Fitzroy Homes for the mentally handicapped, all of which were key dates to be pencilled in. Others include Annual General Meetings of the various charities of which the Princess is President or Patron. As a member of the British Royal Family there are certain dates in the calendar which must always be considered. Should Diana attend the Trooping the Colour, the Buckingham Palace Garden Parties, the Royal Tournament and the State Opening of Parliament? Would it please the Queen if she attended State Banquets in honour of visiting guests? Are there family weddings or christenings that cannot be avoided? One ceremony that she feels obliged to attend is the Remembrance Sunday service at the cenotaph to honour the dead of the two World Wars.

Each engagement must be looked at from the point of view of date, location, and justification. Each venue will have been investigated long before it is put to the Princess, ensuring that Diana will not find herself unwittingly involved in any political or commercial venture. Together Diana, the Prince and their staff, will draw up a basic list of engagements for the following six months' diary. Only one or two will ever be reported in the Press, but between them Charles and Diana can sometimes undertake sixty engagements a month, involving hundreds of miles of travel. The Princess always insists on returning home to her children and tries to select functions that will only detain her during the day, or that will occupy her after the children are in bed. Even now she places her family before duty.

Planning official duties and foreign tours involves far more than simply filling in blank spaces in the diary. Each detail has to be planned down to the last step that the Princess will take. Up to twelve weeks of preparation can go into a two-hour engagement, with itinerary after itinerary being drawn up. Lists of the people who the Princess will meet are compiled and vetted. The Private Secretary will deal with mundane details, such as the cloakroom that should be set aside exclusively for the Princess' use, the type of bouquet that should be presented, and what, if anything, Diana will eat and drink. If the Princess is to dine, officials on a recce will arrive at the venue and have the food cooked and served at a rehearsal to make sure that it fits the requirements exactly. The Princess' office will not provide a list of Diana's likes and dislikes, but they will ask to see the menu and amend it accordingly. The question is always asked, who should the Princess meet, and who should she meet first? If she visits a hospital, who is the host? The Health Minister, the Chairman of the Governors or the Senior Surgeon?

Eventually after weeks of preparation, a final itinerary will be drawn up and it will be photographically reduced to fit in Diana's handbag for consultation:

BUCKINGHAM PALACE

THE PRINCESS OF WALES, PATRON, BRITISH LUNG FOUNDATION, VISITS THE FACULTY OF MEDICINE OF THE UNIVERSITY OF SOUTH-AMPTON AT THE PRINCESS ANNE HOSPITAL AND SOUTHAMPTON GENERAL HOSPITAL, TO SEE RESEARCH PROJECTS AND OPEN A NEW LABORATORY.

Thursday 11 February 1988
Party: The Princess of Wales
          Commander Richard Aylard, RN
          Viscountess Campden
          Inspector Allan Peters

Dress: Day Dress

9.10 a.m. Her Royal Highness departs Kensington Palace
9.32 a.m. Depart Waterloo Station
10.35 a.m. Arrive Southampton Parkway Station
10.55 a.m. Her Royal Highness arrives by car at *Princess Anne Hospital*. Received by Lt. Col. Sir James Scott, HM Lord Lieutenant of Hampshire, who presents:

Lady Scott

Cllr. J. Maynard, Chairman, Hampshire County Council, and Mrs Maynard

Cllr. Mrs I. White, Rt. Worshipful The Mayor of Southampton, and Mr White

Mr P. Robertson, Director of Law and Administration Southampton City Council, and Mrs Robertson

Mr James Hill, MP for Southampton Test, and Mrs Hill

Mr J. Duke, Chief Constable of Hampshire, and Mrs Duke

Lord Lieutenant presents:

Professor Sir Bryan Thwaites, Chairman, Wessex Regional Health Authority

Dr Malcolm Green, Chairman, British Lung Foundation

Mr Peter Davies, Director, British Lung Foundation

Professor Stuart Robertson, Senior Deputy Vice-Chancellor, Southampton University

Professor Charles George, Dean of Faculty of Medicine, University of Southampton

Mrs Sheila Mooney, Senior Assistant Registrar, University of Southampton

Cllr. Mrs Irene Candy, Vice-Chairman, Southampton and South West Hampshire Health Authority

Mrs Lynette Dawkins, Nursery Nurse, presents Her Royal Highness with a posy

11.00 a.m.   In main foyer, Mrs Candy presents:

Mr Tony Shaw, District General Manager

Miss Penny Humphris, Unit General Manager

Mr Arthur Camilleri, Clinical Service Manager for Princess Anne Hospital

Miss Audrey Ebbs, Princess Anne Hospital Manager

Proceed to Special Care Baby Unit (SCBU) via lift

11.05 a.m.   At entrance to SCBU, Mrs Candy presents:
> Professor Alan Jackson, Professor of Human Nutrition
> Professor Colin Norman, Professor of Child Health and Chairman of Combined Hospitals Medical Staffs' Committee

Professor Norman escorts Her Royal Highness to Research Room where he presents:

> Dr Michael Hall, Consultant in Charge of SCBU

Dr Hall gives brief illustrated talk on work of SCBU and the/relevance of research to that work

Dr Hall presents:

> Dr Tony Postle and Dr Frank Kelly, British Lung Foundation grant holders, who outline their research work with aid of poster demonstrations

Dr Hall then presents:

> Mrs Sue Smith, Neonatal Research Sister

Proceed to Intensive Care Area. Dr Hall presents:

> Miss Pam Walton, Clinical Nurse Specialist

Miss Walton conducts Her Royal Highness on tour of ward. View demonstration of Doppler ultrasound in progress in ward

11.30 a.m.   Leave Intensive Care Area. View demonstration of hearing assessment of newborn

11.35 a.m.   Depart Princess Anne Hospital by car

11.40 a.m.   Arrive main entrance to *Southampton General Hospital*.
              Received by Dr Green and Professor George

              Miss Joanne Read, aged 11, presents a posy to Her
              Royal Highness

              Proceed into the hospital foyer and to Medicine I

11.45 a.m.   On arrival at Medicine I Professor George presents:

                      Professor Stephen Holgate, MRC Clinical Pro-
                      fessor of Immunopharmacology
                      Mr Frank Anderson, Senior Chief Technician

              Professor Holgate escorts Her Royal Highness to
              seminar room where he gives a short illustrated talk
              on asthma

11.50 a.m.   Unveil plaque to inaugurate new laboratories

11.55 a.m.   Move to exercise room to see demonstration of
              exercise-induced asthma in a child

12.00   Proceed to large seminar room and view posters and
              demonstrations on research work being undertaken
              in asthma

12.15 p.m.   Leave Medicine I and proceed to East Wing

              Her Royal Highness retires

12.30 p.m.   Join Reception hosted by British Lung Foundation.
              Presentations are made during Reception by Dr
              Green and Professor George

12.50 p.m.   Her Royal Highness leaves Reception. Professor
              George present members of catering staff

Proceed to main foyer and sign Visitors' Book

Professor George takes his leave

12.55 p.m.   Her Royal Highness departs by car

13.16 pm.   Depart Southampton Parkway Station by train

14.18 p.m.   Arrive Waterloo Station

14.30 p.m.   Her Royal Highness arrives at Kensington Palace by car

One can see from the itinerary produced for the Princess' visit to Southampton in February 1988 that every minute of the visit has to be timed exactly. The journey time is worked out to the last minute, and only if Diana remains talking too long at any stage of the proceedings is the planning put out. Her involvement in the planning will always be at the beginning and the end: she is present at the six-monthly planning meeting to decide which engagements she will undertake, and from then onwards her staff take over until a few days before the visit when the Princess will begin to do her homework on the project, the people, and write a speech if necessary, all based on a brief that she will be given by her Private Secretary. On one recent engagement, dignitaries in a line-up were impressed by Diana's knowledge of them and the questions she asked, but when she reached one member who had been added at the last minute about whom she had not been briefed, she had no idea what to say and stumbled. Homework is obviously the main key to the success of an engagement.

Ladies-in-waiting, headed by Miss Beckwith-Smith, will get together once the engagements have been settled to decide who will attend the Princess on each occasion. Traditionally ladies-in-waiting work two weeks on and two weeks off, but those who attend the Princess of Wales are allowed greater flexibility and just as long as an attendant is present, Diana is not concerned how many hours they actually work. Some have children of their own and, like the Princess, appreciate time to spend with them. A schedule is eventually produced that satisfies all concerned.

Ladies-in-waiting are an indispensable part of the team; they are always there in the background, but never upstage the Princess. It has been noted that Diana's attendants are almost deliberately plain and lacking in style whereas Princess Anne's are decidedly pretty. Unlike the Queen's ladies-in-waiting who very often wear classic clothes and unobtrusive colours, Diana's seem to wear clothes that are very much based on the Princess' wardrobe. They will never be leaders of fashion, but they have adopted pie-crust collars, feathery hats, velvet evening dresses, and conspicuous bold colours. They are not copies of Diana, but complement her while remaining forever in her shadow. When Anne Beckwith-Smith was first appointed as lady-in-waiting to the Princess she told journalists, 'I am thrilled, delighted and terribly honoured to be chosen. Will that do?' adopting a tongue-in-cheek spirit that has enabled her to cope with the pressures of her position. She, like Diana's detectives, knows that the Princess' safety on any engagement is paramount and that accompanying her is not without risk.

In the year 1900 the then Princess of Wales, Alexandra, was fired at by an anarchist, named Sapido, aged only fifteen, on a visit to Brussels. Bullets lodged in the cushions of the railway carriage in which she and the Prince of Wales were travelling. One bullet, meant for Alexandra, ended up in the bun of her lady-in-waiting, Charlotte Knollys. All ladies-in-waiting know now that there is an element of risk in their job because of the position Diana holds. When a deranged gunman tried to kidnap Princess Anne in 1974 wounding four men, her lady-in-waiting had to crouch on the ground behind the car to protect herself from being shot. In February 1985 when Diana visited the Broadwater Farm Estate in Tottenham, north London, only weeks before a riot broke out and a policeman was hacked to death, she came face to face with Winston Silcott – the man later convicted of the murder of PC Keith Blakelock. Sensing trouble, aware that here were people prepared to enter the history books for assassinating the future Queen of England, security men bundled Diana and her lady-in-waiting into the royal car and had them back at Kensington Palace before they realized the potential dangers. 'If your name is on the bullet there is nothing you can do about it,' says Prince Charles philosophically, but it is a threat that hangs over any royal engagement. A threat that did not affect Diana in any way until she became a member of the Royal Family. Now it is the major fear in her life.

Becoming a Princess changed Diana's life immeasurably. In gaining a husband, she gained a career. She became an ambass-adress for her country, a representative of the Royal Family. Unlike in any other career she now gets VIP travel throughout the world, a clothing allowance to use the best designers in the country, and five-star treatment wherever she goes. Her success as a member of the Family is that she has not lost her individuality.

'You're so beautiful,' said a seventy-two-year-old woman when Diana visited a hospice in Birmingham. 'Don't embarrass me,' blushed the Princess. Visiting the parents of cot-death babies, the Chairman of the Foundation for the Study of Infant Deaths said, 'She achieved everything we had hoped for ... she knew she would be meeting some devastated people ... she has brought comfort to many people and we are all grateful.' It is a sentiment that has been repeated so many times that if she sometimes lacks the dignity of her mother-in-law, nobody will offer condemnation.

In the early days of duty Diana's phrase was 'Do I have to go?' when given a duty to perform. These are not words that she utters today, having come to terms with her duty. She has learned to cope with aspects of her life that she does not like, by using her position to provide opportunities that she enjoys. This is how she survives and copes with the position she now holds.

Listeners to Capital Radio's early morning show with Graham Dene took little notice one morning in 1987 when he played the song *Uptown Girl* by Billy Joel, dedicated to 'Charles back in Kensington'. At 6.30 that morning Diana had driven herself to the studio and unbeknown to listeners she was sitting quietly in the studio drinking tea and eating sticky buns while her favourite record was played. On a previous occasion she had paid an unscheduled visit to the studios of BBC Radio One. Forsaking the designer wardrobe for a pair of jeans she took a fleeting opportunity to escape from royal life, but it is a paradox of her situation that the very role from which she sometimes runs away turns out to be the key to her places of retreat.

9

Queen Consort

Ultimate acceptance into the Royal Family comes in the shape of the Queen's Personal Order. A miniature of Her Majesty set in diamonds and mounted on a chartreuse yellow ribbon. Only eight members of the Family have been honoured with this symbol. Diana received hers in 1982. It still has not been given to Princess Michael of Kent or the Duchess of York. In the eyes of Elizabeth II it was a sign that the Princess of Wales was part of the Family. It is an emblem that Diana will wear on formal occasions for the rest of her life, even as the Queen and the Queen Mother wear the Personal Order of King George VI.

One day a second Order will be worn on a sash. It will bear the portrait of King Charles III and will mark a new era among the House of Windsor, the beginning of another chapter in the history of the monarchy. When Charles sits on the golden throne in the House of Lords, the official and only throne of England, wearing the Imperial State Crown, at his left hand on a throne one inch lower will be Diana. Queen Consort. On her head she will wear the State Diadem that Elizabeth II now wears on her journeys to Parliament, featured on postage stamps and coins, the most familiar of her crowns. Made for King George IV in 1821 and worn subsequently by Queen Victoria, Queen Alexandra, Queen Mary and Queen Elizabeth (the Queen Mother), it is destined for Diana's head. Then, and only then, will she feel truly royal. The fairytale will be complete.

Although the Prince of Wales appears understandably daunted by the idea of being King, it is a challenge that Diana does not fear. When they drive into the courtyard of Buckingham Palace to take up official residence on that awesome day the last vestiges of freedom will be gone but a veil will in turn be lifted. The darkness of the unknown that haunts the young Princess will be gone, along with the restrictions of the Elizabethan age that now continue to bind her. It was a sheepish Lady Elizabeth Bowes-Lyon who looked from beneath her veil as she walked down the aisle of Westminster Abbey in April 1923, but those eyes brimmed with confidence when as Queen she could 'look the East End in the face' and was the strong support at her husband's side throughout their fifteen-year reign. This is the model that Diana will emulate. When Prince Charles wears the Crown, he and Diana will rule not only the Kingdom but the Family. It is then that she will come into her own. As one journalist said, 'A new Di will dawn!'

The problem that confronts both Charles and Diana at the end of the 1980s is 'where do they go from here?' Unlike Edward VII as Prince of Wales, Charles is not ignorant of his duties as monarch. The Queen has ensured that he has been trained for sovereignty almost from birth, he is a Counsellor of State which gives him the authority to deputize for the Queen whenever she is out of the country. He can carry out investitures, sign official documents that would otherwise bear the monarch's signature and, on the Sovereign's instructions, he could dissolve Parliament. But this is not a full time occupation, it is just a single taste of what is to come.

In April 1988 MP Norman Tebbit caused controversy when he said that Prince Charles felt sympathy for the unemployed in Britain because 'in a way he's got no job.' The Queen Mother has said, 'but he does have a job. He is Prince of Wales,' a very simplistic view that would lead one to ask what a Prince of Wales does, but one cannot question royalty. In a desperate bid to gain credence as heir, Prince Charles has spoken out on emotive issues in recent years to the great consternation of many. As an intelligent human being he looks towards the country that will one day be his and speaks out if he dislikes what he sees, relieving his frustration in speechmaking. The great fear is that the Prince will draw the monarchy too far into politics. Obviously the monarch cannot be indifferent to politics but the key to being a successful King is, in the words of nineteenth-century British economist, Walter Bagehot, to 'warn, encourage and advise'. Elizabeth II has been a successful Queen, and yet we never know what she thinks or feels politically speaking; that is saved exclusively for her Prime Minister and her Government. When Charles becomes King he will be so whichever political party happens to be in power. He has openly expressed left wing tendencies, but as sovereign he will have to remain impartial. This is one of the reasons why the Queen is the only member of the Royal Family who is ineligible to vote.

After speaking out on modern architecture and unemployment the Prince was criticized for 'hawking his anguish around London lunch tables.' He should, it has been said, try to learn from his mother's silence and his father's mistakes. The Duke of Edinburgh has frequently lost the public's respect for speaking his mind, often through a lack of tact. The Princess Royal rarely speaks out publicly on an issue, but when she does it is because she feels very strongly and her words are all the more powerful for their rarity. The words of Prime Minister Clement Attlee to Professor Harold Laski a leader of the 'chattering classes' of his day could as well be put to Prince Charles: 'A period of silence on your part is now in order.'

From the Prince's outbursts to date it appears that his reign might well lead to changing attitudes among the court. Queen Elizabeth II has never given an interview to a journalist and any condemnations on her part have been subtle. In extreme cases her anger is revealed through her Private Secretary or the machinery of the Palace Press Office. Her views will almost always be aired through a third party if they are likely to cause even the slightest controversy. That is not to say that she lacks opinion, neither is she a puppet manipulated by her advisers, but her approach is publicly discreet. Thus she has retained the much vaunted mystique of the monarchy throughout her thirty-six year reign.

A genuine fear is that when Prince Charles is King he will continue to give interviews, go on speaking his mind, and instantly one whole area of mystery will be dispelled. As Queen Consort, Diana will certainly not discourage this new approach. Already she makes no secret of her views, and that will continue with or without a crown. She has never yet created controversies like her husband, but she has occasionally made comments on issues that are potentially explosive. After a year of unrest among the medical profession which led to nurses striking for more pay,

Diana visited a Neurological Unit at the end of 1987 as Patron of the National Hospital for Nervous Diseases. 'Why do they get at nurses?' she asked and spent a great deal of time asking how much nurses earned as part of the National Health Service. It was a sympathetic gesture stemming from obvious concern, but it was a strong political issue into which she could so easily have been dragged as a champion for the nurses' plight.

The whole question of whether or not Charles and Diana should give interviews is highly debatable. Obviously concern that the image of the monarchy could be damaged by an unwise remark is revealed by the fact that Diana has not yet been allowed to give a solo interview on television. Always she has had the Prince by her side, but whereas he maintains a slightly bemused, nonplussed air, the Princess is extremely revealing in her tone. The great emphasis that she places on certain answers says much about her character and feelings, without actually verbally giving much away. She gives the impression that there is so much more that she would really like to say, but . . .

The Prince himself has begun to question whether programmes, such as *In Private, in Public*, conducted by Sir Alastair Burnet in 1985 have any real value. Watched by an estimated 250 million people around the world such exercises feed an obvious appetite for knowledge about Britain's most popular export, but do they in some way tarnish royalty's character? The Burnet programme was intended to be a large public relations exercise, dispelling some of the myths and rumours that had built up in the five years of Charles' and Diana's marriage. It set out to show the Wales as a secure family not on the verge of divorce, it wanted to portray the Prince as an intelligent person with a concern for social issues and not someone who dabbles in the occult, plays around with alternative medicine and shuns Palace food in favour of a vegetarian diet. Diana used the programme, successfully to an extent, to pour cold water on talk of her alleged obsession with clothes, the supposed rift with Princess Anne, and did much to promote the image of working wife and mother, as opposed to empty headed 'Sloane'. At the end of it all the programme seemed to represent a turnaround for royalty. Instead of guarding their privacy they allowed a journalist (albeit a knighted one) into their home; they let cameras, which they normally avoid in private, be trained on them for over 400 hours to produce a film of less than two hours and the trivial questions asked did little to add to the respect and seriousness which the couple should maintain. At the end of the day the Prince scratched his head in disbelief when the main aspect highlighted by the media the day after the programme, was the revelation that he talks to his plants. From the platitudes the public gained little, but the Prince and Princess lost just some of their credibility. Diana's insistence that, yes, she enjoys polo 'enormously', 'no' she is never on a diet, that she did not only enjoy 'pop' music but all the classics too, all smacked of well rehearsed statements. Attacks on various sections of the media, were received like water off a duck's back. Newspapers still continue to print pictures of the Princess looking bored at polo, and will continue also to give details of her so-called diet.

It is sad that the Royal Family today are put in a position whereby they feel a need to have the right of reply. 'Never apologise, never explain' is an adage that they might well learn to adhere to. 'It's never worth saying anything,' says the Princess Royal, 'because whatever you say they will read something into it.' When former detective sergeant Peter Cross sold a story to the Press stating that he had been Anne's lover, the Princess could have taken him to court and sued for damages, but she felt it was best ignored and the revelation very quickly became yesterday's news.

Never before has the heir to the throne felt the need to publicly discuss his private life in front of the cameras. Will Charles and Diana continue to allow cameras into their homes when they are King and Queen? Will no part of Buckingham Palace remain unprobed by the prying lenses of investigative journalists? There is a danger that if too much daylight is let in and the ordinariness of the Royal Family is emphasized then it could well mark the beginning of the end for the monarchy. There is an aura and a divinity that surrounds the Queen that has been maintained by the correct televisual approach. Throughout 1968 cameras were allowed to follow the Royal Family for one whole year to make a film, an historical record directed by Richard Cawston. *Royal Family*, as the film was called, was a revolutionary idea and at the time many questioned the wisdom of showing the Family so intimately. But what was portrayed was very much a team of working royals. One image that people still remember after twenty years is that of Her Majesty working on the red despatch boxes that seemed to dog her every move throughout the year. Behind the scenes views of ceremonial occasions only enlightened us as to the intricacies of tradition. Stories that the Royal Family were filmed preparing a barbecue outside at Balmoral, followed by a formal lunch once the filming had stopped, only added to the mystique. The idea came across that Her Majesty was being shown deliberately doing ordinary tasks merely for the cameras, which instantly highlighted the differences between royalty and their subjects.

It is an exercise that could not be repeated. At the time Richard Cawston's film achieved its aim; it took away some of the remoteness of the Royal Family and appeared to make them more accessible, more identifiable. For many people it was the first time they had heard certain members of the Family speak. At a time when the Royal Family were in danger of becoming an anachronism, when Members of Parliament were starting to discuss whether or not the Family still had any relevance in the late twentieth century, the film brought them to the forefront of the public's imagination. Followed closely by the Investiture of the Prince of Wales, royalty enjoyed a new found popularity.

Since the advent of Diana the Royal Family have needed no such media boost. In many ways we have gone full circle and as we approach the 1990s there is a need to bring us back to a certain level of respect that we had in former days. To show Charles and Diana picnicking beside the River Dee, or breakfasting with Prince William and Prince Harry would not have the impact that it would certainly have had twenty years ago. It would reduce the Windsors to the level of a soap opera family, something they try so hard to avoid. What might have an effect today would be to show the Prince of Wales undertaking a constitutional role, his work as a Privy Counsellor and in the affairs of State, to concentrate to a greater extent on the art of being royal.

Possibly the Prince and Princess of Wales should look to Europe for role models. We have to accept that informality will creep in, but King Juan Carlos and Queen Sofia of Spain seem to have struck an acceptable balance. When Charles and Diana visited Spain in the spring of 1987, Queen Sofia chatted happily to journalists. 'It's been a wonderful visit,' she told a group of reporters as she waved farewell to the Prince and Princess, 'It's all gone very well.' This is not something that Queen Elizabeth would do, but we can well imagine that Diana might in the future. The Spanish Royal Family have managed to draw the fine line between informality which keeps them in touch with their people, and dignity which has earned them respect. In 1981 King Juan Carlos single-handedly stopped an attempted coup by rallying regional military commanders to obey their chief. Like the monarchs of old he took charge at a moment of crisis, like a valiant storybook King.

Britain has the edge over the Bourbon court in that a large amount of pageantry and tradition still remain. The continued success of the British Royal Family in the twentieth century would be a well balanced combination of Charles' upholding of tradition, and the wisdom that has resulted from his training and personal experience, coupled with the personal, informal touch from Diana. This seems to be the way ahead. With careful handling, Diana can maintain the ordinariness of her non-royal background and use it in conjunction with a new-found dignity that will come with maturity.

One example that Diana could follow would be that of former Princess of Wales, Queen Alexandra. A great beauty, Alexandra was alien to the royal court and its workings through her Danish birth and often kicked back at all the protocol. She would always arrive notoriously late, scarcely embracing the adage 'punctuality is the politeness of Princes' and was often unexpectedly informal. Yet she was a greatly respected and successful Queen Consort. Like Diana, Alexandra had style. She created a fashion for chokers, which she used to disguise a scar on her neck resulting from a thyroid operation. Deaf and lame as a result of rheumatic fever during her third pregnancy, she walked forever after with a pronounced limp, which in itself became fashionable. Society ladies adopted the Alexandra walk. Unpretentious, she made no effort to disguise that her hair in later life was not her own and would openly say to guests, 'Is my wig on straight?' I have a photograph taken of Alexandra in 1910, when only recently widowed she had become the Queen Mother. Aged sixty-six in the picture, she looks no more than thirty-six and we are assured that the photograph has not been touched-up, neither was she wearing heavy make-up. On her sixty-second birthday it is recorded that she received a telegram from Admiral Fisher saying: 'Your Majesty is sixty-two today, may you live till you look like it.' She also once commented on her wardrobe: 'I know better than all milliners . . . I shall wear exactly what I like.'

These are words and actions that one can imagine from an aged Queen Diana, who is also destined to remain a beauty. Queen Alexandra spent thirty-seven years of her life as Princess of Wales before becoming Queen Consort, which could well happen to Diana. In thirty years' time Queen Elizabeth II will be ninety-two and it is not beyond the realms of possibility that she could be on the throne at that age.

Part of Diana's success and charm as Princess of Wales has been her unrefined human qualities. She was visibly moved by a fifteen-year-old leukaemia sufferer, Claire Bosworth, who had made a 130-mile journey to London to meet the Princess at the Champion Children's Awards. Despite being blind in one eye and having suffered the emotional trauma of losing her hair through the painful treatment she was undergoing, Claire had managed to pass seven CSE examinations.

'How do you feel?' Diana asked softly, crouching beside the girl's wheelchair. 'I'm just so cross that I can't get out of this chair to curtsey to you,' said brave Claire cheerfully.

A few days after the meeting, news came through that Claire had died. Diana was told while at an engagement in South Wales, and it took several minutes before she could compose herself sufficiently to carry on. The Queen would not have given in to her emotions, but Diana's tears only gained her respect. Knowing how devastated she would be to lose one of her own children she wrote a personal letter in her own hand to Claire's grieving parents.

A few months after the Klosters skiing tragedy in 1988, Diana openly wept in a Soho restaurant during a meal with friends. For some ninety minutes tears streamed down her face as she continued to suffer from the shock of Major Lindsay's death, and she made no attempt to hide her feelings. She may bear the title 'royal' and does try to live up to all that it entails, but she will continue to shun the expected suppression of emotions and nobody can possibly condemn her for it. When the Queen Mother's horse, Devon Loch, collapsed and died inches from the winning post at the 1956 Grand National, the Duke of Devonshire commented on her reaction: 'I hope the Russians saw it. It was the most perfect display of dignity I ever witnessed.' When Prince Charles' horse, Allibar, dropped dead with a heart attack just after he had been riding in preparation for a race at Chepstow, both Diana and the Prince wept uncontrollably as they cradled the horse's head. Such a marked change in reaction from one royal generation to the next can only be applauded.

In the summer of 1987 the Princess of Wales was turned away from St Helier's Hospital in Carshalton where she was visiting a friend who had just had a baby, by a nurse who did not recognize her. 'You can't come in here – it's gone four o'clock,' said twenty-two-year-old nurse Juliet Higgins firmly. One of the most famous faces in the world must have given a wry smile that out of her expected environment she was not recognized. It may even have come as some comfort that she can still walk out in the street without being noticed. The fact is that without being surrounded by an obvious entourage and without the designer clothes, Diana projects the 'girl-in-the-street' image. It is something that she will cling onto for as long as possible and an aspect of her character that endears her to the public. Many a young girl, dressed in the fashions that Diana has influenced, must look up at the Princess of Wales on the balcony of Buckingham Palace and think that in the late twentieth century it is still quite possible to make a fairytale come true.

'I knew that somebody important was going to come, but I didn't know it would be this important,' said a wide-eyed young boy outside London's Great Ormond Street Hospital in December 1987, where Diana had come to visit sick children and distribute Christmas gifts. The child referred not to the Princess of Wales, but to the comedian Jimmy Tarbuck who was dressed as Father Christmas. With great awe the children took presents out of the sack that the white-bearded man in red held out. For once Diana took second place to a fantasy figure, and she was not complaining. She too has a childlike quality and enjoys reliving childhood through Prince William and Prince Harry. Attending William's first ever sports day at Richmond Rugby Club's playing field in London, Diana kicked off her shoes and ran in the parent's race, coming in first. The excitement and sheer joy on her young face was obvious to all. She was equally quick to accept when invited to play tennis in the 1987 Pretty Polly Ladies Double, and in doing so raised £3,000 for Birthright.

Asked to give a recipe for publication in a charity Celebrity Cookbook, Diana quickly sent in her favourite childhood recipe – fudge – and she still retains a childlike glee when she meets her favourite actors and actresses who she has previously seen only on television. One of her treasured possessions is the autograph of Russian dancer Mikhail Baryshnikov, obtained in her pre-Princess days, but if dignity would allow she would still be quite happy to produce an autograph book from her clutch bag at a film première or gala. For someone who has riches and prospects beyond the wildest imaginations of most, it is heartwarming to know that our future Queen still gets the greatest pleasure from the very simplest moments in life. Precious hours spent with her children and nostalgic glimpses of photographs taken in more carefree days, are among her most treasured moments.

In 1984 she delighted in obtaining 800 British Telecom shares when they came on the market. She neither needed the income they might possibly bring, nor the shareholder's reduction in telephone bills, but it was just one more link with humanity, the joy of being able to compete with people in the outside world on the same level and without privileges. Her application went in with everyone else's, she received no special concessions and was allocated the maximum that any individual can own.

On 12 November 1987, Diana returned to her former school, West Heath in Kent. As an old pupil she opened the new Rudge Sports Hall, named after her former headmistress, Miss Ruth Rudge, who was retiring after thirty-seven years at the school. For Miss Rudge, who had taught all three Spencer girls, it must have been a thrill not only to have her most famous ex-pupil present, but to know that she had had some bearing on Diana's character. 'This is an occasion neither of us could have imagined ten years ago,' commented Miss Rudge. Confidently Diana stood at the podium and looked at the girls wearing the uniform that she had herself worn not so very long before. 'In spite of what Miss Rudge and my other teachers may have thought – I did actually learn something,' she said in her opening speech, and of the new hall she quipped, 'perhaps now, when future generations are handed out punishments for talking after lights out, pillow fights and illegal food, they will be told to run six times round this hall. It has to be preferable to the lacrosse pitch or weeding the garden, which I became a great expert at!'

Members of staff looking up at the former 'D. Spencer' must, like so many others, have noticed a remarkable change in her. She has lost the innocence, but not her sincerity; she has gained an interest in social problems, but has not lost her girlish sense of adventure; she is learning self-control, but will never learn to hide her deep-seated feelings. Visiting a hospice in Leeds in 1982 she managed to remain composed throughout the engagement, but broke down in the car on the way home after having met leukaemia sufferers – her own cousin Conway Spencer had died some years earlier of the illness when they were children. Six years on she has learned the poise to cope with the distress.

When Diana first became a bride, her great asset appeared to be what so many called her 'naturalness'. It was a characteristic that many also feared she would lose once sucked into the machinery of royalty. Early commentators boldly stated that she would be forced to grow her hair long to accommodate a tiara, that she would always have to walk three paces behind her husband, forever in his shadow, and that her skittish behaviour would quickly be curbed. One single attempt at putting her hair up received such criticism, that she quickly resorted to her very own style. Respecting her husband's position, she still sometimes outshines him nevertheless. 'I'm afraid I've only got one wife,' the Prince grins on a walkabout when the constant chant is 'Diana, Diana . . .' To see her laugh openly on engagements it becomes apparent that she has not become introspective or dampened by the pressures upon her.

The Diana of seven years ago has gone. She has visibly changed physically. In the last twelve months she has gained twenty pounds in weight. She is not on a diet and in her own words – 'I eat almost everything. I swim every morning and love Harvest Crunch for breakfast.' She has dropped her teetotal habits by developing a taste for Pimms, white wine and champagne. She will never accept the sniping that she receives from the Press, but she is learning to live with it. In 1986 Charles and Diana held a series of private lunches at Kensington Palace for newspaper editors, attempting to safeguard their children's privacy by asking them politely to leave William and Harry alone. Having been wined and dined, one editor still went ahead and printed a paparazzi photograph the very next day of the Princes in the park, effectively bringing to an end any semblance of trust.

Diana has had a liberating and stabilizing effect on Prince Charles; he may have several decades to wait before he finds his true vocation, but for the first time in his life he has as near to a normal family life as he will ever experience. The vital factor in his wife is that she has refused to be swallowed up by convention. She retains individuality, even if it does not always match up to the expectations of a Queen-in-waiting such as the time she rushed excitedly across a room to greet pop singer, Boy George, at a time when he had just publicly admitted that he was taking heroin. Gradually individuality and common sense will come together. She may never have the serenity of the Queen Mother, but she will develop dignity to add to her style.

Together Charles and Diana are shaping the future of the monarchy. Whether good or bad they will carve out a new image for the Royal Family. Queen Elizabeth II would never publicly call herself empty-headed or pull faces at a reception committee, but it could well be that the kicking back at the staid image of royalty might just unsettle some of the dust and reveal a more engaging picture. Diana may not have been born a Princess, but in twenty years time she will have spent more of her life 'royal' than 'non-royal'. In many ways she will have an advantage over her husband in that she will have experienced life on both sides of the fence which will give her a greater understanding of society and a certain credibility in her concern. That she has survived thus far and proven that she is far more than the 'brood mare' that was once suggested, means that she will indeed survive the course. She comes from a family who have given service to the Royal Family since the fourth Earl Spencer became a steward to Queen Victoria's household, and she will continue in that tradition.

On the Queen's sixtieth birthday there were areas of the community that suggested she should step down in favour of Prince Charles, having reached the age of retirement. She did not concede believing, not only that 'Abdication' is a dirty word amongst the Windsors, but that the position of Queen is God-given and cannot be relinquished. This does not mean, however, that abdication is entirely out of the question. She has always said that she hopes to avoid an Edward VII situation in which Queen Victoria refused to allow her heir to take any part in state affairs so that he eventually came to the throne at the age of sixty-two quite unprepared for the role. Already Prince Charles is a Counsellor of State, has been a member of the Privy Council since 1977, is well versed in the constitution and understands the mechanics of the monarchy. Should old age or ill health prevent the Queen from doing her job, she may well decide to step down, or at the least remain Queen in name but create Charles Prince Regent to effectively rule on her behalf. While she is able to continue, however, she most certainly will, and if Her Majesty does cast off the mantle of responsibility it will only be when she feels that Diana is ready to be Queen. That day has not yet dawned, and for as long as she can retain even the slightest sense of immaturity, Diana will avert the evil day.

As she sat on the platform at West Heath School at the end of 1987, the Princess of Wales may have momentarily reflected back to her former life, to the independence and anonymity, the lack of pressure and the freedom to live her days as she chose. But she must have remembered too that there was insecurity and a fear of the future. As she climbed into the car, waving farewell to the pupils amid a barrage of flashbulbs for the return journey to the home, husband and family that are now her life and eternal security, she must have realized that the life she enjoys now is anything but a tragedy.

In the end, liberty will have been a small price to pay.

Appendices

Appendix I

PRINCESS OF WALES FACTFILE

BORN

1 July 1961 at Park House, Sandringham, Norfolk. Weight: 7lb 12ozs

CHRISTENED

30 August 1961 at Sandringham Church (officially St Mary Magdalene) by the Right Reverend Percy Herbert

Names: Diana Frances Spencer
Godparents: John Floyd
             Alexander Gilmour
             Lady Mary Colman
             Sarah Pratt
             Carol Fox

AILMENTS

Chicken-pox
Mumps

CHURCH

Confirmed into Church of England 12 March 1976 by the Bishop of Rochester at Kippington

BRIDESMAID

1969: wedding of cousin Elizabeth Wake-Walker who became a Duckworth-Chad, at St James's, Piccadilly

April 1978: Chief bridesmaid at the wedding of sister Jane, to Robert Fellowes in the Guard's Chapel

EDUCATION

Lessons in the schoolroom at Park House until November 1967 with Miss Gertrude Allen ('Ally')

January 1968: attended Silfield School, King's Lynn, Norfolk, as day girl
  Headmistress: Jean Lowe

September 1970: boarder at Riddlesworth Hall, Norfolk, where she was a member of Nightingale House
  Headmistress: Miss Elizabeth Ridsdale

September 1973–December 1977: Boarder at West Heath School, nr. Sevenoaks, Kent
  Headmistress: Miss Ruth Rudge

January 1978 (six weeks): attended Finishing School – Institut Alpin Videmanette at Château d'Oex, nr. Gstaad

September 1978: three-month cookery course at Elizabeth Russell's school in Wimbledon

JOBS

1978: first paid job looking after Alexandra, baby daughter of Major Jeremy Whitaker and his wife Philippa at their home 'The Land of Nod' in Headley, Hampshire, where she stayed for three months

Returned to London that summer, signing on with two employment agencies – 'Knightsbridge Nannies' who provided babysitting jobs, and 'Solve Your Problems' who more often than not came up with cleaning assignments

January–March 1979: Diana taught very basic dance steps to children under the age of three, at the Vacani Dancing School in London

Autumn 1979: began work at the Young England Kindergarten in St George's Square, Pimlico

During the following twelve months she also looked after a little American boy, Patrick Robinson (work at the Kindergarten permitting)

PROPERTY

On her eighteenth birthday, in July 1979, inherited money left in trust by American great grandmother, Frances Work, and bought a flat at 60 Coleherne Court on the corner of Old Brompton Road, which she moved into with friends Sophie Kimball and Philippa Coaker

DRIVING

Learned to drive with British School of Motoring and passed test in 1978 at the second attempt. First car a Honda Civic bought by her mother

ENGAGEMENT

Announced in *The Times* 24 February 1981

MARRIAGE

29 July 1981 at St Paul's Cathedral

CHILDREN

1   Prince William of Wales (William Arthur Philip Louis) born
    21 June 1982, in the Lindo Wing at St Mary's Hospital,
    Paddington
        Christened by Dr Robert Runcie, Archbishop of Canter-
    bury, in The Music Room, Buckingham Palace on 4 August
    1982
2   Prince Henry of Wales (Henry Charles Albert David) born 15
    September 1984, in the Lindo Wing at St Mary's Hospital,
    Paddington
        Christened by Dr Robert Runcie, Archbishop of Canter-
    bury, in St George's Chapel, Windsor, on 21 December, 1984

RESIDENCES

Kensington Palace, London
Highgrove, Tetbury, Gloucestershire
Althorp, Northampton
Tamarisk, St Mary's, Isles of Scilly

Appendix II

JOINT PATRONAGES

Glasgow Garden Festival

Chester Music Festival

The Wishing Well Appeal for the Redevelopment of Great Ormond Street Children's Hospital

MEMBERSHIPS/FELLOWSHIPS/FREEDOMS

The All England Lawn Tennis	–	Honorary Membership
The British Challenge Cup	–	Honorary Membership
Cardiff	–	Freedom of the City
The Grocers' Company	–	Honorary Freeman
London	–	Freedom of the City
Royal College of Obstetricians and Gynaecologists	–	Honorary Membership
Royal College of Physicians and Surgeons of Glasgow	–	Honorary Fellowship

SPONSORSHIP

HMS *Cornwall*

PATRONAGES – ABROAD

Australian Junior Red Cross Movement	Patron
Barnardo's in Australia	Patron
Barnardo's in New Zealand	Patron
Canadian Red Cross Youth Services	Patron
Chipangali Wildlife Trust, Zimbabwe	Patron
New Zealand College of Obstetricians and Gynaecologists	Patron
The Princess of Wales Children's Health Camp, Rotorua, New Zealand	Patron
Royal New Zealand Foundation for the Blind	Patron

HONORARY MEMBERSHIPS – ABROAD

The Lyford Cay Club, Bahamas, West Indies	–	Joint Honorary Membership
The Royal Guild of St Sebastian, Brussels	–	Honorary Membership
The Variety Club International	–	Honorary Membership

REGIMENTAL

The Royal Hampshire Regiment	Colonel-in-Chief
RAF Wittering	Honorary Air Commodore
The Princess of Wales' Own Regiment (Canada)	Colonel-in-Chief
The Royal Australia Survey Corps	Colonel-in-Chief

Appendix III

OFFICIAL OVERSEAS VISITS
(most were with The Prince of Wales)

1983

Australia	20 March–17 April
New Zealand	17–30 April
Canada	14 June–1 July

1984

| Norway | February (solo visit) |

1985

Australia	27 October–8 November
Fiji	8 November
USA (Washington and Palm Beach)	9–13 November

1986

Austria/Vienna	14–16 April
Canada	30 April–7 May
Japan	8–13 May

Oman	10–14 November
Qatar	14–16 November
Bahrain	16–17 November
Saudi Arabia	17–19 November

1987

Portugal	11–14 February
France	14 February
Spain	21–26 April
France (Cannes)	15 May
Germany	1–7 November

1988

Australia	25 January–3 February
Thailand	3–5 February

Appendix IV

DIARY OF ENGAGEMENTS JANUARY 1987–JULY 1988

January

15   As Patron of Help the Aged, attended the première of *Short Circuit* at the Leicester Square Theatre, London

20   Visited the Tadworth Court Hospital for Children, Tadworth, Surrey

22   As President of Dr Barnardo's, visited St John's Community Day Care Centre, 2–4 St John's Crescent, London SW9

27   Opened the new Special Unit for Deaf/Visually Handicapped children at Whitefield School, MacDonald Road, London E17

February

4   Accompanied the Prince of Wales who, as President of The Prince's Trust, attended the première of the film *Mosquito Coast* in aid of the Trust at the Odeon Theatre, Haymarket, London SW1

5   p.m. Attended a concert given by the London Philhar-
           monic Orchestra, together with children from the Lon-
           don Borough of Tower Hamlets, at the Royal Festival
           Hall

           p.m. Accompanied the Prince of Wales who, as Patron of
           the Royal Society of Asian Affairs, attended the Society's
           Annual Banquet at the Savoy Hotel, London WC2

11–14   Accompanied the Prince of Wales on a visit to Portugal
           at the invitation of His Excellency the President of
           Portugal, visiting Lisbon and Oporto during their
           programme

14   p.m. Accompanied the Prince of Wales at the launch of
           the first Airbus A320 passenger aircraft at Toulouse

23   Attended a performance of *High Society* in aid of Help the
           Hospices at the Victoria Palace, Victoria Street, London
           SW1

24   As Patron of London City Ballet, attended a luncheon at
           the Grocers' Hall, Princes Street, London EC2

26   As Royal Patron of the British Deaf Association, and
           accompanied by the Prince of Wales, attended the
           première of *Children of a Lesser God* in aid of the British
           Deaf Association and the Variety Club of Great Britain,
           at the Empire, Leicester Square, London WC2

                              March

4   Visited Fashion Services for the Disabled, Saltaire
           Workshops, Ashley Lane, Shipley, West Yorkshire

6   Accompanied the Prince of Wales, who as President of
           the Royal Jubilee and Prince's Trusts, visited training by
           the Prince of Wales Community Venturers in Birming-
           ham

                              215

11   a.m. As Patron of Help the Aged, visited the Tynemouth Village Day Centre, Holy Saviour Church Hall, Manor Road, Tynemouth

        p.m. As Patron of Birthright, attended a luncheon at the Gosforth Park Hotel, High Gosforth Park, Newcastle-upon-Tyne

12   As Patron, Pre-School Playgroups Association, opened the Association's new headquarters at 61–63 King's Cross Road, London WC1

13   As President of Dr Barnardo's, visited High Close School, Wiltshire Road, Wokingham, Berkshire

17   Attended a gala performance of the jazz ballet *Night Creature* by the London Festival Ballet, at the Hippodrome, Leicester Square, WC2

27   As President of Dr Barnardo's attended a Centenary Concert in aid of the charity, at St David's Hall, Cardiff

April

1   a.m. As Royal Patron of the British Deaf Association, visited the sheltered housing scheme for the deaf on Tulketh Brow, Preston, Lancashire

        a.m. Visited the West View Leisure Centre, Preston

3   a.m. As President of Dr Barnardo's, visited the Barnardo School of Printing at William Baker House, Mead Lane, Hertford

        a.m. Opened Spencer Close, a new centre for the mentally handicapped adjacent St Margaret's Hospital, Epping, Essex

216

7   As Patron of the National Rubella Council, attended a luncheon at Marlborough House to mark World Health Day

9   Opened the new AIDS unit at the Middlesex Hospital, Mortimer Street, London W1

10   Represented Her Majesty the Queen at the Sovereign's Parade, Royal Military Academy, Sandhurst, Camberley, Surrey

29   Attended a children's party on board the Cunard Line's ship *Queen Elizabeth 2* at sea

30   Attended a dinner with British and American cancer surgeons at the Grosvenor House Hotel, Park Lane, London W1

May

4   Accompanied the Prince of Wales, who as President of the Wildfowl Trust, attended the World Wildlife Fund Banquet, in aid of the Wildfowl Trust and the British Wildlife Appeal, at Hampton Court

5   As Patron of Red Cross Youth, presented the national awards for the British Red Cross Young Community Champion Competition at the Café Royal, 60 Regent Street, London W1

8   As Patron of Gloucestershire Cricket Club, attended a dinner at the Cheltenham Town Hall, Imperial Square, Cheltenham, Gloucestershire

12   a.m. Opened the new Enterprise Units and the new factory of the Landywood Group Limited at Holly Lane, Great Wyrley, South Staffordshire

         p.m. Visited Oak House, Bentons Lane, Great Wyrley, South Staffordshire

14 Attended the British Paraplegic Sports Society Ball at Osterley Park, Osterley, Middlesex

19 As Patron of the National Hospitals for Nervous Diseases, visited Maida Vale Hospital, 4 Maida Vale, London W9

20 Presented the 1987 Construction Achievement Award to Contractor Cementation International and Architect YRM International Partnership at a luncheon at the Inn on the Park, Hamilton Place, London SW1

21 a.m. As Patron of the Malcolm Sargent Cancer Fund for Children, opened the new Regional Children's Cancer Unit and the new CAT Scanner at the Alder Hey Branch of the Royal Liverpool Children's Hospital, Liverpool

  a.m. As Patron of the British Lung Foundation, attended the launch of the Foundation's North West Branch at the Liverpool Medical Institution, 114 Mount Pleasant, Liverpool

28 As President of Dr Barnardo's, visited Fulford Family Centre, 1 Fulford Road, Hartcliffe, and the Young People's Centre at 114 Whitehall Road, Bristol

June

3 Presented the prizes at the National Art Collections Award dinner at the Savoy Hotel

4 Accompanied the Prince of Wales who, as Colonel, Welsh Guards, took the Salute at Beating the Retreat by the Massed Bands, Corps of Drums, Pipes and Drums of the Household Division by floodlight on Horse Guards Parade

5   Admitted as an Honorary Fellow of the Royal College of Obstetricians and Gynaecologists at 27 Sussex Place, Regent's Park, London NW1

       Evening. Accompanied the Prince of Wales, who as President of the Prince's Trust, attended a rock concert in aid of the Trust at Wembley Arena

9   As President of Business in the Community, attended a Design and Marketing Conference in Nottingham

10   a.m. As President of Dr Barnardo's, visited Nechells Centre, 40 Rupert Street, Birmingham

       a.m. As President of Dr Barnardo's, visited the Barnardo Shop and Shops Training Centre at 724–726 Stratford Road, Sparkhill, Birmingham

15   Attended the Toscanini Memorial Concert in aid of the Musicians' Benevolent Fund and the Casa Verdi at the Royal Albert Hall, London SW7

23   As Patron of the National Hospitals for Nervous Diseases, attended a reception at Guildhall, London EC2

24   As Patron of Birthright, attended the *Woman* Golden Jubilee Concert at the Palladium Theatre, London W1

25   a.m. As Patron of Help the Aged, visited a sheltered housing scheme run by the charity at 'Southdene', Huddersfield

       Visited the Huddersfield Royal Infirmary, in connection with the Asian Mother and Baby Campaign

29   Accompanied the Prince of Wales, who, as President of the Prince's Trust, attended the world charity première of the film *The Living Daylights* in aid of the Trust, at the Odeon Theatre, Leicester Square

30   As Patron of the London City Ballet, attended an evening entertainment in aid of London City Ballet and the Purcell School, at Charleston Manor, West Dean, nr. Seaford, Sussex

July

4   Accompanied the Prince of Wales who, as President of the Prince's Trust, attended a Genesis concert in aid of the Trust, at Wembley Stadium

6   As President of Dr Barnardo's, visited the Merthyr Tydfil Centre, 56 High Street, Pontmorlais, Merthyr Tydfil, Mid-Glamorgan

        a.m. As Patron of Help the Aged, attended a reception at Cardiff Castle for staff and volunteers of Help the Aged in Wales

        p.m. As Patron of the Gloucestershire County Cricket Club accompanied the Prince of Wales as Patron of the Glamorgan County Cricket Club, to attend a cricket match between the two clubs at Sophia Gardens, Cardiff

7   Accompanied the Prince of Wales to open the extended and modernized Brixton Police Station, 367 Brixton Road, Brixton

        Evening. Accompanied the Prince of Wales who, as Patron of the Royal Society for Nature Conservation, attended a Gala performance of *Romeo and Juliet* in aid of the Society's British Wildlife Appeal and the London Festival Ballet Development Trust at the London Coliseum to mark the European Year of the Environment

9   p.m. Visited the Royal Air Force Hospital, Ely, Cambridgeshire

Evening. Opened the Flower Festival organized by the National Flower Clubs of Great Britain in support of Ely Cathedral and attended Evensong

22   a.m. Received the Honorary Freedom of the City of London, Guildhall, London EC2, accompanied by the Prince of Wales

p.m. Accompanied the Prince of Wales who, as President of the Mary Rose Trust and Life Member of the Variety Club of Great Britain, attended the film première of *Superman 4* in aid of the Mary Rose Trust and the Variety Club of Great Britain at the Odeon Theatre, Leicester Square

28   Opened the Princess of Wales' Conservatory at The Royal Botanic Gardens, Kew, Surrey

29   Presented a new Guidon of the 13th/18th Royal Hussars (Queen Mary's Own) at Tidworth Garrison

30   Accompanied the Prince of Wales as Duke and Duchess of Cornwall, attended the Golden Jubilee Celebrations of the Cornwall Federation of Young Farmers' Clubs and the Pageant on the occasion of the 650th anniversary of the Duchy of Cornwall at Trewithen, Cornwall

August

No engagements

September

9   Accompanied the Prince of Wales on a visit Caen in Normandy to attend a Commemorative Service on the 900th Anniversary of the death of William the Conqueror. Their Royal Highnesses also marked the Anniversary by visiting Bayeux to see the Bayeux Tapestry

17   As Patron of the Guinness Trust, visited the Trust's estate at Fulham Palace Road, Hammersmith

20   Attended the Festival of National Parks in Chatsworth Park, Derbyshire

21   Attended a service to commemorate the centenary of the Queen's Nursing Institute at Westminster Abbey. Subsequently attended a reception in the Abbey gardens, organized by the *Nursing Times*, to meet nurses attending the 2nd International Primary Health Care Conference

22   Visited Lingfield Hospital School, Lingfield, Surrey

23   Visited the Spelthorne St Mary Treatment and Rehabilitation Centre for Women Alcoholics at Milton Road, Harpenden, Hertfordshire

24   As Patron of the British Sports Association for the Disabled, attended a luncheon in aid of the British team for the 1988 Seoul Paralympics, at the Grosvenor House Hotel, Park Lane, London W1

28   Attended a Gala Evening to commemorate the twenty-fifth Anniversary of the founding of the Elizabeth Fitzroy Homes for the Mentally Handicapped at Claridges Hotel, Brook Street, London W1

29   a.m. As Patron of Help the Aged, visited the Age Concern Day Centre, Atherton Street, Durham

          a.m. As Royal Patron of the British Deaf Association, visited Durham University to see project work associated with higher education for the deaf

30   Opened the Paediatric Cardiac Intensive Care Unit of Russell Brock Ward at Guy's Hospital, St Thomas' Street, London SE1

Appendix IV

October

1   Attended a Reception in aid of the International Spinal Research Trust, at Grocers' Hall, London EC2

8   Visited the Royal Ballet School, Talgarth Road, Barons Court, London W14

9   a.m. As Patron of Turning Point, visited Sherwood House, Rotherham, South Yorkshire

      p.m. Visited the offices of the Doncaster and District Association for the Welfare of the Disabled at Guild House, Christ Church Road, Doncaster, South Yorkshire

13   a.m. Opened the new offices and workshops of the South Lincolnshire Enterprise Agency at Station Road, Grantham, Lincolnshire

      a.m. Opened the new Community Health Clinic, Grantham, Lincolnshire

14   As Patron for the National Hospitals for Nervous Diseases, visited the National Hospital Rehabilitation Centre, Great North Road, Finchley, London N2

20   As Patron of Turning Point, visited Suffolk House, Slough Road, Iver Heath, Buckinghamshire

21   As Patron of Help the Aged, attended the charity's Gold and Diamond Appeal at Christie's, King Street, London SW1

23   As Colonel-in-Chief, The Royal Hampshire Regiment, attended the Laying-Up of the old 1st Batallion Colours in Winchester Cathedral

27   As Patron of Birthright, attended a Birthright Gala Evening held at Garrard, 112 Regent Street, London W1

November

1   Accompanied the Prince of Wales on visit to Berlin to attend the Première of the Royal Ballet

2–7   Accompanied the Prince of Wales on Official Visit to the Federal Republic of Germany

7   Evening. Attended the Royal British Legion Festival of Remembrance together with the Queen and Duke of Edinburgh and the Prince of Wales

12   a.m. Opened the Rudge Sports Hall at West Heath School, Sevenoaks, Kent

a.m. As President of Dr Barnardo's, opened the Knotley School, Springfield Gardens, West Wickham, Bromley

13   a.m. As Patron of Help the Aged, visited the Bridges Community Project, Hadnock Road, Monmouth, Gwent

a.m. As President of Dr Barnardo's, visited the '175' project, Chepstow Road, Newport, Gwent

16   Attended the departure from Heathrow Airport of the British Airways staff 'Dreamflight to Disneyworld' for children with special needs

Evening. Accompanied the Prince of Wales when they attended a charity performance by Barry Humphries of his new show *Back with a Vengeance* in aid of the Royal Marsden Hospital Cancer Fund, at the Strand Theatre, Aldwych, London WC2

18   Opened the St Ann's Shopping Centre, Harrow, Middlesex

23   As Patron of the National Rubella Council, visited the factory of Park Cakes, Oldham, Greater Manchester, in connection with National Rubella Awareness Week

25   With the Prince of Wales attended the Anglo-Spanish Society Bi-annual Ball at Syon House, Brentford, Middlesex

26   As Patron of The National Hospitals for Nervous Diseases, opened Chandler House, Wakefield Street, London WC1

December

3   Distributed Christmas presents at Great Ormond Street Children's Hospital, London WC1

4   a.m. Opened the Drugs Detoxification Unit at Northern Road, Cosham, Portsmouth, Hampshire

p.m. As Patron of Help the Aged, opened the new head office of McCarthy and Stone plc at Homelife House, Oxford Road, Bournemouth

Evening. Accompanied the Prince of Wales who, as President of the Prince's Trust, attended a Royal Gala Evening in aid of the Trust at the London Palladium, 8 Argyll Street, London W1

7   Attended the Gala Première of *Dancers* in aid of the St Mary's Save the Baby Fund and the National Society for the Prevention of Cruelty to Children, at the Canon Cinema, Shaftesbury Avenue, London WC2

10   a.m. Opened the new Community Hospital at Heanor Road, Ilkeston, Derbyshire

p.m. Visited the factory of the Royal Crown Derby Porcelain Company Limited, Osmaston Road, Derby, and opened an extension to the company's museum

16   As Patron of the British Lung Foundation, and accompanied by the Prince of Wales, attended a Gala Première of *Cinderella*, in aid of the charity, at the Royal Opera House, Covent Garden

January 1988

19   Opened the Maternity Unit, Antenatal and Special Care Baby Unit, St Helier Hospital, Carshalton, Surrey

21   As Patron of Turning Point, visited the charity's head office at Cap House, Long Lane, London EC1

25–3 Feb   Accompanied the Prince of Wales on visit to Australia, where they visited New South Wales, Victoria, South Australia and the Northern Territory

February

3–5   On their return from Australia, the Prince and Princess of Wales made a two-day visit to Thailand as the guests of Their Majesties The King and Queen of Thailand in connection with celebrations to mark the King's sixtieth birthday

10   As Patron of Dr Barnardo's, visited the West Beckton Children's Community Centre, Lawson Close, London E16

11   As Patron of the British Lung Foundation, visited the Faculty of Medicine of the University of Southampton at the Princess Anne Hospital and Southampton General Hospital, to see research projects and open a new laboratory

15   Opened the Children's Society's Youth Link project at 98 Church Hill Road, Handsworth, Birmingham

17   Together with the Prince of Wales, opened the 'Suleyman the Magnificent' Exhibition at the British Museum, London WC1

24   a.m. Opened the new premises of the National Institute for Biological Standards and Control at Blanche Lane, South Mimms, Hertfordshire

        a.m. Opened Watford Chater Junior School, Addiscombe Road, Watford, Hertfordshire

25   Accompanied the Prince of Wales who, as President of The Prince's Trust, attended the film première of *The Last Emperor* in aid of the Trust at the Odeon Theatre, Leicester Square

March

14   Lunched with the senior officers of the Metropolitan Police Royalty and Diplomatic Protection Department, New Scotland Yard, London SW1

        Evening. Held a reception during London Fashion Week at Kensington Palace, London W8

16   a.m. As Patron of Birthright, attended a fitness festival in aid of the charity at the Holywell Leisure Centre, Fron Park, Clwyd

Lunched at Theatre Clwyd, Mold, on behalf of the Dr Barnardo Centenary Appeal in Wales

22 Evening. As Patron, London City Ballet, attended a Gala Performance at Sadler's Wells Theatre, London EC1

23 a.m. Visited the Headquarters and College of the National Marriage Guidance Council, Herbert Gray College, Little Church Street, Rugby, Warwickshire

24 Visited the Childline offices at Faraday Building, Queen Victoria Street, London EC4

25 a.m. As Patron of the Guinness Trust, visited Boyd Court, one of the Trust's estates, at Downshire Way, Bracknell, Berkshire

29 a.m. Launched the Brigg Regeneration Project in Brigg, South Humberside

a.m. Opened the new terminal building at Humberside International Airport, Brigg, South Humberside

a.m. Opened the new factory extension of Falcon Cycles, Bridge Street, Brigg, South Humberside

p.m. Opened the King Edward Street New Enterprise Centre, Grimsby

31 a.m. Attended a luncheon organized by Capital Radio in aid of 'Help A London Child' at the Café Royal, Regent Street, London W1

April

14 Opened the Maltings Shopping Centre, St Albans, Hertfordshire

15 p.m. As Patron, Gloucestershire County Cricket Club, attended a Gala performance of *Song and Dance* at the Bristol Hippodrome

17 a.m. Started the London Marathon, Blackheath, London

19 a.m. Opened the Bradwell Hospital for the Elderly, Bradwell, Newcastle-under-Lyme, Staffordshire

  p.m. As Patron of Turning Point, opened the organization's Stoke-on-Trent Drugs Service in the Hope Street Centre, Hanley, Staffordshire

20 Evening. As Patron of London City Ballet, attended a dog racing evening, in aid of the charity, at Wembley Stadium

21 Evening. As Patron of, The Malcolm Sargent Cancer Fund for Children, attended a concert given on behalf of the Fund at St Nicholas Church, Newbury, Berkshire

23 a.m. Attended the commissioning of HMS *Cornwall* at Falmouth Docks, Cornwall

26 a.m. Officially opened the new Day Centre at St Helena's Hospice, Myland Hall, Barncroft Close, Colchester, Essex

  p.m. Visited the homes of the Essex Voluntary Association for the Blind at 19–21 The Esplanade, Frinton-on-Sea, Essex

27 Evening. Attended the Gala première of *Wall Street* in aid of the AIDS Crisis Trust at the Odeon Cinema, Haymarket, London W1

28 a.m. Visited Fairfield School for physically and visually handicapped children, Trinity Avenue, Northampton

p.m. Opened the new extension to Saxby Brother's Factory, Wellingborough, Northamptonshire

29   With the Prince of Wales, as Patrons of the Glasgow Garden Festival, formally opened the five-month event at Prince's Dock, Glasgow

May

3   p.m. As Patron, British Red Cross Youth, named a British Rail 125 locomotive *The Red Cross* at Paddington Station, London W2

4   a.m. As Patron, British Sports Association for the Disabled, attended the South West Region Junior Games at Norton Manor Camp, Taunton, Somerset

10   Evening. As Patron, Birthright, opened the Birthright Mother and Child Exhibition at the Lefèvre Gallery, Bruton Street, London W1

11   a.m. Opened the new Leisure Pool at Weybourne Road, Sheringham, Norfolk

12   Evening. As Patron, The National Hospitals for Nervous Diseases, attended a Gala Performance of *The Magic Flute*, in aid of the charity, at the London Coliseum, St Martin's Lane, London WC2

14   p.m. Attended the Football Association Challenge Cup Final at Wembley Stadium

16   Evening. Attended a reception to mark the twenty-fifth year of the National Children's Bureau at 8 Wakley Street, London EC1

17   a.m. Visited The Royal Ballet School, White Lodge, Richmond Park

18   a.m. As President, Dr Barnardo's, visited The Chester Families Project, Hoole, Chester

With the Prince of Wales, opened St Luke's (Cheshire) Hospice Day Care Centre at Grosvenor House, Ways Green, Winsford, Cheshire

19   Evening. As Patron, Scottish Chamber Orchestra, attended a Scottish Gala Evening at Guildhall, London EC2

24   Evening. As Patron, National Rubella Council, attended a reception at the Martini Terrace, New Zealand House, London SW1

25   a.m. Opened a Mother and Child Unit which is an extension of the drug rehabilitation unit at Ashley Copse, Smannel, nr. Andover, Hampshire

p.m. As Colonel-in-Chief, The Royal Hampshire Regiment, visited the Regimental Headquarters at Serlses House, Southgate Street, Winchester

26   a.m. As Patron, British Lung Foundation, visited the Department of Thoracic Medicine at the Royal Free Hospital, Hampstead, London NW3

31   a.m. Visited the counselling centre run by the London Marriage Guidance Council on the Doddington Estate, Battersea Park Road, London SW11

June

1   a.m. As President, Wales Craft Council, visited the Council's offices at Severn Street, Welshpool, Powys

7   a.m. As Patron, British Lung Foundation, visited the Chest Medicine Unit at Papworth Hospital, Cambridge,

and subsequently visited the Assisted Ventilation Unit at Newmarket General Hospital, Exning Road, Newmarket, Suffolk

9   p.m. Attended the departure of the Handicapped Children's Boat Trip, organized by the Miss Deptford's Carnival Fund, from Greenwich Pier, London SE10

11   Attended The Queen's Birthday Parade

13   Evening. As Patron, The Wishing Well Appeal, attended the Wishing Well Tennis Classic at the David Lloyd Racquet Club

17   a.m. Received an Honorary Fellowship of the Faculty of Dental Surgery of the Royal College of Surgeons of England, at the Diplomates Ceremony held at the College, Lincoln's Inn Fields, London WC2

21   Evening. Accompanied the Prince of Wales, as President of The Prince's Trust, to the film première of *Crocodile Dundee II* in aid of the Trust at the Empire Theatre, Leicester Square

23   Visited the 13th/18th Royal Hussars (Queen Mary's Own) on Salisbury Plain, Wiltshire

24   p.m. As Patron, The Wishing Well Appeal for the Redevelopment of Great Ormond Street Children's Hospital, attended a luncheon for the charity at Stowell Park, Northleach, Gloucestershire

30   a.m. Opened the new Fish Market at Newlyn, Cornwall

       p.m. Opened the new Renal Unit at the Royal Cornwall Hospital, Truro, Cornwall

July

4   a.m. Opened the Mother and Baby Unit at City Roads, (Crisis Intervention), William Hart House, City Road, London EC1

5   p.m. As Patron, Help the Aged, attended the charity's Annual Meeting at the Institute of Education, University of London, Bedford Way, London

7   p.m. Opened 'The New Designers' Exhibition and presented the *House and Garden* Design Awards at the Business Centre, Islington Green, London N1

15   Evening. Attended a charity dinner at Flintham Hall, Newark, Nottinghamshire

16   Evening. Accompanied the Prince of Wales as Joint Patrons of the Wishing Well Appeal for the redevelopment of Great Ormond Street Children's Hospital, attended a concert at Wembley Stadium

20   a.m. Presented the 1988 Digital Dance Awards at Sadlers Wells Theatre, Roseberry Avenue, London N1

21   a.m. As Patron, the British Deaf Association, visited the Northern Counties School for the Deaf in its 150th year, at Great North Road, Newcastle-upon-Tyne

        a.m. As President, Dr Barnardo's, visited the Youth Training Scheme, at South Parade and The Base at The Esplanade, Whitley Bay, Tyne & Wear

28   p.m. With the Prince of Wales attended the matinée performance of the 1988 Royal Tournament at Earls Court

Bibliography

Aronson, Theo. *Royal Family – Years of Transition* (John Murray, 1983)

Ashdown, Dulcie. *Princess of Wales* (John Murray, 1979)

Barry, Stephen P. *Royal Service* (Macmillan, 1983)

Barry, Stephen P. *Royal Secrets* (Villiard, 1985)

Battiscombe, Georgina. *The Spencers of Althorp* (Constable, 1984)

Brown, Craig and Cunliffe, Lesley. *The Book of Royal Lists* (Routledge & Kegan Paul, 1982)

Colville, John. *Footprints in Time* (Collins, 1976)

Courtney, Nicholas. *Sporting Royals Past and Present* (Hutchinson/ Stanley Paul, 1983)

Crabtree, Constance, The Dowager Lady. *The Secret Journals* (Columbus, 1988)

Duncan, Andrew. *The Reality of Monarchy* (Heinemann, 1970)

Edgar, Donald. *Palace* (W H Allen, 1983)

Graham, Tim. *On the Royal Road* (Weidenfeld & Nicolson, 1984)

Grunfield, Nina. *The Royal Shopping Guide* (Pan Books, 1985)

Hall, Trevor. *Royal Family Yearbook* (Colour Library Books, 1983)

Hamilton, Alan. *The Royal Handbook* (Mitchell Beazley, 1985)

Holden, Anthony. *Charles, Prince of Wales* (Weidenfeld & Nicolson, 1979)

Honeycombe, Gordon. *The Year of the Princess* (Michael Joseph, 1982)

James, Paul. *The Royal Almanac* (Ravette London, 1986)

James, Paul. *Anne: The Working Princess* (Pan, 1988)

James, Paul and Russell, Peter. *At Her Majesty's Service* (Collins/ Fontana, 1987)

James, Sue. *The Diana Look* (Orbis, 1984)

Junor, Penny. *Diana, Princess of Wales* (Sidgwick & Jackson, 1982)

Keay, Douglas. *Royal Pursuit* (Severn House, 1983)

Lacey, Robert. *Princess* (Hutchinson, 1982)

Lowry, Suzanne. *The Princess in the Mirror* (Chatto & Windus, 1985)

Maclagen, Michael and Louda, Jiri. *Lines of Succession* (Orbis, 1984)

Martine, Roddy. *A Royal Tradition* (Mainstream Publishing, 1986)

Rose, Kenneth. *Kings, Queens and Courtiers* (Weidenfeld & Nicolson, 1985)

Storey, Harriet. *Diana, The Children's Princess* (Michael Joseph, 1984)

Wade, Judy. *Charles and Diana: Inside a Royal Marriage* (Eden, 1987)

Ziegler, Philip. *Crown and People* (Collins, 1978)

Index

237

Index

Index

Stephenson, Pamela, 47
Stewart-Richardson, Mary-Ann, 58
Straker, Sophie (née Kimball), 45, 58
Stratton, Judy, 165

Tarbuck, Jimmy, 198
Tebbit, Norman, 191
Tennant, Lady Anne, 107
Thatcher, Margaret, 40
Tilly, Sheila, 34
Tinker, Jack, 47
Tollemache, Lady Alexandra, 58
Tonga, King and Queen of, 150
Trangmar, Simon, 169
Trestrail, Michael, 32
Tryon, Lord Anthony, 59, 60
Tryon, Lady ('Kanga'), 59–61, 76, 79, 94

Vacani, Madame Betty, 164–5
Van Der Post, Sir Laurens, 94
Van Velden, Jan, 144
Vestey, Lord and Lady, 76, 135
Victoria, Queen, 104, 150, 190, 202

Walker, Catherine, 152, 153, 159
Wallace, Anna, 74–7, 94
Wallace, Ruth, 115
Ward, Jane, 71
Waterhouse, David, 54
Wellesley, Lady Jane, 71, 94
Wernher, Lady Zia, 56

West Heath Boarding School, 2, 38, 72, 150, 163, 199, 202
Westminster, Duke and Duchess of, 56
Whitaker, James, 73
Whitaker, Major Jeremy, 163
Whiteland, Paddy and Nesta, 36–7, 61–2
Wilde, Oscar, 1, 162
William, Prince, of Wales, 7, 16, 17, 24, 34, 39, 44, 101, 102, 107–14, 117, 135, 136, 139, 171, 178, 179, 199, 201
Windsor, Duchess of (Wallis Simpson), 2, 28, 92, 99, 149
Windsor, Duke of (Edward VIII), 99, 101
Windsor, Lord Frederick, 115
Windsor, Lady Gabriella, 115
Windsor, Lady Helen, 49–50
Winter, Major John, 34
Work, Frances, 163
Wogan, Terry, 135

York, Duchess of (née Sarah Ferguson), 3, 10, 12, 22, 48–55, 65, 83, 90–91, 114, 116, 136, 138–9, 145, 160, 190
York, Duke of (Prince Andrew), 3, 90, 99, 100, 108, 114, 136, 138
Young England Kindergarten, 9, 74, 79, 102, 131, 165

Zavaroni, Lena, 45